THE
GOLD AND
FIZDALE
COOKBOOK

THE
GOLD AND
FIZDALE
COOKBOOK

Arthur Gold and Robert Fizdale

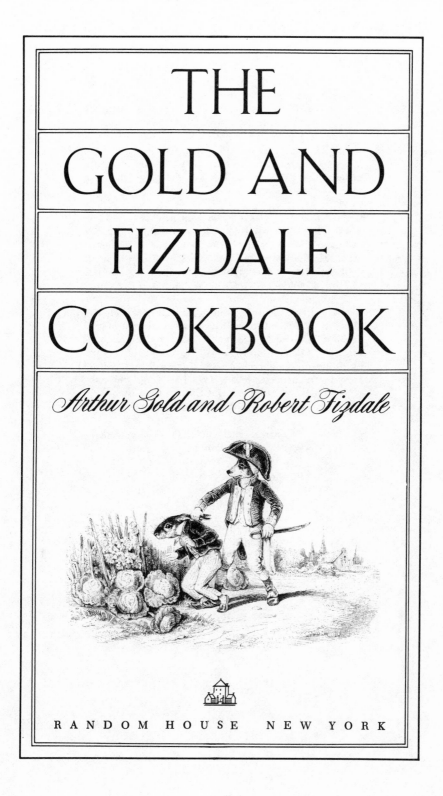

RANDOM HOUSE   NEW YORK

We want to thank Condé Nast for permission to reprint
material that originally appeared in the pages of *Vogue*
and *House and Garden* magazines.

Grateful acknowledgment is also made to William Morrow
& Co., Inc., for permission to include the recipe for
"Chicken Breasts with Leeks and Truffles," adapted
from *The Cuisine of Fredy Girardet* by Fredy Girardet
with Catherine Michel, published by William Morrow &
Co., Inc. Copyright © 1982 by Editions Robert Laffont,
S.A. English Translation © 1984 by William Morrow & Co., Inc., and the recipes for "Chocolate Mousse
Cake" and "Coffee Custard Sauce," adapted from *Michel
Guérard's Cuisine Gourmande* by Michel Guérard, published by William Morrow & Co., Inc. Copyright © 1978
by Editions Robert Laffont, S.A. English Translation ©
1979 by William Morrow & Co., Inc. Originally published under the title *La Cuisine Gourmande*.
Used with permission.

Library of Congress Cataloging in Publication Data
Gold, Arthur.
The Gold and Fizdale cookbook.
1. Cookery. I. Fizdale, Robert. II. Title.
TX715.G6112   1984   641.5   83–19255
ISBN 0–394–50414–3

Manufactured in the United States of America
Typography and binding design by J. K. Lambert
24689753
First Edition

CONTENTS

INTRODUCTION

A devouring passion for cooking reached epic heights in the 1960s and '70s. The passion was kindled by a trio of ladies whose books became a gleaming new *batterie de cuisine*. To begin with, there was the coolly elegant dowager duchess of English cooking Elizabeth David. Determined to save the English from their own cooking, Miss David presented French and Italian country recipes with cosmopolitan flair. Spiked with literary reference and anecdote, her books lightened the guilt of the cultivated reader who felt uneasy reading a cookbook. One finds dog-eared copies of her books nestled between Coleridge and Euripides on the bookshelves of many a self-respecting intellectual.

Then came our friend Alice B. Toklas, whose Parisian gossip was as rich as her food. Miss Toklas combined elegant recipes with captivating autobiographical fragments that ranged from poodles to Picasso, from Gertrude Stein to chicken in wine. Alice was both kind and imperious. One day, we were helping her prepare a *boeuf bourguignon* in her Paris apartment. Did she know, we asked, that a bit of dried orange peel was a fine addition to the stew? "My dears," she snapped with good-natured contempt, "any Australian schoolgirl knows *that*!"

Last but far from least, in marched Julia Child, who codified and clarified French cooking and dubbed it an art. Encouraged by these three culinary Graces—along with the wise James Beard, the urbane Craig Claiborne, and the captivating M.F.K. Fisher—people armed with cookbooks stormed their kitchens determined to equal or surpass the virtuoso feats of professional chefs or the cooks they could neither find nor afford. "Downstairs" became the new "upstairs" of the rich and the not-so-rich.

The passion for food continued to grow. The gratifications of good eating, after all, have certain advantages, even over the physical pleasures of love. One can enjoy eating three times a day, one can enjoy eating by oneself and one can enjoy food's constant satisfactions from innocent childhood to sophisticated old age.

It was Julia Child who first suggested we write about cooking. One summer evening she came to dine at our house on Long Island. "Julia Child coming to dinner! Good God! What to make?" We knew that when the good lady was invited to dinner she was apt to be submerged by an avalanche of elaborate dishes. Should we give her a simple hamburger? Of course, we decided, that was the civilized thing to do. But when the great day came—we are, after all, pianists who thrive on applause—we set out to cook an impressive Moroccan dinner: eight kinds of hors d'oeuvres and a *pastilla*, that pungent pigeon pie encased in flaky filo pastry. We even invented a complicated praline cake for the occasion. We were rewarded when Julia, sweetly unproprietary about cooking, told us that Moroccan food was new to her. With Down East practicality she added, "But you must write about food." Write about food we did when shortly afterwards *Vogue* magazine, somewhat to our surprise, invited us to be their cooking columnists. All that was ten years ago—and here we are.

But first a confession. Cooking is not our profession. Our kitchen does not bristle with an arsenal of gadgets. We do not own a restaurant stove, a convection oven, or an electric flour sifter. Sometimes we misplace our meat thermometer and our food processor is often silent. For us, preparing food is pleasure, therapy, and diversion. Above all, cooking is a way to please our friends and ourselves. And is there a more pleasant way to spend an evening than lingering over a leisurely meal with good company, good wine, and easy laughter?

Our cooking is international, unpretentious *cuisine bourgeoise*, simplified and lightened. We now eat more vegetables, salads, fish, and fowl—and less meat. Some of the recipes in this book are either quickly prepared or calorie-conscious, or both. Most of us who enjoy cooking do not want to spend hours in the kitchen, although from time to time that too can be an absorbing occupation.

Bourgeois cooking, of course, implies French cooking. But times have changed. Now it is more likely to mean relatively simple food, often with a country accent, not only from France but from all over the world. Traveled as we all are, who among us does not want to re-create the bistro and trattoria dishes of France and Italy, the aromatic subtleties of Morocco and the Middle East, and the satisfying food of Russia and Middle Europe? To say nothing of the Maryland crab cakes, the Maine chowders, the soul-stirring gumbos of Louisiana and the heartwarming perfection of an apple pie from almost anywhere in America. As Lin Yutang said, "What is patriotism but the love of the food one ate as a child?"

Even the great French practitioners of *la nouvelle cuisine* (a cuisine whose star we devoutly hope is on the wane) have told us that what they really dream of and live on is the great home cooking of France.

"There is no *nouvelle cuisine*," Paul Bocuse announced to us, "there is only *la bonne cuisine*."

The origin of recipes, like that of folk sayings and jokes, is a mystery. Our recipes come from friends, from cooks who worked in the houses where we lived in France and Italy, from great chefs we have interviewed whose food we have eaten and re-created, and, of course, from the hundreds of cookbooks that we have read, the way others read Agatha Christie.

In reading a mystery story we accept the author's solution, but when we read a recipe we often change the plot midway. Alter the ingredients, shift the emphasis, and you will create a dish that is quite different from the one the author intended. We hope you will feel free to do the same with our recipes. If you like more or less seasoning, lemon, onion, cream, butter, oil, etc., indulge yourself. Tasting, after all, is one of the pleasures and imperatives of successful cooking.

Recurrent fond memories are barometers of taste. One of our most memorable food experiences occurred years ago on our first trip through France. We were driving from Paris to Provence with Germaine Tailleferre, the only woman member of the group of French composers known as *Les Six*. Four of "The Six"—Poulenc, Auric, Milhaud and Tailleferre—were to write two-piano music for us. Musically the composers differed, but they were as one on the subject of food.

Bons vivants, they all ate like gods. To dine with them made us understand and love their music even more. Sensuous harmonies, nostalgic melodies, spicy dissonance melting into delicious consonance, drama and excitement, infectious gaiety, *joie de vivre*—all these qualities were as present in their food as in their music.

On the way down to Provence, Germaine thought it might be amusing to stop for lunch at the restaurant her retired Parisian butcher ran on the banks of the Rhone. When we approached the modest little place, as appealing as a Corot painting, with its three tables set out under an ancient thick-waisted elm, we knew that pleasure lay ahead. After enthusiastic greetings, our host got down to serious matters.

"What would you like to eat?" he asked, all hospitality. "The whitebait is superb at this time of the year." Whitebait would be splendid, we agreed. In no time at all we found ourselves in Monsieur Duffrand's bulky rowboat, watching him net the tiny fish. Fifteen minutes later we were seated at the river's edge sipping the local Mâcon Blanc and admiring the beauty of the day. The table setting was every bit as stimulating as the wine: a starchy white linen cloth, the largest napkins ever seen, butter-yellow dishes, a bowl of jonquils, and sparkling wineglasses. Everything was designed to heighten the joys of the meal.

Blue skies with an occasional floating cloud as white and billowy as an eiderdown, witty company and the feeling of well-being, all contributed to the bucolic lunch we remember so happily. The menu? A tray of the minuscule crisp fish with fried parsley and great wedges of lemon, followed by wild asparagus dressed with *sauce sabayon* and ending with a warm pear *tarte Tatin* glossily coated with caramel.

This ingenuous but original menu and the ease of its presentation gave us as much pleasure as the magnificent dinner we had that night chez Point at La Pyramide in Vienne.

Our aim in this cookbook is to share with you the countless dishes—simple or complicated, innovative or traditional—that we have enjoyed through the years. Our book is a culinary reminiscence. The recipes, like objects one collects, are mementos—of the good places we have visited, the good food we have eaten and the good friends who shared it with us.

THE
GOLD AND
FIZDALE
COOKBOOK

COOKING WITH

BALANCHINE

$\mathcal{O}$f all our friends, George Balanchine was in the highest sense a bon vivant. The sensual pleasure he found in food and wine was surpassed only by the delight he took in shaping the bodies of his magnificently trained dancers to the myriad designs of his ballets.

The great choreographer said of himself, quoting the Russian poet Vladimir Mayakovsky: "I am 'not a man, but a cloud in trousers.'" Certainly this Magician, this Prospero of the Dance, was as elusive, as immaterial, and as ever-changing as a cloud. Unlike the wise cat in the Russian legend who spoke in verse when he turned to the left and in prose when he turned to the right, Balanchine, no matter which way he turned, always spoke his personal poetry. The telegraphic omission of "the" and "a" from his Russian-accented conversation intensified the impatient swiftness of his thought. Silent and pensive at times, he was also capable of suddenly releasing a devastating avalanche of irony, wit, opinion (prejudiced and otherwise), paradox, and, above all, flights of fancy open to as many interpretations as his ballets.

Born in St. Petersburg, the son of what might be called a mixed marriage, Balanchine had an impassive aloofness and Oriental elegance that may have been a heritage from his Georgian father, while his idealistic love of music and dance and his extraordinary generosity and hospitality could have come from his Russian mother. His daily life, like ballet itself, was one of constant motion. When he was not creating ballets or rehearsing his dancers, he was apt to be gardening, puttering about the house, or cooking. It was a very moving experience to watch the creator of *Serenade* and *Agon, Concerto Barocco,* and *The Four Temperaments* peel carrots and slice potatoes with the same intensity he gave to his choreography. To all of his activities he brought a confident, uninterrupted flow of ideas and an intense concentration, the concentration of genius that we have witnessed in only three people: Stravinsky, Picasso, and Balanchine himself.

Curiously enough, this most urbane of men was brought up as a country boy on a farm near the Russian-Finnish border. He used to recall the constant snowfall (which he so touchingly included in his ballet *The Nutcracker*), the horse-drawn sleds with jingling bells, the long winter walks on skis over fifteen-foot snowdrifts. He remembered with nostalgia the half-buried wooden hut, filled in winter with huge blocks of ice from the frozen lake. There food was stored—whole salted cabbages which "when cut, fell away like silk," sauerkraut, tiny pickled cucumbers.

And in summer there was the vegetable garden "as big as city block where we grew everything; nah-turally, there were no stores." Then there was mushroom hunting deep in the pine and birch forests and the search for wild berries. But most of all, he remembered poking his nose into the kitchen to see what his mother and the cook were preparing—the cook who received as her yearly wages twenty rubles in gold coins.

Like Proust's madeleine, *gogl-mogl,* a frothy mixture of egg yolks whipped with sugar, evoked Balanchine's childhood for him. "At bedtime my brother, my sister, and I sat around Mama in a semicircle. She had a glass of *gogl-mogl* and a spoon. While she fed one, the other two watched to see who got the biggest spoonful. We were like little birds in a nest fed by the mama bird."

GOGL-MOGL

❧

3 SERVINGS

6 *egg yolks*
6 *tablespoons sugar*
½ *teaspoon vanilla*

Put all the ingredients in the top of a double boiler over simmering water. Beating continuously, heat until light, fluffy, and somewhat thick. Pour into a bowl or into wineglasses and chill.

Several years ago, when our studio was being painted, Balanchine and his wife, the enchanting ballerina Tanaquil Le Clercq, suggested, "Why don't you come here to rehearse on our two pianos?"

"We can play piano together," George added, "cook a little, this and that. Will be cozy."

Fortunately for us, the painting dragged on for weeks and we spent our days chez Balanchine. Our concerts may have suffered, but our cooking improved enormously as we spent a little time each day alternately playing duets with Balanchine, a marvelous pianist, and the rest of the time cooking, eating, and discussing food.

One day in a characteristic burst of enthusiasm George said, "Let's open wonderful, lovely restaurant, like famous, fahn-tah-stic restaurant in St. Petersburg. It was like palace. There were little Chinese boys with pigtails in silk trousers but barefooted, running, running, running like hell. Silent. It was fahn-tah-stic service." (Balanchine's ideal waiter was one who followed Prospero's injunction to Ariel: ". . . appear, and pertly./No tongue! all eyes! be silent.")

"Then in entranceway big buffet table with hundreds of hors d'oeuvres and in the center huge, *huge* silver bowl filled with best beluga caviar. We will have same thing. First, everybody eats as much as they want; then they go into dining room and order dinner."

With somewhat less enthusiasm we said, "It sounds marvelous, but wouldn't it be terribly expensive?"

"No! No! Not expensive!" said Balanchine, looking shrewd and practical. "Free! All caviar and hors d'oeuvres absolutely free! Will be excellent."

Even we realized this was impractical, to say the least, and plans for the restaurant were abandoned. Instead, George described in mouth-watering detail the voluminous menu the restaurant would have had, and each afternoon we all cooked our way through the staggering list of dishes.

"First," said George, "in our Roosky Cordon-Bluesky, we make *bitki* and mushrooms with *kasha*—but we make nice crusty *kasha*, not mushy mess most people make. This one goes down like nothing." *Kasha* (buckwheat groats) is a Russian staple eaten at breakfast as porridge in its "mushy" state and at other meals in its "crusty" version as a garnish to soup or meat.

BITKI
(Russian Meat Patties with Mushroom Sauce)

∼

5 SERVINGS (10 patties)

PATTIES

1	*stick (¼ pound) butter*
4	*tablespoons (¼ cup) vegetable oil*
1	*cup finely chopped leeks*
½	*cup finely chopped onions*
1¼	*pounds ground chuck*
1–1½	*teaspoons Dijon mustard*
	Salt and freshly ground pepper to taste
	A pinch or two of curry powder
4	*dashes of Worcestershire sauce*
1	*cup finely chopped fresh dill*
1	*egg, lightly beaten*
1	*cup fine bread crumbs (half to be used for breading)*
	or more if needed

MUSHROOM SAUCE

1	*pound mushrooms, cut into ¼-inch slices*
2–3	*tablespoons butter*
	Salt and freshly ground pepper to taste
1½	*cups sour cream*

Heat 3 tablespoons of the butter and 1 tablespoon of the oil in a heavy pan. Add the leeks and onions. Sauté them over low heat, stirring often, until they are limp and golden. Transfer them to a large bowl. When they are cool, add the meat, mustard, salt, pepper, curry, Worcestershire sauce, 2 or 3 tablespoons of the chopped dill, the egg, and ½ cup of the bread crumbs.

Combine all the ingredients thoroughly with your hands. Divide into ten equal portions (about ⅓ cup each). Roll the patties in the bread crumbs. Flatten them to a thickness of about 1 to 1½ inches. Heat most of the remaining butter and oil in the pan and arrange the patties. Leave enough room between the patties so that you can turn them easily. Sauté them over medium heat, adding more butter and oil as needed. Turn them once. They should be crisply browned on both sides. *Bitki* are best when cooked medium or well done. Transfer them to a platter, cover them lightly with foil and keep them warm in a low oven while you make the sauce.

In a frying pan, sauté the mushrooms in the butter for 4 to 5 minutes. Season with salt and pepper. Add ½ cup of the sour cream.

Place the remaining cup of sour cream in the pan in which the *bitki* were sautéed and cook over low heat for a minute or two, scraping all the brown bits into the cream. Add the mushrooms. Taste and correct the seasoning. Stir over the heat till piping hot. Sprinkle with the remaining dill and pour the mushroom sauce over the *bitki*.

A SUGGESTED MENU

(*see Index for recipes*)

EGGPLANT ORIENTALE

BITKI WITH KASHA

WATERCRESS AND RADISH SALAD

RUSSIAN CHEESE PASTRIES

wine: FLEURIE OR MERCUREY, LIGHTLY CHILLED

KASHA
(Buckwheat Groats)

❧

4–5 SERVINGS

1   *cup finely chopped onions*
2   *tablespoons butter*
1   *egg, lightly beaten*
1½ *cups whole-grain buckwheat groats (be sure
     to buy the whole-grain groats—absolutely
     essential)*
2   *cups beef broth*
   Salt and freshly ground pepper to taste

Preheat the oven to 350°.

Sauté the onions in the butter over medium heat, stirring often, until they are golden brown. Reserve. Put the buckwheat groats in a heavy frying pan over medium heat with no fat in the pan. Stir constantly for a few minutes until the groats are toasted and give off a nutty aroma. Add the beaten egg and stir until every grain is coated.

Bring the broth to a boil. Pour just enough of it into the pan to cover the groats. Bring the broth back to a boil. Transfer the pan to the oven.

From time to time, add more boiling broth (or water) to keep the groats covered. When a crust forms on top, remove the skillet from the oven and stir, scraping the bottom and turning the crust under. Taste the *kasha* after 20 minutes. It should have the consistency of rice cooked *al dente*. From now on, add just enough broth to keep the *kasha* from sticking. Dry it in the oven until a crust forms two or three more times, turning the crust under each time. (Cooking time: approximately 1 hour.) Remove from the oven, add salt and pepper and stir in the sautéed onions. Return to the oven until a final crust is formed. Serve with *bitki* (see page 6).

VARIATION: Soak ½ cup dried mushrooms in warm water for 20 minutes. Drain and dry them. Chop them, along with ½ cup fresh mushrooms, and sauté them in 3 tablespoons of butter. Add to the *kasha* at the same time as the onions. Excellent with roast lamb.

TIP: For a delicious salad, mix cold leftover *kasha* with chopped red or green pepper and toss with vinaigrette.

While he showed us how to prepare *kasha*, George told us about the first meal he ever cooked. It was for Diaghilev and dancers of the Ballets Russes in Monte Carlo. Balanchine, only twenty, was already a choreographer for the legendary ballet company. His first menu was an ambitious one.

"I made fillet of sole—came out mushy; chicken cutlets—mushy; soufflé—mushy. Everything looked like *kasha*; was awful!"

Diaghilev, always elegant, turned as he left to the table, where most of the food remained uneaten, and, bowing courteously to each platter in turn, said, "*Kasha* number one, *kasha* number two, *kasha* number three, and thank you, George!"

Reminiscing about the Diaghilev days that evening at dinner, one of the guests, a ballerina, was trying to place the year in which her husband first danced a leading role in one of Balanchine's ballets.

"It was the year your husband jumped into bed with Diaghilev," said Balanchine.

"He never jumped into bed with Diaghilev," said the indignant ballerina, "and besides . . . if he did . . . it was the year after."

Balanchine smiled enigmatically, heaped a second serving of *kasha* onto every plate and, in a triumphant stage whisper, said to us, "It was the year before; and, anyway, he never could jump!"

The *kasha* served with *bitki* and mushrooms was preceded by the following dish.

EGGPLANT ORIENTALE

❧

4–6 SERVINGS

2   *medium-size eggplants*
2   *cloves garlic, finely chopped*
1   *cup finely chopped dill*
½   *cup finely chopped parsley*
½   *cup finely chopped onions or scallions*
¼   *cup lemon juice or vinegar*
¼   *cup sunflower-seed oil*
    Salt and freshly ground pepper to taste

Bake the unpeeled eggplants in a 350° oven for 1 hour, or until they are really soft. Scoop out the pulp and combine it with the remaining ingredients. Mix well and chop fine. Season with salt and pepper and chill.

VARIATIONS: Do as the Armenians do and add ½ teaspoon of cinnamon and 2 tablespoons of crumbled dried mint. Or try the Persian version, adding 2 large ripe tomatoes and 2 small green peppers, all finely chopped.

All these eggplant dishes are excellent served as a first course on lettuce leaves or in hollowed-out tomatoes, accompanied by buttered thinly sliced dark bread or with Near Eastern Melba Toast.

NEAR EASTERN MELBA TOAST

With a very sharp knife, separate the upper and lower crusts of pitas, the small, flat circular Near Eastern breads. Cut each crust into 2-inch strips. Butter them liberally and sprinkle with sesame seeds, salt, and pepper. Dry in a 300° oven until delicately browned.

VARIATION: In place of sesame seeds, use finely chopped chives or curry powder.

Another wonderful melba toast can be made with English muffins. Put the muffins into the freezer for 30 minutes. It will then be possible to cut each muffin into several extremely thin slices. Butter and season. Dry in the oven until browned.

GEORGIAN CORIANDER SAUCE

༄

Balanchine roasted lamb very simply, preferably on a spit, but with it he served this most exotic and fragrant sauce.

2 cups chopped coriander (available at Oriental or
    Latin-American groceries)
½ cup chopped fresh herbs
    (parsley, dill, basil, or tarragon)
½ cup chopped scallions
½ cup walnuts
2 or more cloves garlic, finely chopped
6 cooked prunes, pitted and chopped
¼ cup lemon juice or vinegar
1 cup walnut oil or more if needed
    Salt, pepper, and cayenne pepper to taste

In a mortar or wooden bowl, mash together the herbs, walnuts, garlic, and prunes. Stir in the lemon juice, oil, and seasoning.

TIPS: Coriander sauce, like Italian pesto, can be made in summer and successfully frozen for six months.

To make an extraordinary green mayonnaise, stir 1 cup coriander sauce into 2 cups mayonnaise.

In the Caucasus, coriander sauce is ever-present. It is served with hors d'oeuvres of cold sautéed eggplant slices and thickly sliced ripe tomatoes, and in kidney-bean and potato salads. It is used on fish, roast meat, chicken, and "best of all," Balanchine used to say, "on sliced leftover white meat of turkey or any other nice leftovers."

Speaking of leftovers, we are reminded of a persistent acquaintance of Balanchine's who had been hinting regularly that he would like to be invited to dinner. When he telephoned one morning, we were amused to hear George's end of the conversation. "What am I doing? Well, as a matter of fact, we're cooking tonight's dinner. You'd like to come? I hope you like leftovers. Yes? You do? Good! Come tomorrow."

CHICKEN STEW
WITH CORIANDER SAUCE

❧

Inspired by Balanchine's love of coriander, we invented this dish, which pleased our friends and even won the approval of the master.

4 SERVINGS

1 *cup sliced onions or leeks*
¼ *cup olive or French peanut oil*
1½ *cups canned Italian-style tomatoes, drained and*
       mashed
2 *cloves garlic, mashed*
    Salt and freshly ground pepper to taste
1 *2½-pound chicken, cut in eighths*
1½ *cups dry white wine*
2 *cups chicken broth*
1 *bay leaf*
    Georgian Coriander Sauce (see page 11)

In a covered heavy casserole, cook the onions slowly in the oil for 10 minutes, stirring frequently. Add the tomatoes and garlic. Cook, uncovered, for 10 minutes. Salt and pepper the chicken and put it in the casserole. Spread some of the vegetables over the chicken. Cover and cook for 10 minutes. Add the wine, broth, and bay leaf, and bring to a simmer. Simmer for 20 minutes, or until the chicken is tender. Remove from the heat and stir in 1 cup of coriander sauce.

Serve with boiled potatoes and pass any remaining coriander sauce separately.

When we asked George what he would choose if he were on a desert island and could have only one dish, before we could complete the question he answered, "Potatoes! Nah-turally! Nice, excellent, fahn-tah-stic hot boiled potatoes—crunchy, crisp—like sugar." Then after a moment's reflection, he added plaintively, "Could I have a little oil, a little chopped parsley, and a nice cold bottle of Roederer Cristal champagne?"

Since Balanchine usually spent every evening during the ballet season at the New York State Theater, some of his best meals were after-theater suppers. One that was unforgettable consisted of *borschok*, a ruby-red, beet-flavored clear consommé, and seven kinds of *piroshki*, those delicious Russian pastries.

BORSCHOK BALANCHINE
(Clear Beet Soup)

෴

The secret of this soup is baking the beets.

8–10 SERVINGS

8   *large or 12 small beets, tops removed*
6   *cups beef broth, homemade if possible*
6   *peppercorns*
1   *bay leaf*
1½ *teaspoons wine vinegar*
1½ *teaspoons sugar*
    Salt and freshly ground pepper to taste
½   *cup Madeira*
2   *lemons, sliced*

Wash the beets. Bake them wrapped in aluminum foil for 1 hour, or until they are tender. Cool, peel, and grate them. Put the broth, peppercorns, and bay leaf in a pot and bring to a boil. Add the grated beets, vinegar, and sugar. Stir and simmer for 10 minutes. Strain the soup. Add salt, pepper, and the Madeira. Serve in cups, a lemon slice in each.

Balanchine's most elaborate meal of the year was always the Russian Easter midnight supper. For days before this great feast, his every spare moment between rehearsals and performances was spent rushing home to see if the yeast dough was rising for the *kulich* and if the *paskha* was draining properly in its flower pot. Had the sturgeon jelled in its aspic? Had the pheasant arrived for the Salade Olivier? What about the tearful grating of the horseradish?

It was dazzling to see the swiftness and cool dispatch with which he completed these elaborate dishes. Of course, between bouts of cooking there was a great deal of rushing back to the theater to supervise his ballets.

After the moving Russian Orthodox Church service, Balanchine and his friends would return to his apartment where the traditional three kisses were exchanged, champagne was poured, and everyone gathered round the sumptuous buffet table.

One Easter, one of the strangers somehow made it known to George that he had no place to go after the service. With true Russian hospitality, Balanchine invited him to come along to his party where the unknown guest soon proved to have an impressive capacity for celebration. Fragrant hyacinths, bottles of iced vodka, and bowls of caviar stood at each end of the buffet. We all returned to the candlelit table time after time but no one more assiduously than Mr. X. After a while it became quite clear that he had had too much to drink. When he poured himself what must have been his tenth vodka, Balanchine tactfully suggested that perhaps he had had enough. To which Mr. X cheerfully replied, "Well, how about a beer?" In desperation, George said there was no beer. Mr. X seemed astonished. "Whaddaya mean, no beer?" he said. "You're Mr. Ballantine, aren't you?"

Enthralled though he was by this particular case of mistaken identity, Balanchine said, "My friend, you've had a lot to eat and a lot to drink. In fact, you've had a wonderful time. Now you're happy, maybe you should go home." He spoke with such gentle authority that Mr. X took no offense. "I guess you're right," he mumbled. And bestowing a few nontraditional Easter kisses—and a few well-placed pinches— on several of the beautiful women present, he calmly, if unsteadily, departed.

At another such evening, Stravinsky, the composer that Balanchine most admired and to whose music he created many of his greatest masterpieces, asked if he could see Mourka's famous leaps. (Balanchine had trained his cat, Mourka, to do spectacular balletic leaps and *tours en l'air*.) We all gathered in a solemn circle, Mr. and Mrs. Stravinsky in the seats of honor. Balanchine appeared, a ball of crumpled newspaper in his hand, leading the cat into the room.

We had seen George at many an opening night, cool as a cucumber, completely confident of himself and his dancers. Now for the first time we saw him visibly nervous. Tanaquil whispered to us mischievously, "I hope Mourka rises to the occasion!"

We all held our breath. George threw the ball of paper high into the air. The prodigious Mourka leaped higher than ever before. He seemed to remain in the air for a full minute, defying gravity à la Nijinsky, and then landed lightly on velvet paws to tumultuous applause and bravos led by the beaming Stravinskys. Another Balanchine triumph! From then on the evening was a great success, and we all addressed ourselves to the delicious food.

We felt we had been awarded the diploma of the Cordon Bleu, as Tanny and George had asked us to contribute their favorite salad, created by a French chef in the service of Czar Nicholas II.

SALADE OLIVIER, GEORGE BALANCHINE

℘

8–12 SERVINGS

1   cucumber, peeled
1   dill pickle (German style; that is, pickled without
       garlic)
     The meat of 1 3-pound roast chicken (or roast
       pheasant), cubed
4   boiled potatoes, peeled and sliced
1   cup cooked peas, well drained
¾   cup mayonnaise
½   cup sour cream
4   teaspoons Dijon mustard
     Salt and freshly ground pepper to taste
4   hard-boiled eggs, quartered
2   tablespoons capers, drained
24   black and green olives, pitted and halved
4   ripe tomatoes, quartered

Slice the cucumber and the pickle in quarters lengthwise, then in thin slices crosswise. Mix them with the chicken, potatoes, and peas. Mix the mayonnaise, sour cream, and mustard together. Add to the salad and toss well. Season with salt and pepper. Garnish with the eggs, capers, olives, and tomatoes.

On the festive table, next to the sturgeon in aspic were bowls of cucumber salad. The cucumber plays a comically important role in Russian life. To one of us who had finally given up smoking at Balanchine's insistence, he said, "Excellent! When you were smoking, you looked like an old dill pickle. Now you look like a nice young cucumber!"

Balanchine always felt that shopping for cucumbers was a serious business that required great skill and lightning action. "I watch big, fat ladies fighting to get biggest, fattest cucumbers which are lousy and I stand behind them, like eagle, on my toes. Then, when I see tiny, green, firm young cucumbers, I swoop down and pounce on them and fly home."

Balanchine had a childlike love of desserts, which he immortalized in his ballet *The Nutcracker*. The décor of the last act of the ballet is, indeed, a monument to his sweet tooth, a child's paradise of sweets. With the help of designer Rouben Ter-Arutunian, all imaginable kinds of puddings, pies, jellies, cakes, and cookies in captivating candy colors tumble in marvelous profusion out of cornucopias and are piled high on giant pagoda-like epergnes.

One Christmas we took three very young children to see their first performance of *The Nutcracker*. Afterwards we took them backstage to meet the choreographer. What a pleasure it was to watch the playful yet serious consideration with which Balanchine showed them the props. He seated them on the children's thrones, put them in the reindeer sleigh, and finally led them into and under the skirts of the gigantic Mother Ginger costume.

Happy in their hiding place, the children refused to come out, until Balanchine, like a magician, tugged at a pulley that lifted the costume high into the air exposing the three giggling children. It would be difficult to say who was more delighted, Balanchine or his young guests.

PLANNING

MENUS

Never eat more than you can lift.
MISS PIGGY

$\mathcal{P}$lanning menus is much like planning concert programs. Begin with a light, stimulating first course which—like Scarlatti sonatas—invites your guests to settle in expectantly for an evening's pleasure. A modulation to the main course, which should be—like a Beethoven or Brahms sonata— full of drama and excitement. The salad and cheese, like a group of Stravinsky pieces, cleanses the palate or "scours the maw" as Rabelais said, and will lead the diner into a virtuoso dessert which sends your guests home singing— what else?—your praises. Alas, there are always food cranks among our friends. Let us hope that when they come to dine your difficult guests have the charm and talent of Lord Byron. Samuel Rogers tells this story about the Romantic poet:

When we sat down to dinner I asked Byron if he would take soup? 'No, he never took soup.'—'Would he take fish?'—'No, he never took fish.'— Presently I asked if he would eat some mutton? 'No, he never ate mutton.'— I then asked if he would take a glass of wine? 'No, he never tasted wine.' —It was now necessary to inquire what he *did* eat and drink; and the answer was, 'Nothing but hard biscuits and soda-water.' Unfortunately, neither hard biscuits nor soda-water were at hand; and he dined upon potatoes bruised down on his plate and drenched with vinegar.—My guests stayed till very late discussing the merits of Walter Scott and Joanna Baillie. —Some days after, meeting Hobhouse, I said to him, 'How long will Lord Byron persevere in his present diet?' He replied, 'Just as long as you continue to notice it.' I did not then know, what I now know to be a fact— that Byron, after leaving my house, had gone to a club in St. James's Street, and eaten a hearty meat-supper.

A few things to remember: Many dishes—and it is wise to decide on them *before* planning your menu—are as good, or better, reheated just before dining. Prepare these dishes the preceding day if you can. Other dishes can be made ahead of time except for the finishing touches. Only one dish at a meal should be spicy and strong or rich and creamy. In winter, when most of our houses are sadly overheated, all dishes do not have to be hot or even warm. One of our favorite menus for friendly suppers is hot okra and tomato soup, cold steak, a salad, and quince crisp. Three or four courses are not always necessary. A few well-chosen canapés, a satisfying main course, excellent cheese, crusty bread, fruit and, most important, entertaining company can make for a memorable evening's meal. Remember what the poet said:

> Oh, bother your books and all their receipting,
> The proof of the pudding is in the eating.

ABOUT WINE

"I rather like bad wine," said Mr. Mountchesney, "one gets so bored with good wine." Disraeli, in his novel *Sybil,* had a point—as he so often did. There is poetry in wine and science in the making of it, but what lofty double-talk, what miasmal mists, surround the subject. Only Zen Buddhism, LSD, Jerzy Grotowski, and Bob Wilson elicit such mystic euphoria.

Although most of us are not as jaded as Mr. Mountchesney, legendary French wines at legendary prices would be as out of place with plain American food as a dress by Madame Grès on Bette Midler. In general, most country food, no matter how good, is better partnered by a simple companionable wine. So save your Corton-Charlemagne, your Château Margaux, and your Dom Perignon for those nights when you dazzle your guests with the suavest, most subtly complicated French dishes. With simpler French, American, or Italian food, it seems to us, you can drink deliciously appropriate, less expensive wines that will enhance the food, brighten the conversation, make you as lovable as you are loving, and even quench your thirst.

For the French, *vin ordinaire* for everyday use is second nature. In the Midi, a modest rosé, such as a Rémy-Pannier Rosé d'Anjou, is drunk with the aromatic *pissaladière, bourride,* and *bouillabaisse.* Or try the Tavel Vin Rosé Château d'Aqueria. Either wine would be splendid with a chicken sandwich or a lobster salad.

In Brittany, a reasonably priced Muscadet is considered *comme il faut* with anything from a *langoustine* to a buckwheat crêpe. Both the Château de la Bidière and the Château de Briacé Muscadets are as refreshing as a dip under a green, white-fringed Atlantic breaker. Invigorating with fresh oysters, New England clam chowder, or a delicately steamed fish.

It goes without saying that Spanish wines, such as the Rioja whites or full-bodied reds, are best with any Spanish dish. They are excellent with Moroccan food as well.

With your own favorite pasta or risotto, you cannot do better than a Villa Antinori Chianti Classico or Bianco Secco, wonderful wines for drinking day after day. Perfect with veal *scaloppine* or fish soup Italian style are the Soaves, Verdicchios, and white Brolios. Or Prosecco if you can find it.

As for those epicures, the Chinese, *they* know that great French wine does not suit their food. Dry Spanish or Italian white wine is their wise Oriental answer—or ice-cold Chinese beer.

What to drink with American cuisine is a more complicated question. We remember once being given, on a great ranch in the Southwest, a superb dish of chili con carne with a Romanée-Conti. It was like mating a handsome gorilla with a Tanagra figurine. Mexican beer or the too little known Rhone Valley reds, such as a chilled Gigondas or Juliénas, would have been ideal with the spicy chili. But why not go native and serve an excellent American wine such as a Pinot Noir?

In France, red Beaujolais is now often served *not* at room tempera-

ture, not even at the *correct* room temperature—that of a chilly French
château or stone farmhouse, not of an overheated American apartment—but cold, really cold. The American influence, no doubt. Try a
chilled Beaujolais-Villages with a perfectly roasted Long Island duck-
ling or with barbecued spareribs, and you have the best of both worlds.

By extension, we like to serve one of our favorite dessert wines, a
Château Nairac Sauternes straight from an hour or two in the freezer—
gold flakes in a crystal glass. At that temperature it is difficult to
distinguish this wine from Château d'Yquem, our absolute favorite
despite its lordly price. Not only are these dessert wines perfect at
the end of a meal but their sweetness makes a surprisingly inspired
counterpoint to the dark richness of *pâté* of foie gras or chicken livers
when served at the beginning of a meal.

Few of us have the perfect controlled-temperature space for storing
wine. Why not let a reliable wine dealer do the storing for you, and
buy your wine as you need it? One is forever reading about making
the perfect little wine cellar out of an apartment closet, but the in-
genious writers never tell their readers what to do with their leftover
clothes. One advantage of the simpler, more robust wines is that they
are not as exigent about their surroundings as the great aristocratic
wines, which, like aging French countesses, require constant pampering
and suffer from the slightest *courant d'air*.

Red or white? The color line is fast disappearing. Only the most
delicate white-fleshed fish beg for dry white wines. Serve them with
Alsatian Riesling or the surprisingly dry Sicilian white Corvo, Duca di
Salaparuta. Try a French Chablis, a Billaud Simon, dry as mountain
air, or two of our Italian favorites, Pinot Grigio and Gavi. Both these
Italian whites are better than many a French wine at comparable
prices. And only the reddest of red meats, a rare steak or roast beef,
demands a red wine. You cannot go wrong with a French Mercurey
Louis Latour or Château Grand-Puy Ducasse. Of course you can
stimulate your patriotic feelings with an American Cabernet Sauvignon,
excellent with rare beef.

Otherwise you are on your own. Salmon, mackerel, or fresh tuna
are just as good or better with a light red Beaujolais such as a Saint-
Amour or a Château de la Chaize in place of white wine. However, if
you prefer white wine throughout a meal, try a Kriter, a sparkling
cousin to champagne, or a Pouilly-Fumé. A reasonable solution, in
fact, is to serve one wine before, during and after dinner. Gone, or at
least going, are proper French meals preceded by an apéritif, accompanied by two white wines and three reds in an ascending scale

of greatness and followed by a choice of Cognac, Armagnac and white *eau de vie*: *framboise, poire,* or *mirabelle*. The traditional non-chilled, freshly squeezed orange juice that appeared at the end of the evening was not only a signal that the party was over and the hosts were ready for bed but a suggestion, not unreasonable in the circumstances, that perhaps the guests had drunk enough.

Even in America, a company dinner in the good old days was preceded by cocktails and highballs, was served with at least one white and one red wine, and was followed by serious drinking. But now, in both countries, wine has become *the* apéritif, usually white wine, with or without the drop of *crème de cassis,* the black-currant liqueur that turns a glass of wine into a roseate *Kir.* Iced champagne with *crème de cassis* becomes a *Kir royale,* and a royal treat it is.

Less known is the *Communard,* although the French have been drinking it since the days of the Paris Commune in 1870. It is made like a Kir but with a chilled *red* wine, usually a new Beaujolais, plus a dash of crème de cassis. We first tasted this variation in a working-men's bistro in Lyons and were so enthusiastic that we ordered it in the dining room of the Ritz on our return to Paris. At the word *Communard* the waiter turned pale and looked uneasily out of the window to reassure himself that the barricades had not been raised again. Regaining his composure, he sniffed haughtily as he turned back to us and said, "Messieurs, at the Ritz we call it the Chamonix." By either name, a delightful way to begin a meal.

Since taste in wines is a very personal matter, a wine-tasting party is the quickest and most amusing way to become acquainted with wines you do not know. Chill the whites in advance and open the reds. Provide ten of your friends with cheese and crackers and ask them to join you in tasting ten different bottles of wine. At the end of the evening, you will know a good deal more about wine, about one another, and about which ones—friends and wines—you find most stimulating.

Salut! Skal! Za zdorov'e! Prosit! Cin-cin! and Cheers!

FIRST COURSES

Hunger is the best sauce in the world.
CERVANTES
Don Quixote

The first course should be a light promise of serious things to come. It was not always thus. Certainly, the French during the Belle Epoque, and the Russians in Czarist times, felt otherwise. The Russian *zakuska*, the buffet banquet that accompanied drinks before dinner, was a gourmand's glorified cocktail party. Before World War I, even the French considered it chic. They called it *hors-d'oeuvre à la russe* and took it to their hearts—and stomachs.

We can be nostalgic about the good old days, but alas—and hurrah—they are over. Though we are no longer titans of the table, there are few things more agreeable than a dinner that spans the evening hours. (And nothing more disagreeable than having your dish snatched away before it has been quite finished.) Leisure, after all, is the bouquet garni of the gastronome.

We find vegetables, savory and amusingly prepared, one of the most pleasant and prettiest ways to introduce a meal. Try something as simple as leeks on toast or, if you are in the mood, as complicated as our artichoke and spinach pie, and we think you and your guests will agree. And you will have added another arrow to your gastronomic bow.

AN ARTICHOKE–SPINACH PIE FOR JASON
(Torta di Carciofi e Spinaci)

∽

6 SERVINGS

6   *artichokes or 6 well-drained canned artichoke*
      bottoms
1   *cup vegetable or peanut oil*
1½ *cups thinly sliced onions*
    Salt and freshly ground pepper to taste
1   *clove garlic, finely chopped*
1½ *pounds fresh spinach*
1   *cup ricotta*
½   *cup freshly grated Italian Parmesan cheese*
3   *tablespoons pine nuts (pignoli), lightly toasted*
    in the oven
8   *eggs*
12 *filo leaves (available at specialty shops)—keep*
    refrigerated until ready to use

Preheat the oven to 425°.

To prepare the artichoke bottoms, pull off the outer leaves of the artichokes, cut off the inner leaves, stems and all traces of the thistle-like "chokes," and discard them. Slice the artichoke bottoms as thin as possible, then cut the slices in half.

Heat ¼ cup of the oil in a heavy pan. Add the artichokes and onions. Season with salt and pepper. Sauté over medium heat, stirring often.

Add more oil if needed. Cook until the onions are limp and the artichokes are crisp but tender. Stir in the garlic for the last minute of cooking.

Meanwhile remove the coarse stems from the spinach. Wash it thoroughly, pat it dry and chop it coarsely. When the onions and artichokes are ready, add the spinach and cook for 3 to 4 minutes, stirring, until it wilts. Set aside to cool.

Put the ricotta, Parmesan, pine nuts, and 2 eggs in a large bowl. Beat until well combined. Season with salt and pepper. Add the cooled vegetable mixture and stir it in thoroughly.

Rinse two clean dish towels in cold water and wring them out so that they are just slightly damp. Lay one towel on a wooden board. Place the filo leaves on it and cover them with the other towel. Work with one filo leaf at a time and keep the others covered, or they will become brittle.

Brush the bottom and sides of the pie plate lightly with oil. Lay 1 filo leaf on the bottom of the pie plate so that it hangs over the side by 2 inches. Brush it lightly with oil. Add 5 more leaves, one by one, giving the pie plate a small turn before you add each leaf so that the overhanging leaves will be evenly distributed. Brush each leaf with oil before adding the next.

Spread the filling evenly in the pie plate. Press a small soup ladle into the filling to make 6 depressions large enough to hold a raw egg. The depressions should be evenly spaced, 1 inch from the outer edge. Break an egg into each depression very carefully. Season the eggs with salt and pepper. Carefully fold the overhanging leaves over the filling. Cover the pie with the remaining 6 filo leaves, working as before, distributing them evenly and oiling each one as you go. Tuck the overhanging edges down inside the pie plate. The last leaf should be broken into large pieces, placed on top, then brushed with oil.

Bake for 10 minutes. The crust should be brown and the eggs set but not hard. Serve warm (not hot) or at room temperature. A remarkable dish!

CAPONATA

∾

6 SERVINGS

About ¾ cup olive oil
1 large onion, coarsely chopped
2 cloves garlic, passed through a garlic press
      or peeled and finely chopped
   Salt and freshly ground pepper to taste
   About 2 tablespoons sugar
1 cup ripe tomatoes, peeled, seeded, and coarsely
      chopped
1 medium-size eggplant, about 1 pound,
      unpeeled, cut into strips 2 inches by 1 inch
1½ cups green and yellow peppers cut into 1-inch strips
1½ cups hearts of celery cut into 1-inch slices
2 tablespoons wine vinegar
2 tablespoons currants or raisins
2 tablespoons pine nuts (pignoli)
¼ cup capers, drained
¼ cup whole pitted Italian green olives
3 tablespoons chopped fresh basil

In a large heavy skillet, heat 2 tablespoons of the oil. Add the onion and garlic, season with salt, pepper and a pinch of sugar, and sauté, stirring often, until tender but not browned. Add the tomatoes and cook, stirring occasionally, until you have a thick sauce. Remove the contents of the skillet with a slotted spoon to a large bowl.

Add some more oil to the skillet and sauté the eggplant till lightly browned. Season with salt and pepper and press out some of the oil with a spatula. Remove the eggplant with a slotted spoon to the bowl containing the onion-tomato mixture.

Sauté the peppers and celery in the same skillet with a little added oil if necessary for 5 minutes. Return the contents of the bowl to the skillet. Stir in about 1½ tablespoons of sugar, salt and pepper to taste, and all the remaining ingredients except the basil. Adding more oil if necessary, cook everything together over low heat for 20 to 30 minutes, or until the vegetables are cooked but still somewhat crisp. Taste and correct the seasoning. The caponata should have a subtle sweet-and-sour taste. Add more salt, pepper, sugar, or vinegar as desired. Remove from heat and mix in the chopped fresh basil.

Serve hot, cold, or tepid. Equally delicious at all temperatures, whether eaten as a first course or as an accompaniment to a roast, broiled meat or fowl, or with an omelet.

PERSIAN EGGPLANT CAKE

6–8 SERVINGS

2   *medium-size eggplants*
    Seasonings: 1 teaspoon each salt, freshly
        ground pepper, and turmeric, or
        more to taste
½   *cup chopped walnuts*
4   *eggs*
4–6   *tablespoons butter*

Bake the eggplants at 375° for about 45 minutes, or until tender when pierced with a fork. When they are cool, peel them and mash the pulp. Add the seasonings, walnuts, and eggs, mixing them in thoroughly. Melt the butter in a large cast-iron frying pan. Spread the eggplant mixture in the pan, flattening the top. Bake at 350° for 30 minutes, or until the mixture holds together. Cut into wedges and serve hot or at room temperature. The eggplant cake keeps well in the refrigerator for 2 to 3 days. When serving, let it warm to room temperature or reheat it in a little butter.

"PIZZA" WITH EGGPLANT CRUST

❧

6 SERVINGS

CRUST

Salt
6   *rounds of unpeeled eggplant, ¾ inch thick*
3   *tablespoons flour*
4–6 *tablespoons olive oil*
    Freshly ground pepper

TOPPING

6   *thick tomato slices, as near in size to the eggplant*
       slices as possible
12 *flat anchovy fillets*
12 *black Italian olives, pitted and halved*
1   *teaspoon freshly ground pepper*
1   *tablespoon chopped fresh oregano or basil*
       (or 1 teaspoon dried)
2   *tablespoons grated imported Parmesan cheese*
6   *thin slices mozzarella cheese, at room temperature*

Sprinkle salt generously on the eggplant slices. Cover them with a dish and a heavy weight. After 30 minutes, press out the bitter juices and drain. Wipe the slices dry and dredge them with flour. Fry them in hot oil until golden brown. Season generously with pepper but sparingly with salt.

Arrange the eggplant slices in one layer in an oiled baking dish. Cover each of them with a tomato slice. Decorate each slice with 2 anchovy fillets, crisscrossed, and 4 olive halves placed between the anchovies. Sprinkle with pepper (but no salt), oregano or basil, and Parmesan cheese. Cover each "pizza" with a slice of mozzarella, bake at 325° for 10 to 15 minutes, or until the mozzarella has melted. Serve as a first course or with veal chops.

ROASTED BABY EGGPLANT, WORD OF MOUTH

∽

8–10 SERVINGS

2½ *pounds baby Italian eggplants, quartered*
2 *large onions, thinly sliced*
2 *large cloves garlic, finely chopped*
½ *cup vegetable or olive oil*
   Salt and coarsely ground pepper
¼ *cup red wine vinegar*
¼–½ *cup chopped fresh basil or dill*

Preheat the oven to 400°.

Place the eggplants on an oiled shallow baking pan. Cover with the onions and garlic. Drizzle with the oil. Season with salt and pepper. Bake for 35 to 45 minutes, turning occasionally until the eggplants are well browned and tender. The skins should be crisp. Cool slightly, then toss with the vinegar. Garnish lavishly with the chopped basil or dill. Serve chilled or at room temperature.

BRAISED LEEKS ON TOAST, FRED LAZARUS

∽

2 SERVINGS

4 *small leeks, about ¾ inch in diameter*
2 *slices good white bread*
4 *tablespoons butter*
2 *shallots, finely chopped*
   Salt and freshly ground pepper
2 *cups chicken broth*
2 *teaspoons finely chopped fresh chives*
2–3 *tablespoons freshly grated Parmesan or Gruyère*
     cheese, or a mixture of both

Trim the beard end of each leek and cut it the same length as the bread. Cut the leeks in half lengthwise and wash them under running water, holding the leaves apart so that all the dirt is washed away. Tie the two halves of each leek together with string.

Heat 2 tablespoons of the butter in a heavy skillet just large enough to hold the leeks in one layer. Sauté the shallots until golden. Arrange the leeks on top of the shallots in a single layer. Season with salt and pepper to taste and add broth to cover. Cover the skillet and simmer over low heat for about 15 minutes, or until the leeks are tender. Remove the leeks and shallots with a slotted spoon and drain them well on paper towels. Toast the bread lightly, butter one side of each slice, then sprinkle it with chives. Untie the leeks and arrange them, cut side down, on the toast. Sprinkle with the shallots and the grated cheese. Dot with butter. Trim the toast so that none of it is exposed. Heat under the broiler, watching carefully so that the cheese does not burn. Serve hot as soon as the cheese has browned.

SUSANNA AGNELLI'S LENTIL PURÉE WITH PROSCIUTTO ROLLS

❧

8–12 SERVINGS

Lentils Provençale (see page 272)
24   *thin slices prosciutto, mortadella, or ham*
Parsley for garnish

Prepare lentils provençale. When it is ready, discard the bay leaves, then purée in two batches in a blender or food processor. Taste for seasoning, adding salt and freshly ground pepper if needed. Reheat it. The purée should have the consistency of a thick paste. If it is too thin, return it to the pot and cook it, stirring, over medium heat until it thickens, then put a tablespoon or two of purée on each slice of prosciutto and roll it up. Put any remaining purée on an ovenproof platter, arrange the prosciutto rolls on top, and keep warm in a low oven. Garnish with parsley and serve.

MUSHROOM SNAILS

❧

A delightful substitute for *snails à la bourguignonne.* A fine dish for those who won't eat snails but love garlic butter.

6 SERVINGS

6 *very large mushroom caps (reserve stems for another use)*
1 *stick (¼ pound) butter, softened*
2 *cloves garlic, finely chopped*
4 *tablespoons finely chopped parsley*
2 *tablespoons finely chopped chives*
   Salt and freshly ground pepper to taste
2 *tablespoons butter*
1 *tablespoon peanut oil*
6 *¾-inch slices of French bread*

Preheat the oven to 400°.

Wipe the mushroom caps clean with a damp paper towel. Mash together the butter, garlic, parsley, chives, salt, and pepper, and use this mixture (which, of course, is the classic stuffing for snails) to fill the mushroom caps. Bake in a buttered baking dish for 7 to 10 minutes, or until the mushrooms are cooked but still hold their shape and the filling has melted.

Meanwhile, heat the 2 tablespoons of butter with the oil and fry the bread slices till browned on both sides. Serve one mushroom and one slice of bread to each person.

VARIATION: For an attractive presentation that takes just a few more minutes, cut the slices of bread 1 inch thick and scoop out just enough of the center of each slice so that you can set a filled mushroom cap into the hollow. In this procedure, fry the flat side of the bread until browned. Then brush a little melted butter on the scooped-out side, set the mushrooms into the hollows and serve.

RED PEPPER QUICHE

∽

An unusual quiche from Word of Mouth, one of New York's finest caterers.

6 SERVINGS

Pie crust (see pastry recipe for Seafood Chowder Pie,
   page 159)
1   *medium-size onion, thinly sliced*
4   *tablespoons butter*
2   *sweet red peppers, cut into thin strips*
1½ *cups grated Gruyère cheese*
4   *eggs*
1   *cup heavy cream*
½   *cup milk*
¼   *cup chopped fresh herbs (parsley, dill, tarragon)*
1   *teaspoon salt*
¼   *teaspoon cayenne pepper*

Preheat the oven to 350°.

Line a 9-inch pie plate with pie crust.

Sauté the onion in 2 tablespoons of the butter until browned. Set aside. Heat the remaining 2 tablespoons of butter till sizzling. Sauté the pepper strips quickly over high heat until they blister. Layer the crust with the cheese, the onions, and then the peppers.

Whisk together the eggs, cream, milk, herbs, and seasonings, and pour this mixture over the peppers. Bake for 45 minutes. Serve warm.

ROASTED PEPPERS WITH MOZZARELLA
(Peperoni Arrostiti con Mozzarella)

∽

4–6 SERVINGS

6   *bell peppers (red, green, or both)*
2   *small mozzarella cheeses, cut into ¼-inch slices*
    Salt and freshly ground pepper to taste

1   *teaspoon dried oregano or more to taste*
½   *cup olive oil*

Char the peppers according to the directions given for Roasted Peppers (see page 279). Discard the stems, seeds, and membranes.

Cut each pepper into 4 wide strips and drain them on paper towels. On a large platter, alternate the pepper strips with the mozzarella slices, overlapping them. Season with salt, pepper, and oregano. Pour the olive oil over all. Serve at room temperature.

VARIATION: Instead of peppers, use 4 small zucchini. Wash the zucchini and dry them well. Trim the ends. Cut them, unpeeled, into ¼-inch slices. Sauté them in 3 tablespoons of olive oil until tender but not soft. While they are hot, put them into a large bowl with the mozzarella slices. Add additional olive oil if needed, and season with salt, pepper, and oregano. Toss together, and serve at room temperature.

ROASTED PEPPERS AND ANCHOVIES

ᕼᘰ

4–6 SERVINGS AS A MAIN COURSE, MORE IF PART
OF A MIXED ANTIPASTO OR BUFFET

1   *can flat anchovies with a little of their oil*
6   *red or green sweet peppers, charred according to the
      procedure for Roasted Peppers (see page 279)*
    Juice of 1 lemon
    Freshly ground pepper

GARNISH

1   *hard-boiled egg, finely chopped*
4   *tablespoons finely chopped parsley*
1   *tablespoon capers, drained*

Drain the anchovies, reserving the oil. Cut the peppers into 1½-inch strips and arrange them on a serving dish. Sprinkle them with a little of the anchovy oil, the lemon juice, and pepper to taste. Lay the anchovy fillets over the peppers. Garnish with chopped egg, parsley, and capers.

PINZIMONIO
(Fresh Vegetables with Anchovy Dip)

❧

4 SERVINGS

A platter of mixed raw vegetables such as carrots,
celery, endive, fennel, and red and green peppers
cut into long narrow strips; cauliflower and
broccoli florets; tender young green beans and
asparagus tips

ANCHOVY DIP

16	*anchovy fillets with a little of their oil*
10	*capers, well drained*
1–1½	*teaspoons Dijon mustard*
1	*teaspoon freshly ground pepper*
4	*tablespoons wine vinegar*
1	*tablespoon finely chopped parsley*
1	*cup olive oil*

Blend all the anchovy-dip ingredients in a food processor until well blended. Or mash the anchovies and capers in a wooden bowl or a mortar, and stir in the mustard, pepper, vinegar, and parsley. Mix well. Gradually add the oil, beating constantly, until the sauce has the consistency of heavy cream.

Provide each guest with a small bowl of sauce and pass the platter of fresh vegetables.

SARDINES IN LEMON SHELLS

❧

6 SERVINGS

6	*large lemons*
2	*cans sardines*
1	*hard-boiled egg, finely chopped*

2–3 *tablespoons mayonnaise or more to taste*
   A 1-inch ribbon of anchovy paste (or 1–2 anchovies,
      finely chopped)
   A splash of vodka
   Salt and freshly ground pepper
2 *tablespoons finely chopped fresh chives or scallions*
2 *tablespoons finely chopped fresh parsley*

Cut a third off the top of each lemon. Squeeze and strain the juice from the lemon tops and reserve it. With a curved grapefruit knife, cut out most of the pulp from the lemon "shells" and reserve. Drain off most of the oil from the sardine cans and put the sardines with a bit of their oil into a mixing bowl. Mash them with the egg. Stir the mayonnaise and anchovy paste together and add to the sardine-egg mixture. Stir in the vodka. Season to taste, using little or no salt and a generous amount of pepper. Add the reserved lemon juice and a little of the reserved pulp to taste. Stir in the chives.

Cut a thin slice from the bottom of each lemon so that it will stand upright. Heap the sardine mixture into the lemon shells and garnish with the chopped parsley.

Refrigerate until ready to serve. Serve with thin buttered slices of dark bread.

For a simpler preparation, eliminate the lemon shells and spread the sardine mixture on small squares of dark bread.

Perfect with drinks.

SFORMATO OF ARTICHOKES AND CARROTS

✺

Sformato is an old-fashioned Italian vegetable dish rarely found in restaurants and virtually unknown here. It provides the comfort of a pudding without the anxiety of a soufflé. The word *sformato* means unmolded. As you remove it from its mold, do not be alarmed when it collapses with a soft Italian sigh, rather like the ending of a Mozart aria. It is meant to collapse.

Sformati can be made from a variety of vegetables, singly or combined. Usually eaten separately as a first course and sometimes garnished with chicken livers, they can also be served with roast meat.

6 SERVINGS

  6 *artichoke bottoms, freshly boiled or 1 7¾-ounce can*
        artichoke bottoms (available in specialty shops)
  1 *cup sliced carrots*
  1 *tablespoon butter*
1½ *tablespoons flour*
  1 *cup light cream*
  3 *eggs, separated*
  2 *tablespoons freshly grated Parmesan cheese*
  1 *teaspoon salt*
 ½ *teaspoon freshly ground pepper*

Preheat the oven to 375°.

If you use canned artichoke bottoms, rinse them in cold water. Drain and dry them on paper towels. Boil the carrots until tender. Drain and dry. Purée the artichokes and carrots together in a food processor or pass them through a food mill.

Heat the butter in a small heavy saucepan over medium heat until it foams. Add the flour and cook, stirring for 1 minute. Remove from the heat. Heat the cream just to the boiling point and add it to the butter-flour mixture. Beat with a wire whisk to blend thoroughly. Return the saucepan to the heat and bring to a boil, stirring constantly. Boil for 1 minute, stirring, then remove from the heat and let it cool for a minute or two. Whisk in the egg yolks, cheese, salt, and pepper until well combined.

Stir the sauce into the puréed vegetables and mix well. Beat the egg whites until stiff and fold them in carefully. Butter and lightly flour a soufflé or charlotte mold, shaking out the excess flour. Pour in the mixture. Place the mold in a pan of hot water and bake for about 40 minutes, or until a knife inserted into the *sformato* comes out clean. Remove the mold from the oven and let it rest for a minute. Unmold carefully onto a warm round platter. Also excellent as a main course for lunch, with or without tomato sauce.

TOMATO SAUCE

  2 *pounds very ripe tomatoes*
 ½ *medium-size onion, finely sliced*
  5 *basil leaves, minced, or 2 teaspoons dried*
  1 *bay leaf*
  1 *rounded teaspoon tomato paste*

½   *cup dry white wine or vermouth*
    Salt and freshly ground pepper to taste
    A pinch of sugar or more to taste

With a sharp knife, cut a shallow cross on the round end of each tomato. Plunge the tomatoes into a pot of boiling water for 30 seconds. Remove with a slotted spoon. Peel them with a sharp knife as soon as they are cool enough to handle. Cut them in half crosswise and squeeze out the seeds. Chop the tomatoes coarsely and place them in a heavy-bottomed saucepan over high heat. Cook, stirring often, for 5 minutes. (No butter is needed.)

Add all the remaining ingredients. Cook, stirring often, for about 15 minutes, or until the mixture begins to thicken. Reduce the heat to low and continue to cook, stirring occasionally, until the sauce is quite thick. Discard the bay leaf. Taste and correct the seasoning.

SFORMATO OF BROCCOLI

⌒

8 SERVINGS

1   *large bunch broccoli (enough to make 2 cups purée)*
    Salt, freshly ground pepper, and nutmeg to taste
2   *tablespoons butter*
2   *large shallots, very finely chopped*
1½ *tablespoons flour*
1   *cup milk*
6   *egg yolks*
8   *egg whites*
1¼ *cups freshly grated imported Parmesan cheese*

Wash the broccoli, trim and discard the tough ends, and separate into florets. Cook in boiling salted water for 15 minutes, or just until tender. Drain and purée in a food mill or food processor. Season with salt, pepper, and nutmeg. Measure 2 cups of purée and put it in a large bowl to cool.

Preheat the oven to 375°.

Melt the butter in a small heavy saucepan over medium heat and sauté the shallots in it for 2 to 3 minutes. Stir constantly, taking care not to let them brown. Add the flour and cook, stirring constantly, for exactly 1 minute. Remove from the heat. In another pan, heat the milk. Add the warm milk to the flour-butter mixture, return to the heat and cook, stirring, till it is completely smooth. Season with ½ teaspoon each of salt and pepper. Stir into the broccoli purée along with the egg yolks and ¼ cup of the grated cheese. Taste and correct the seasoning. Beat the egg whites until stiff and fold them in carefully.

Butter a 2-quart ring mold or soufflé dish and coat it lightly with flour, inverting and tapping it to shake out any excess flour. Spoon the mixture into the mold. Set the mold in a pan of hot water and bake for 30 to 40 minutes, or until a knife inserted into the *sformato* comes out clean. Let the *sformato* sit for a minute, then run a knife around the edges and unmold it onto a warm, round serving platter. Serve with melted butter and the remaining cheese as a first course or as an accompaniment to fried chicken or baked ham.

VARIATIONS: Substitute for the broccoli 2 cups of spinach purée to which you have added a bit of crumbled crisply fried bacon and a good squeeze of lemon juice. Bake in a soufflé dish. Unmold and serve with poached eggs.

Or make a *sformato* of peas using 2 cups of puréed cooked peas to which you have added a slice of finely chopped ham or prosciutto. Excellent with chicken livers sautéed in butter and sprinkled with finely chopped fresh chives.

SHRIMP AND
CELERY VINAIGRETTE

❦

6–8 SERVINGS AS PART OF AN ASSORTED ANTIPASTO

1   *pound shrimp*
¾   *cup julienned celery (use the tenderest stalks)*
¼   *cup finely chopped parsley*

VINAIGRETTE SAUCE

6   *tablespoons olive oil*
2   *tablespoons lemon juice or wine vinegar*
    Salt and freshly ground pepper to taste
1   *2-inch ribbon of anchovy paste or*
        1 teaspoon Dijon mustard
1   *teaspoon fennel seeds, ground to a powder*

Boil the shrimp for 2 to 3 minutes. Cool, drain, peel, and devein them. Do not refrigerate. Put them in a bowl with the julienned celery and parsley.

Beat together with a fork all the ingredients for the vinaigrette sauce, rubbing the anchovy paste against the sides of the bowl with the back of the fork to dissolve it. Pour the sauce over the shrimp. Marinate for 20 to 30 minutes before serving.

VARIATION: Substitute fennel for the celery.

TURKEY GUACAMOLE

Since the Aztecs not only domesticated the wild turkey but cultivated the avocado, this is a natural combination.

6–8 SERVINGS

2   *large, very ripe avocados*
1   *small onion, finely chopped*
1   *ripe tomato, peeled, seeded, and finely chopped*
    Optional: 1 clove garlic, finely chopped; crisp bits of
        bacon; fresh coriander or basil, finely chopped
3   *tablespoons lime juice*
1   *tablespoon olive oil*
    Salt and chili powder to taste
    Leftover white meat of roast turkey, thinly sliced

Peel the avocados and reserve one of the pits. Mash the avocados and combine them with the rest of the ingredients except the turkey. (Or purée the ingredients in a food processor.) Bury the avocado pit in the mixture to prevent discoloration and refrigerate until ready to use. Spread the guacamole on the turkey slices and serve as a first course.

VARIATION: Use cold poached salmon instead of turkey.

FRESH TOMATO ASPIC

6–8 SERVINGS

4   *pounds very ripe tomatoes, peeled, seeded, and*
    coarsely chopped (enough to make 4 cups of pulp)
5   *basil leaves or 1½ teaspoons dried basil*
1   *teaspoon celery salt*
½   *teaspoon freshly ground pepper*
2–3 *drops Tabasco sauce*
2–3 *drops Worcestershire sauce*
    Juice of 1 lemon
2   *tablespoons (2 envelopes) unflavored gelatin,*
    dissolved in ½ cup cold water

Purée in a blender or food processor all the ingredients except the lemon juice and gelatin. Put 1½ cups of this mixture into a large bowl. Stir in the lemon juice and gelatin. Bring the remaining purée to a boil and simmer over low heat for 3 minutes. Add it to the cold purée and stir well. Cool to room temperature, stirring occasionally. Rinse a glass bowl or decorative mold with cold water, leave it wet, and pour in the tomato purée. Chill in the refrigerator for a few hours, or until it is set. Run a knife around the edges of the mold; set the mold in hot water for a few seconds, dry it, invert onto a platter and serve.

VARIATION I: Garnish with cooked shrimp, cucumber slices, and chopped basil.

VARIATION II: Use a ring mold, and when serving, fill the center with celery rémoulade, made by dressing julienned celery root—blanched for 1 minute if you like—with a mustardy mayonnaise thinned with a little heavy cream.

GRATIN OF TOMATOES
AND ZUCCHINI

$\backsim$

A fine first course for a summer meal.

4–6 SERVINGS

4 *tablespoons olive oil*
1 *clove garlic, peeled*
12 *ripe plum tomatoes, halved horizontally*
2 *scallions, chopped*
  Salt, pepper, and sugar to taste
2 *medium-size zucchini, thinly sliced*
2 *tablespoons fresh basil, finely chopped*
1 *teaspoon wine vinegar*
2 *tablespoons fresh bread crumbs (easily made in a*
  blender or food processor)
1–2 *tablespoons sweet butter*

Preheat the oven to 375°.

Heat half the oil with the garlic in a heavy frying pan. Remove the garlic before it turns brown and discard it. Add the tomatoes, cut side down, and the scallions. Season to taste with salt, pepper and a bit of sugar. Sauté for 5 minutes over medium heat.

In another heavy pan, heat the remaining oil and add the zucchini slices and the basil. Season with salt and pepper and cook over fairly high heat, stirring frequently for 2 to 3 minutes.

In a gratin dish large enough to hold all the vegetables, arrange first a layer of half the tomato-scallion mixture with its oil, then half the zucchini-basil mixture with its oil. Repeat the process. Sprinkle the vinegar and the bread crumbs over all and dot with butter.

Bake for 10 to 15 minutes, or until the zucchini are tender but still crisp and the crumbs are lightly browned. Baste with the oil from time to time. Before serving, cool to room temperature. If there is too much liquid, remove it with a bulb baster.

STUFFED ZUCCHINI

❧

4–8 SERVINGS, AS PART OF AN ASSORTED ANTIPASTO

4   *fairly large zucchini, washed carefully*
    About 4 tablespoons butter
    Salt and pepper to taste
1   *cup Meat Sauce, Bolognese Style (see below)*
¼   *cup freshly grated Parmesan cheese*
1   *cup beef or chicken broth*

Preheat the oven to 350°.

Slice the zucchini in half lengthwise. Parboil for 1 minute. Scoop out the centers with a curved grapefruit knife, leaving a shell about ⅛ inch thick. Be careful not to pierce the skin. Chop the pulp and reserve. Drain the shells upside down on paper towels.

Butter the sides and bottom of a large baking dish. Arrange the zucchini close together. Season them very lightly with salt and pepper. Fill the cavities with the meat sauce mixed with ½ cup of the reserved chopped zucchini. Sprinkle with Parmesan cheese and dot with butter. Pour ¼ inch of broth into the baking dish, adding more as it cooks away.

Bake for about 30 minutes, or just until the zucchini is cooked but still firm enough to hold its shape. Serve hot or at room temperature.

MEAT SAUCE, BOLOGNESE STYLE
(Salsa alla Bolognese)

❧

This traditional sauce is one of the best known of all spaghetti sauces. In Bologna a little heavy cream is often stirred into it before serving. It is always accompanied by grated cheese. In many parts of Italy it is also used (always with grated cheese) in or over baked vegetables, such as zucchini, squash, green peppers, onions, and beets, all of which are served warm or at room temperature as part of an antipasto.

ABOUT 2 CUPS

4 tablespoons butter
2 tablespoons olive oil
1 cup chopped onion
4 slices prosciutto, finely diced, or 2 slices blanched
    lean bacon
1 carrot, diced
1 stalk celery, diced
1 bay leaf
1 pound ground beef (chuck or round steak)
1 large clove garlic, crushed in a garlic press
1 cup red wine
3 tablespoons chopped fresh Italian (flat-leaf) parsley
3 tablespoons chopped fresh basil or 2 teaspoons dried
1 teaspoon salt
1 teaspoon freshly ground pepper
3 cups very ripe tomatoes, peeled, seeded, and coarsely
    chopped, or 3 cups imported Italian canned
    tomatoes, chopped
2 tablespoons tomato paste
1 cup beef broth
Optional: ½ cup heavy cream

Melt the butter and oil in a large heavy pan. Add the onions, prosciutto
or bacon, carrot, celery, and bay leaf. Cook over low heat, stirring
often, until the onions are translucent. Push everything to one side,
add the chopped beef to the exposed part of the pan, and cook, breaking the meat up, just until it loses its color. Add all the remaining
ingredients except the beef broth and cook, stirring occasionally, for
1 hour or more. Add a little of the beef broth from time to time so that
the sauce does not dry out. Taste and correct the seasoning.

ZUCCHINI AND ANCHOVIES

∾

In Italy this dish is often served surprisingly cold.

4–6 SERVINGS

6 *small zucchini (4 to 5 inches long)*
1¾ *cup chicken broth*

VINAIGRETTE SAUCE

5 *tablespoons olive oil plus 1 tablespoon oil from the*
  anchovy can
2 *tablespoons wine vinegar*
  Salt and freshly ground pepper to taste
12 *flat anchovies*
2 *tablespoons minced parsley*
1 *hard-boiled egg, finely chopped*

Wash the zucchini and cut them in half lengthwise. Put them into boiling chicken broth. Lower the heat and simmer for 5 minutes, or until they are tender but still firm. Drain and reserve the broth for another use.

Mix the ingredients for the vinaigrette. While the zucchini are still warm, marinate them in the vinaigrette for 1 hour. Arrange them like the spokes of a wheel on a round platter. Refrigerate. Lay an anchovy fillet on each, sprinkle with the parsley and chopped egg, and serve.

SOUP

*R*ecipes are like blueprints: bare outlines for the dishes we construct. While the baker of cakes and pastries must follow a plan as precisely as a bridge-builder or face collapse and disaster, soup-makers can be as playfully baroque as they please. Would you like to add celery or coriander and a bit of chopped salami to your lentil soup? Do, and the results will be fine. Do you have fresh mint in the garden? Put it in your tomato soup and it will add luster. Or float some nasturtium petals on the surface for an edible and visual surprise.

One day when we were making sorrel soup a young neighbor came by and offered us some fish he had caught. "Why not a fish and sorrel soup?" we wondered. In went some carrots, then the fish and sorrel. The inspiration was sound, the soup a marvel. A few weeks later we found ourselves in Brittany, where we discovered that the dish we thought we had invented was a soup Breton fishermen have been making for years. Proof, if any was needed, that there is no new sorrel soup under the sun.

The soup pot is a natural recipient for leftovers. Last night's unfinished salad of greens or tomatoes, fennel or grated carrots, can be chopped and added to the pot. The oil and vinegar in the salad will enhance the flavor and add a Mediterranean flourish to a vegetable soup. A leftover ham bone will do wonders for a bean soup. And how satisfying it is to add slivers of leftover vegetables, chicken, shrimp, or a bit of rice or pasta to a clear consommé.

Some cookbooks take for granted that our houses are run like restaurants, that there are always chicken, beef, and fish stocks in the freezer and a crockful of *glace de viande* in the refrigerator. Of course any dish benefits from these pure ingredients, and they are well worth the effort. But many of us do not have the time or the patience for such kitchen ideals. Good canned chicken or beef broth make an adequate substitute for homemade stock, but be wary of adding more salt. Certainly canned broths do nicely in highly seasoned soups even if they do not always stand on their own. Leaving them a few hours in the refrigerator makes it easy to remove the fat. We have made excellent fish soups with bottled clam broth and must confess that we have fooled some rather finicky gourmets with such ready-to-use ingredients.

One of our favorite menus for busy or lazy days requires no cooking or heating between courses. It begins with soup as the only hot course, followed by cold steak, veal, ham, or meat loaf—that *pâté américain*—a salad and a perfectly baked apple. The soup can be made ahead of time and reheated. The meats can be leftovers neatly sliced, decoratively arranged, and surrounded by a choice of condiments, mustards, chutneys, and *cornichons*. Or they can be cooked in the morning and served at room temperature. In either case they will be sitting on the sideboard, blessedly ready to be served.

FISH STOCK
(Court-Bouillon)

⌒〵

ABOUT 2 QUARTS

2–3   *pounds fresh fish heads, bones, and trimmings from
any white-fleshed fish*

2   *stalks celery, cut up*
1   *medium-size onion, peeled and quartered*
1   *quart dry white wine*
6   *peppercorns*
    A few sprigs of parsley
1   *bay leaf*
2   *teaspoons salt*

Combine all the ingredients with 1 quart water in a large pot. Bring to a boil. Lower the heat and simmer for 20 minutes. Strain through a moistened cheesecloth-lined sieve. If not used immediately, the stock can be stored in the refrigerator or freezer, then defrosted and used as needed.

FISH FUMET: Boil fish stock, uncovered, over medium heat until reduced to a third of its original volume.

BEEF BROTH
(Beef Stock)

෴

ABOUT 2 QUARTS

2   *pounds lean beef, top or bottom round*
2   *pounds beef bones, including 1 marrowbone cut into*
        2-inch pieces and tied in cheesecloth
1   *tablespoon salt*
2   *carrots*
½   *small white turnip*
1   *parsnip*
2   *leeks*
1   *stalk celery*
1   *medium-size onion stuck with 1–2 cloves*
1   *clove garlic*
1   *sprig thyme or 1 teaspoon dried*
6   *peppercorns*
1   *bay leaf*

Put the beef and the bones in a large pot. Add 3½ quarts of cold water. Bring to a boil. Skim the surface carefully. Add the salt, vegetables, garlic, thyme, peppercorns, and bay leaf, and reduce the heat to a very low simmer. (The bubbling should hardly be visible.) Simmer for about four hours. Skim off the surface fat. Strain the broth through a sieve lined with four layers of moistened cheesecloth. When the broth has cooled, refrigerate it for 4 hours. Skim off the fat once again before using. The broth can be stored in the freezer.

CHICKEN BROTH
(Chicken Stock)

❧

ABOUT 2 QUARTS

4   *pounds chicken parts (necks, backs, legs, and thighs)*
1   *pound gizzards*
1   *large onion, peeled and stuck with 6 cloves*
6   *peppercorns*
2   *leeks, thoroughly cleaned and coarsely chopped*
2   *carrots, peeled and cut in half*
2   *stalks celery, cut in half*
1   *teaspoon salt*

Wipe the chicken parts with a damp cloth. Wash and trim the gizzards. Put all the ingredients in a 6-quart pot and add 3½ quarts cold water. Bring to a boil over moderately high heat. Skim off the scum that forms on the surface. Cover, reduce the heat, and simmer for 2 hours. Never allow it to boil.

Strain the soup through a sieve lined with four thicknesses of dampened cheesecloth. Allow the soup to cool, then refrigerate it overnight. Remove all the fat that has congealed on the surface with a spatula or spoon. Bring to a boil and simmer, uncovered, for 30 minutes.

You now have a chicken broth, or stock, that is delicious but somewhat murky. It can be clarified to make a clear consommé. Clarified or not, it can be used for many purposes: cooked again with the addition of various vegetables and herbs, used as a base for cream soups, to poach a chicken in, or to be served as it is.

CHICKEN CONSOMMÉ
(Clarified Chicken Broth)

⌒

You will need cold Chicken Broth (see page 48), 1 egg white and 1 egg shell for each quart of broth.

Skim the cold broth of all surface fat and put it in a heavy pot. Beat the egg whites lightly with a whisk and crush the egg shells. Add the egg whites and shells to the pot and whisk constantly while you bring the broth to a boil. Transfer the pot to a cold burner, then simmer the broth over the lowest heat for 15 minutes, without stirring.

Line a large sieve with four thicknesses of dampened cheesecloth and place it over a large bowl. Agitating the broth as little as possible, pour it slowly and carefully through the sieve. One quart makes 4 servings.

BLACK BEAN SOUP

⌒

6 SERVINGS

1½   *cups black beans, soaked overnight (or as indicated on the package)*
2   *onions, coarsely chopped*
2   *tablespoons olive oil or bacon drippings or salt-pork fat*
1   *teaspoon tomato paste*
1   *tablespoon chopped parsley*
1   *bay leaf*
1   *teaspoon dried thyme*
1   *teaspoon dried sage*
¼   *cup Madeira or sherry*
   Salt to taste
   A dash of cayenne pepper
6   *slices lemon*

Drain the beans and put them in a pot with 6 cups of cold water. Bring to a boil, reduce the heat, and simmer. Sauté the onions in the oil over low heat until they are translucent but not browned. Add them to the beans along with the tomato paste, parsley, bay leaf, thyme, and sage. Cook, covered, for 3 hours or longer, until the beans are soft. Add more water as needed if the soup becomes too thick. Add the Madeira and simmer for 5 minutes. Discard the bay leaf. Add salt and cayenne pepper. Purée in a blender or food processor. Return to the heat for a minute or two and serve garnished with lemon slices.

EUGENIA DOLL'S BORSHCH

Mrs. Henri Doll, wife of the distinguished French inventor, or Genia Delarova, as she is known in the world of the dance, is one of New York's most delightful hostesses. From the time of her first marriage to Leonide Massine when she was one of the leading dancers of the Ballets Russes de Monte Carlo, she has been celebrated for her after-ballet parties. Makarova, Nureyev, Baryshnikov, and Rostropovich are among the many friends who find her house a haven of superb Russian food and hospitality.

Borshch should be prepared a day in advance or, at the latest, in the morning of the day you plan to serve it. This hearty soup can be served as an entrée or a main course.

You will need an 8- to 10-quart soup pot.

8–10 SERVINGS

12   medium-large beets, 6 whole and unpeeled and
     6 peeled and sliced
1   ham bone with some meat on it or ¼ pound smoked
     ham butt
2–3   beef marrow bones, each one tightly wrapped in
     cheesecloth and tied with string
2   pounds brisket of beef
2   onions, peeled and stuck with cloves
4   carrots, peeled
1   white turnip, peeled

2 *stalks celery*
½ *cup parsley*
6 *peppercorns*
3 *bay leaves*
   Salt to taste
2 *tart apples, washed but not peeled*
2 *large tomatoes*
1–1½ *heads cabbage, cored and shredded*
1 *tablespoon vinegar*
1 *tablespoon lemon juice*
1 *tablespoon sugar*
¾ *cup chopped fresh dill*
1 *pint sour cream*
   Optional: 8–10 peeled, boiled potatoes; ½ cup chopped
      fresh parsley or chives

Bake the unpeeled whole beets in a 375° oven for 1 to 1½ hours, or until they are tender. Set them aside in a cool place. In a large soup pot, put the ham bone, the beef marrow bones, the brisket of beef, the sliced beets, onions, carrots, turnip, celery, parsley, peppercorns, bay leaves, and a little salt. Add 2½ to 3 quarts of water or a little more if needed to cover all the ingredients. Bring to a boil, then lower the heat and simmer, covered, for 2 hours or longer, until the brisket is very tender.

During the cooking, carefully set the apples and tomatoes on top of the soup. Let them steam until they are tender, then remove them with a slotted spoon. Purée them together in a food mill and set aside in a cool place.

When the meat is tender, stop the cooking. Discard all the vegetables. Set the bones and meat aside in a cool place. Strain the soup through a sieve lined with several thicknesses of dampened cheesecloth into a large bowl. Refrigerate overnight or for at least 4 hours. Carefully remove all the fat that has accumulated. Return the soup to the large pot. Cut the ham off the bone and into small pieces. Carefully remove the marrow from the beef bones and cut it into thin slices. Discard the bones.

If you would like to serve the soup first, followed by the brisket as a second course, return the brisket to the soup pot in one piece. Otherwise, cut it into ½-inch slices on the bias—that is, against the grain of the meat—and then into ½-inch cubes. Add them to the pot along with the pieces of ham or pork and the sliced marrow.

Add the puréed tomatoes and apples, the shredded cabbage, vinegar, lemon juice, and sugar and cook for 10 minutes. Meanwhile peel the reserved baked beets and cut them into julienne strips. Add them to the borshch. Bring the soup back to the boil and cook until the cabbage and beets are tender. Add the chopped dill and serve with sour cream passed separately. If this substantial soup is to be the main course of a meal, you may put a hot boiled potato sliced in half on each soup plate before adding the borshch.

If you prefer to serve the beef as a second course, slice it thinly against the grain and serve it with hot boiled potatoes rolled in chopped parsley or chives. Dijon mustard as well as dill pickles or *cornichons* should be served with the meat.

BOUILLABAISSE OF PEAS

Everyone knows *bouillabaisse*, that glory of France which is at its authentic best in Marseilles. Less well known but equally authentic are the garden cousins of that noble fish soup, *bouillabaisse* of spinach or peas. The two vegetables are readily available in America, whereas the *rascasses* and other Mediterranean fish are not. Modest Provençal soups, they are every bit as good as and immeasurably easier to make than the *bouillabaisse* of fish and seafood.

4–6 SERVINGS

1	onion, finely chopped
¼	cup olive oil
1	tablespoon butter
5–6	small, waxy new potatoes, peeled and thinly sliced
1	quart Chicken Broth (see page 48)
2–3	pinches saffron
2	cloves garlic, minced
3	cups shelled peas
	Bouquet garni (made by tying together a bay leaf and a few sprigs of thyme and parsley)
	Croutons: 4–6 slices French bread lightly fried in butter on both sides

In a large heavy-bottomed pot, sauté the onion in the oil and butter until translucent but not browned.

Add the potatoes and cook them for 5 minutes. Heat the chicken broth and steep the saffron in it for 10 minutes. Add the broth to the onions and potatoes, then add all the remaining ingredients except the croutons. Cook for 10 or 15 minutes, or until the potatoes and peas are tender. Discard the bouquet garni. Place a crouton in each soup dish, pour the soup over it and serve.

A SUGGESTED MENU

(see Index for recipes)

BOUILLABAISSE OF PEAS

RED PEPPER QUICHE

ENDIVE SALAD WITH ALMOND DRESSING

APPLE CRISP

wine: PINOT GRIGIO

BOUILLABAISSE OF SPINACH

◡

A rustic soup from Provence.

4–6 SERVINGS

2 *pounds fresh spinach*
1 *quart Chicken Broth (see page 48)*
3 *pinches saffron*
1 *medium-size onion, chopped*
1 *fennel bulb, finely chopped (reserve a few sprigs of the feathery green tops)*
¼ *cup olive oil*
3–4 *medium-size potatoes, thinly sliced*
2 *cloves garlic, finely chopped*
   Salt and freshly ground pepper to taste
   Croutons: 4–6 slices French bread cut about ¾ inch thick, and lightly fried in butter or olive oil on both sides
   Garnish: 4–6 eggs, poached or hard-boiled and chopped; chopped fennel sprigs

Carefully wash and trim the spinach, discarding any bruised leaves. Shred it coarsely.

Bring the chicken broth to a boil. Add the saffron. Turn off the heat, cover, and let the saffron steep in the hot broth for 10 minutes.

In a large heavy-bottomed pot, sauté the chopped onion and fennel in the oil over low heat, stirring often until they are limp but not browned. Add the spinach, and cook, stirring, until it wilts. Add the chicken broth, potatoes, garlic, salt, and pepper. Bring to a boil, then lower the heat. Cover and cook just until the potatoes are tender, then lower the heat to a simmer.

To serve, place a fried crouton at the bottom of each soup bowl, carefully place a poached egg on it, then ladle the soup over it. Sprinkle with some chopped fennel sprigs. For a lighter soup, garnish with chopped hard-boiled eggs.

COLD APPLE–ONION SOUP

ᑯᑌ

4 SERVINGS

1   *small onion, peeled and quartered*
1   *medium-size tart apple, peeled and quartered*
4   *cups Chicken Broth (see page 48)*
    Freshly ground white pepper, salt, and curry powder
       to taste
4   *tablespoons sour cream*
1   *tart apple for garnish*

Place the onion and the apple in a food processor and blend until very smooth. Put this purée into a pot. Add the chicken broth and the seasonings and simmer 10 to 15 minutes, or until the onion and apple are cooked. Let cool for 10 minutes. Return to the processor, add the sour cream, and blend until well combined. Chill in the refrigerator for several hours. Garnish with thin slices of unpeeled apple arranged like the spokes of a wheel.

COLD CUCUMBER–YOGURT SOUP

 ❧

2–4 SERVINGS

½   cup currants or raisins
⅓   cup coarsely broken walnut meats
1   cup yogurt
1   cup light cream
1   hard-boiled egg, finely chopped
1   clove garlic, minced
¼   cup scallions, finely chopped
1   cucumber, peeled and diced
    Salt and freshly ground pepper to taste
    Garnish: 3 tablespoons fresh dill, finely chopped,
        or 1 tablespoon dried

Soak the currants or raisins in water for a few minutes till they are plump. Drain and put them in a bowl with the walnuts. Stir in the yogurt, cream, egg, garlic, scallions, and cucumber. Add 1 cup of cold water, season, and stir. Refrigerate for several hours. Serve garnished with dill.

VARIATION: For a lighter soup use two cups of yogurt and omit the cream.

COLD SPINACH SOUP

 ❧

4–6 SERVINGS

1   small onion, coarsely chopped
1   pound spinach or 1 package frozen chopped spinach
1½   tablespoons sugar
3   lumps of sour salt (citric acid) or
        1 teaspoon vinegar
½   teaspoon salt

½   teaspoon freshly ground pepper
3   tablespoons lemon juice
2   eggs
½   cup sour cream
2   tablespoons chopped fresh dill
    Garnish: 2 eggs, hard-boiled and chopped; half a
        cucumber, peeled and diced; 6 radishes, sliced;
        and 3 scallions, sliced

Bring 4 cups of water to a boil in an enamel-lined pot. Add the onion, and cook over medium heat for 10 minutes. Add the spinach and cook 4 to 5 minutes. Add the sugar, sour salt, and pepper and let cool in the pot until tepid. In a small bowl, lightly beat together the lemon juice and the eggs. Spoon a little of the tepid spinach broth into the egg-lemon mixture, stirring constantly so that the eggs do not curdle. Repeat this process, adding more broth to the egg mixture until the small bowl is full. Now pour it all back into the pot, stirring constantly. Pour into a serving bowl and cool. Add the sour cream, mashing it against the sides of the bowl to remove the lumps. Refrigerate for 2 to 3 hours before serving.

When ready to serve, correct the seasoning, adding more lemon juice, salt, pepper, or sugar as needed. Stir in the dill. Top with the garnishes or pass them separately.

CREAM OF SPLIT PEA SOUP
(Potage aux Pois Cassés)

ᖇ

8–10 SERVINGS

1   pound split peas
1   quart Chicken Broth (see page 48)
¼   pound salt pork, cut into 12 pieces, or a ham bone
        with some ham on it
2   medium-size onions, chopped
3   leeks, white part with a bit of the green, carefully
        washed and coarsely chopped
3   medium-size potatoes, peeled and sliced
    Salt and freshly ground pepper to taste

2 cups heavy cream
2 tablespoons butter

Soak the split peas in cold water to cover for 1 hour. Drain and put them in a soup pot with 1 quart of water, the chicken broth, salt pork, onions, leeks, and potatoes. Season lightly with salt and pepper. Bring to a boil, lower the heat, and simmer gently, covered, for 1½ to 2 hours, or until the peas are well cooked.

Remove the pieces of pork or the ham bone, then pass the soup through a *chinois*, the French cone-shaped strainer. Or purée the soup in several batches in a blender or processor fitted with the knife blade. Discard the salt pork. If using a ham bone, cut the ham into small pieces and add them to the soup after it is puréed.

Return the soup to the pot, bring to a boil, stir in the cream, and simmer for 3 to 5 minutes. Taste and correct the seasoning. Stir in the butter, and serve very hot.

GENIA'S SIMPLE FISH SOUP

❧

8 SERVINGS

3 tablespoons vegetable oil
2 onions, peeled and chopped
6 carrots, peeled and cut into 1-inch pieces
6 stalks celery, cut into 1-inch pieces
   Salt and freshly ground pepper to taste
1 clove garlic, peeled and put through a press
8 small potatoes, peeled and cut in half
3 ripe tomatoes, peeled, seeded, and coarsely chopped,
      or 1 cup canned Italian plum tomatoes
1½ quarts Fish Stock (see page 46) or clam broth
2 cups dry white wine
2 bay leaves
1 teaspoon fennel seed
1 tablespoon saffron
3 pounds halibut, monkfish, or striped bass fillets,
      skinned and cut into 1½-inch pieces
½ cup chopped fresh parsley

In a large heavy pot with a tight-fitting lid, heat the oil with the onions, carrots, and celery. Season with salt and pepper. Cook over low heat, stirring occasionally, until the onions are limp but not browned. Add the garlic, potatoes, tomatoes, fish stock, wine, bay leaves, fennel seed, and saffron. Simmer, covered, for 20 to 30 minutes, or until the potatoes and carrots are tender. Add the fish. Press it down until it is submerged. Cover the pot and turn off the flame. Let the fish soup rest for 10 minutes. No further cooking is necessary. Sprinkle with parsley and serve.

FISH WATERZOOIE
(A Flemish Fish Soup)

Waterzooie (which means "water on the boil") is the bouillabaisse of Belgium. Not often found on restaurant menus, it is nonetheless one of that country's most famous dishes.

6–8 SERVINGS

COURT BOUILLON

3	pounds heads (with gills removed), tails, and bones from any white-fleshed fish
1	cup sliced onions
1	cup chopped celery
1	bay leaf
2–3	sprigs parsley
6–8	peppercorns, crushed
2	cups dry white wine
2½	quarts water

4	tablespoons butter
1½	cups finely chopped leeks
1½	cups finely chopped celery
8	small potatoes, peeled and halved
3	pounds assorted white-fleshed fish (such as freshwater pike, perch, and whitefish or saltwater monkfish, tilefish and sea bass, cleaned, trimmed and cut into ½-inch-thick slices

1   pound eel, skinned and cut into 2-inch lengths
    Bouquet garni (made by tying together in a piece of
       cheesecloth a peeled clove of garlic, a few sage
       leaves, a few sprigs of parsley, and, if available,
       2 parsley roots, coarsely chopped)
1   quart mussels, soaked and scraped clean with beards
       removed
¾   cup heavy cream
    Juice of 1 lemon
4   egg yolks
    Salt
    Freshly ground pepper

Bring all the court bouillon ingredients to a boil in a large pot. Lower
the heat and simmer for 20 minutes. Strain over a large bowl, pressing
down hard with the back of a spoon to extract the flavor from the
fish and vegetables before discarding them. Set the court bouillon
aside.

Melt the butter in a large casserole and sauté the leeks and celery
in it, stirring often, until the vegetables are soft but not browned.
Meanwhile boil the potatoes just until they are tender. Drain and keep
them warm in a low oven. Lay all the fish and the eel on the vegetables and add the bouquet garni. Reserve 1½ cups of the court bouillon.
Pour the remaining court bouillon into the casserole. Bring to a boil,
lower the heat immediately and simmer for about 8 minutes, or until
the fish flakes easily when tested with a fork. With a slotted spoon
remove the fish and the eel to a warm platter. Discard the leeks and
celery. Moisten the fish and eel with a little court bouillon, cover with
foil, and keep warm in a low oven.

In the meantime, steam the mussels in the reserved 1½ cups of court
bouillon until they open. Remove them from their shells and add them
to the fish platter. Strain the mussel liquid through a cheesecloth-lined
sieve back into the casserole.

Boil the liquid in the casserole over high heat till it is reduced by
a third. Remove it from the heat.

Whisk the cream, lemon juice, and egg yolks together. Whisking
steadily, gradually pour in 1 cup of the hot fish broth. Return the
cream mixture to the casserole, whisking constantly. Put the casserole
over low heat and cook, stirring often, until the broth has thickened.
Do not allow it to boil, or it will curdle. Season to taste with salt and
pepper. Pour a little of it over the fish on the platter. Serve at once

in soup dishes, adding a boiled potato and some of each kind of fish to every portion. Sometimes the soup is served first, followed by the fish and potatoes moistened with a little of the soup.

VARIATION: 2 teaspoons of curry powder (or more to taste) added to the soup after it has thickened makes a dish that is ethnically incorrect but surprisingly delicious.

A SUGGESTED MENU

(see Index for recipes)

FISH WATERZOOIE

ENDIVE SALAD WITH LEMON DRESSING

CHOCOLATE MOUSSE CAKE, MICHEL GUÉRARD

wine: CHABLIS

CHICKEN WATERZOOIE

One of Belgium's great culinary traditions: a Flemish chicken dish halfway between a soup and a stew.

8 SERVINGS

1	*6–8 pound capon, cut into 8 pieces*
	Salt and freshly ground pepper to taste
4	*tablespoons butter*
4	*leeks, carefully cleaned and cut into ½-inch slices*
4	*carrots, sliced*
4	*stalks celery, sliced*
1	*onion, sliced*
4	*sprigs parsley*
	Seasonings: ½ teaspoon thyme, ½ teaspoon nutmeg,
	3 cloves
4–5	*cups Chicken Broth (see page 48)*
4	*egg yolks, beaten with ¼ cup heavy cream and*
	2 tablespoons lemon juice

3 *tablespoons chopped parsley*
  Optional and not traditional: 1–2 cloves garlic,
      passed through a garlic press
  Garnish: 2 lemons, thinly sliced

Lightly season the capon with salt and pepper. Melt the butter in a heavy casserole. Spread the vegetables and parsley over the bottom of the casserole and sprinkle them with salt and pepper. Add the capon and seasonings. Cook over low heat for 10 minutes. Heat the broth and pour it over the capon just to cover. Cover the casserole and simmer for 1 hour, or until the capon is tender. Remove the capon. Discard all bones and skin. Cut the capon into strips about 1 inch by 2 inches. Place them on an ovenproof platter. Moisten them with 1 cup of the broth, and keep them warm in a low oven.

When the broth in the casserole has cooled somewhat, strain it through a sieve into a large bowl, pressing down on the vegetables before discarding them. Return the broth to the casserole and add the mixture of egg yolks, cream, and lemon juice, very gradually, stirring constantly. Cook over lowest heat until the soup thickens a little. Return the pieces of capon to the casserole. Add the parsley and garlic. Serve in soup plates. Garnish each portion with a slice of lemon.

FROSTY LEMON VELVET SOUP

❧

4 SERVINGS

1 *large or 2 small lemons*
4 *cups Chicken Broth (see page 48)*
4 *tablespoons rice*
  About ¼ cup light cream
  Freshly ground white or black pepper
  Garnish: 2 tablespoons chopped fresh chives;
      1 hard-boiled egg, finely chopped

Using a swivel-bladed vegetable peeler, peel the lemon rind into the thinnest strips possible—avoid the bitter white pith. Cut the peeled lemon in half and juice it. Put the lemon peel and juice into a pot with the broth and rice. Simmer, covered, for about 25 minutes, or until the rice is very soft.

Pour the soup through a strainer into a large bowl. Pick out and discard the pieces of lemon peel. With the back of a large spoon, press the rice through the strainer into the soup (the rice will give the soup its velvety texture). Blend until smooth in several batches in a blender or food processor.

Pour the soup into a glass serving bowl. When it is tepid, stir in the cream, tasting as you go, to make sure that the soup retains its strong lemon flavor. Chill, covered, in the refrigerator for a few hours or overnight. When the soup is very cold, add a bit of pepper. It should not need salt. Garnish with chopped chives and egg before serving.

ICED GUACAMOLE SOUP

❧

6–8 SERVINGS

3 tablespoons butter
1½ cups minced onions
4 cloves garlic, passed through a press
¼ cup diced green peppers
3 eggs, separated
2 very ripe avocados, peeled and pitted
1 cup tomato purée
1 tablespoon tomato paste
1 teaspoon Worcestershire sauce
4 teaspoons chili powder
2 teaspoons each salt and freshly ground pepper
   Optional: ½–1 cup cream

Melt the butter in a large pot over medium heat. Add the onions, garlic, and peppers. Cook, stirring often, until tender. Add 5 cups of water and bring to a boil. Lower the heat and cook, covered, for 10 minutes. Purée in a blender in two batches. Add unbeaten egg whites. Purée another few seconds, then return the mixture to the pot off the heat.

Without washing the blender container, put in the egg yolks and all the remaining ingredients and run the blender until well mixed. With the blender running, gradually add 1 cup of the hot soup mixture. Then pour it all back into the pot. Cook over low heat, stirring constantly, until the soup is slightly thickened. Do not boil. Cool, then refrigerate. If you like, stir in the cream. Correct the seasoning and serve.

OUR FAVORITE
HOT MUSHROOM SOUP

$\backsim$

6–8 SERVINGS

   2 *tablespoons dried mushrooms*
   1¾ *cups chopped leeks (the white part only)*
   4 *tablespoons butter*
   1¼ *pounds fresh mushrooms*
   ¼ *cup chopped fresh dill or tarragon*
   1 *clove garlic, put through a garlic press*
   1 *teaspoon nutmeg*
   3 *tablespoons chopped fresh coriander or parsley*
   1 *bay leaf*
      Salt and freshly ground pepper to taste
   5 *cups Chicken Broth (see page 48)*
   1 *4-inch piece of French bread, broken into pieces*
   1 *cup cream*
      Optional: 1 tablespoon Madeira

Soak the dried mushrooms for 30 minutes in just enough warm water to cover them. Wash the leeks well and dry them. Sauté them in the butter in a heavy pot until wilted. Drain the dried mushrooms through a very fine sieve. Reserve the liquid. Rinse the mushrooms to wash off any sand and chop them fine.

Wipe the fresh mushrooms clean with a damp cloth and chop them coarsely. Add the fresh and dried mushrooms to the leeks and sauté them together.

When the mushrooms begin to sweat, add the dill, garlic, nutmeg, coriander, bay leaf, salt, and pepper. Cook, stirring, for another minute. Add the chicken broth, the bread, and the reserved liquid from the dried mushrooms. Simmer for 20 minutes. Discard the bay leaf. Let the soup cool somewhat, then purée it in two batches in a blender or food processor until it is smooth. Return it to the pot and add the cream and Madeira. Taste and correct the seasoning. Reheat, but do not boil.

VARIATION I: Add to the pot a cup of shredded sorrel leaves along with the herbs and spices.

VARIATION II: Add a small can of imported German Steinpilz mushrooms, drained and coarsely chopped, along with the fresh and dried mushrooms.

OUR FAVORITE
COLD MUSHROOM SOUP

6–8 SERVINGS

4–5   *dried mushrooms*
1½   *pounds fresh mushrooms*
5   *cups Chicken Broth (see page 48)*
1   *scallion, white part only, coarsely chopped*
1   *medium-size potato, boiled, peeled, sliced*
  Salt and freshly ground pepper to taste
3   *egg yolks*
¾   *cup cream*
2   *tablespoons chopped fresh herbs, such as*
    dill, tarragon, or chives
  Optional garnish: ½ cup sour cream

Soak the dried mushrooms for 20 minutes in just enough hot water to cover. Drain and rub them clean with your fingers. Wipe the fresh mushrooms clean with a damp cloth. Trim the stems. Put 1 cup of the broth in a food processor or blender and heat the remaining broth in a large pot. Add to the broth in the food processor both kinds of mushrooms, the scallion, potato, salt and pepper. Purée, then pour the mixture into the hot broth in the pot. Simmer 10 to 15 minutes and remove the pot from the heat.

In a small bowl, beat the egg yolks with a whisk, then beat in the cream. Whisking continuously to avoid curdling, very gradually beat in about 1 cup of the hot soup. Pour this mixture back into the pot. Cook over medium heat, stirring constantly, until hot. Do not let it boil.

Pour the soup into a serving bowl and chill for several hours. When it is cold, taste and correct the seasoning. Cold soup requires more seasoning than hot. Serve sprinkled with chopped herbs and garnish with dollops of sour cream if you like.

INSTANT COLD SOUPS

We have discovered a way to make truly "instant" cold puréed vegetable soups. There is no washing, no peeling, no cooking, and no waiting for the soup to chill. The method is so quick that it will fill you with the delicious sense of pleasures too easily won. Simply take a package of frozen vegetables (such as peas, beans, or cauliflower), break it up into several pieces, if frozen solid, with a strong, sharp knife. Put some cold liquid (tomato juice, chicken or beef broth, buttermilk, cream, milk or yogurt, or a combination) into the container of a food processor with the knife blade. Add the chunks of vegetables *in their raw and frozen state* and some seasonings. A bit of lemon juice or chopped onion, salt and pepper. Process—and there you are. You can, of course, use home-frozen vegetables. The uncooked puréed vegetables have a startlingly fresh, garden taste. What is more, you have not cooked a single vitamin out of them.

INSTANT ICED CREAM OF
CAULIFLOWER SOUP

◜◞

4 SERVINGS

1   package frozen cauliflower
2   cups buttermilk
1   cup chicken or beef broth
1   medium-size potato, boiled, peeled, quartered, and
       kept in the refrigerator until cold
2   scallions, white part only, coarsely chopped
    Salt and pepper to taste
2   tablespoons chopped fresh chives or parsley

Remove the cauliflower from the freezer 15 to 20 minutes before
using. Keep the buttermilk, broth, potato, and scallions in the refrigerator until ready to use. Break the frozen cauliflower into chunks.
Place the buttermilk and broth in the container of a food processor.
Add all the other ingredients except the herbs. Put the cauliflower in
last. Purée until smooth. Serve at once, generously sprinkled with
chopped chives or parsley.

INSTANT ICED GREEN-BEAN SOUP

◜◞

4–5 SERVINGS

1   package frozen French-style green beans
2   cups buttermilk
2   cups tomato juice
    Salt and freshly ground pepper to taste
1   scallion, white part only, coarsely chopped
2   tablespoons chopped fresh basil or 2 teaspoons dried
    Optional: 1 egg yolk

Keep the ingredients cold until you are ready to prepare the soup.
Break the frozen green beans into chunks. Put all the ingredients in

the container of a food processor, adding the beans last. Blend till smooth and serve immediately.

INSTANT ICED LIMA BEAN SOUP

6~୬

4–6 SERVINGS

3 cups tomato juice
2 cups plain low-fat yogurt
1 package frozen lima beans
½ teaspoon curry powder
  Salt and freshly ground pepper to taste
2 tablespoons chopped fresh parsley or chives

Keep the tomato juice and yogurt in the refrigerator until ready to use. Do not defrost the beans completely but remove them from the freezer 15 to 20 minutes before using. Break the frozen beans into chunks. Put the tomato juice, yogurt and beans in the container of a food processor. Add the curry powder, salt and pepper, and blend to a smooth purée. Bits of lima-bean skin give the soup the texture of a French soup puréed through a food mill. Serve at once, garnished with chopped parsley or chives.

INSTANT ICED PEA SOUP

6~୬

4–5 SERVINGS

1 package frozen peas
2 medium-size potatoes, boiled, peeled, and cut into
    chunks
2 cups beef or chicken broth (or 1 cup each)
1 cup light cream
  Salt and freshly ground pepper to taste
2 tablespoons finely chopped fresh mint or tarragon,
    or 2 teaspoons dried

Do not defrost the peas. Keep the potatoes, broth, and cream refrigerated. Break the frozen peas into chunks. Put the broth and the cream into a food processor, and add the peas and potatoes. Blend until you have a smooth purée. Taste for salt and pepper. Serve at once, sprinkled with chopped mint or tarragon.

VARIATION: To make a light but sustaining lunch of this soup, add 1 or 2 whole eggs or egg yolks before blending.

MALAGUEÑA SOUP

4 SERVINGS

1   *very ripe Spanish melon, cantaloupe, or honeydew melon*
4   *slices stale French or Italian bread or stale "home-style" white bread, trimmed of crust*
2   *tablespoons whole blanched almonds*
2–3 *small cloves garlic*
2   *tablespoons olive oil*
2   *teaspoons vinegar (imported sherry vinegar is very good)*
    Salt, freshly ground pepper, and hot red pepper flakes to taste
2   *cups ice cubes*

With a melon-ball cutter, scoop out the melon and refrigerate. Put the bread in the container of a food processor using the knife blade. Add the almonds and garlic. Process for a few seconds until the bread, almonds, and garlic are finely ground. With the motor running, pour in the oil and vinegar. Scrape the mixture into a serving bowl and season with salt and pepper. Stir in the ice cubes and add the melon balls to the bowl. Stir occasionally. Serve when the ice is almost melted.

ONION SOUP, LYONS STYLE
(La Vraie Gratinée Lyonnaise)

၆~ၥ

The difference between this soup and the onion soup familiar to us all is the enriching addition of eggs and cream.

8–10 SERVINGS

6 *tablespoons butter*
2 *tablespoons French peanut oil*
2 *pounds yellow onions, thinly sliced*
   Salt, pepper, sugar to taste
2 *tablespoons flour*
2 *quarts beef consommé*
   Bouquet garni (made by tying together a bay leaf
      and a few sprigs of parsley and thyme)
8–10 *thin slices French bread*
⅔ *cup grated imported Gruyère cheese*
2 *egg yolks*
⅔ *cup light cream*
¼–⅓ *cup cognac, port, or Madeira*

Melt 3 tablespoons of the butter with the oil in a large ovenproof pot. Add the onions. Sauté, covered, over low heat for 15 minutes, stirring often. Add salt, a few generous twists of pepper, and a good pinch of sugar. Raise the heat to medium and cook, stirring often, for 30 minutes, or until the onions are a deep golden brown. Sprinkle them with the flour and cook, stirring constantly, for 2 minutes. Add the consommé and the bouquet garni and bring to a boil. Lower the heat and simmer, covered, for 30 minutes. Discard the bouquet garni.

Toast the bread in a moderate oven until golden brown. Remove it from the oven and raise the oven heat to 450°. Spread the toast with the remaining 3 tablespoons of butter and sprinkle it with grated cheese. Put it into the hot oven for 6 to 8 minutes, or until the cheese is nicely browned. Reserve.

Meanwhile purée the soup in a blender. You will have to do this in several batches. Return it to the pot. In a small bowl, whisk together the egg yolks, the cream, and the cognac. Beat a little of the hot soup into this mixture and, stirring continuously, empty the bowl into the pot. Place the pieces of toast in individual soup bowls, ladle in the soup, and serve.

QUICK SCALLOP SOUP

4–5 CUPS, OR 2–3 BOWLS

1   *cup finely diced potatoes*
½   *cup finely minced onion*
2   *cups Fish Stock (see page 46) or clam juice*
     A pinch of salt
     Freshly ground pepper to taste
1   *cup fresh bay scallops (approximately ½ pound)*
2   *tablespoons sweet butter*
¼   *cup heavy cream*
2–3 *tablespoons finely chopped fresh dill, chives, or*
     watercress

Place the potatoes, onion, fish stock, salt, and pepper in a heavy saucepan and bring to a boil. Cover and cook over medium heat for 10 minutes, or until the potatoes are soft.

Meanwhile, pick over the scallops and remove any black bits. Do not wash the scallops. Add them to the soup as soon as the potatoes are soft. Reduce the heat immediately so that the soup simmers. Do not let it boil, as that would toughen the scallops. Cook, for 2 to 3 minutes, covered. Remove from the heat. Stir in the butter until it melts, then the cream. Return to the heat for a few seconds. The soup must not boil once the cream has been added. Pour into a warmed tureen, sprinkle with chopped herbs, and serve at once.

QUICK VICHYSSOISE

⌒〜⌒

6–8 SERVINGS

4–5 scallions, white part only
  2 medium-size potatoes, boiled, peeled, and quartered
  3 cups light cream or 1 cup buttermilk and 2 cups light
      cream
  2 cups Chicken Broth (see page 48)
      Salt and freshly ground white pepper to taste
2–3 tablespoons chopped fresh dill or chives

Put the scallions in a food processor with the knife blade and blend
until finely chopped. With the motor running, add the potatoes and
all the other ingredients except the dill. Process until smooth. Chill
in the refrigerator for several hours. When ready to serve, taste and
correct the seasoning. Sprinkle with chopped dill or chives.

SLAVIC SUMMER SOUP

⌒〜⌒

An unusual soup, as refreshing to the eye as to the palate.

6–8 SERVINGS

  1½ pounds fresh young beets with their tops,
        chopped together
2–3 tablespoons vinegar
1–2 tablespoons sugar
  1½ teaspoons salt
        Freshly ground pepper to taste
    1 bay leaf
    1 bunch of fresh dill, tops and stems minced separately
1½–2 cups sour cream
        Optional: 1 cup cold beer

GARNISHES
1   pound shrimp, peeled, boiled, and halved
2   medium-size cucumbers, peeled, seeded, and diced
4   scallions (white part with a little of the green),
        thinly sliced
2   hard-boiled eggs, finely chopped
6   radishes, thinly sliced

Put the beets and the beet tops in a pot with 7 cups of cold water. Bring the water to a boil. Cook, uncovered, for 10 minutes. Reduce the heat to medium. Add the vinegar, sugar, salt, pepper, bay leaf, and minced dill stems. Cook, covered, for 30 minutes. Discard the bay leaf and transfer the soup to a large bowl.

When the soup has cooled, stir in the sour cream and the beer. Refrigerate for 2 to 3 hours. When serving, put an ice cube in each soup plate along with some of each of the garnishes. Sprinkle each portion with the remaining dill.

CHINOOK CHOWDER
(Smoked Salmon
and Sorrel Chowder)

~

Not only did the American Indians in the Northwest smoke peace pipes, but they also smoked their own magnificent Columbia River salmon, which they then made into soup with wild sorrel. In the unlikely event that you have some leftover smoked salmon on hand, it can be used in this recipe based on an old American Indian dish.

6–8 SERVINGS

3   tablespoons butter
1⅓   cups diced potatoes
1   cup diced onion
       Freshly ground pepper to taste
6   cups Fish Stock (see page 46) or clam juice
¼   pound smoked salmon, thinly sliced, then cut into
        bite-sized pieces with scissors
1   cup tightly packed fresh sorrel or spinach leaves
       Optional: 2 tablespoons light cream

In a heavy saucepan, melt the butter over low heat. Add the potatoes and onion. Season generously with pepper, but use no salt. Cook, stirring, about 5 minutes, or until the onions are limp but not browned. Add the fish stock and 3 cups of boiling water. Cook until the potatoes are soft. Add the salmon and the sorrel or spinach. Cook over low heat for 2 to 3 minutes, or until the spinach is wilted. Taste for seasoning and add more pepper and a bit of salt if needed.

When ready to serve, remove from the heat and stir in the cream if you like.

SPINACH EGG-DROP SOUP
(Stracciatella di Spinaci)

The Italians call this soup *stracciatella*, which means rag, because of the raglike effect you get when you drop the egg-cheese mixture into the boiling broth. The addition of spinach makes for a less known version of a classic Italian dish.

4–6 SERVINGS

3½ cups homemade Beef Broth (see page 47) or
    Chicken Broth (see page 48)
1 pound fresh spinach, trimmed and washed, or 1
    10-ounce package frozen chopped spinach
1 egg
1 cup grated Parmesan cheese
    Salt and freshly ground pepper to taste

Boil 1 cup of the broth. Add the spinach and cook over high heat until it is soft but still bright green. Remove the spinach with a slotted spoon and set aside. Add the remaining broth to the pot and bring to a boil.

Meanwhile, beat the egg lightly with a fork. Beat in ¼ cup of the cheese. When the broth is boiling, pour in the egg-cheese mixture, stirring constantly for a few seconds until it cooks into "rags." Add the reserved spinach and the salt and pepper. Cook for 1 minute and serve. Pass the remaining cheese separately.

Stracciatella can, of course, be made without the spinach.

SORREL AND POTATO SOUP

⌒

While sage symbolizes the domestic virtues, rosemary is for remembrance, parsley for joyful victory, and mustard, surprisingly, for indifference, sorrel—that waywardly wild and acid herb—signifies affection. Mention sorrel to a Frenchman and he will be sure to sigh a gustatory "Ah! J'adore la soupe à l'oseille." Ask a Pole or a Russian about this sour-grass plant and he will wax nostalgic about icy, pale-green shchav, a sorrel soup decorated with sharp spring onions, fiery red radishes, and the dandelion-yellow yolks of hard-boiled eggs, all adrift in a sea of sour cream.

How versatile sorrel is! Even when tempered with butter and thick cream, it makes an astringent purée, a perfect foil for veal or pork, chicken or fish. Blended with fresh sweet peas, lemony sorrel makes an ideal green purée to fill mushroom caps. And it adds a tangy counterpoint to an omelette paysanne, along with cubed bacon, diced potatoes, chopped shallots, and pepper.

It is difficult to imagine a more inviting sight than quartered hard-boiled eggs (or poached eggs, for that matter) on a bed of this companionable herb. Try sorrel risotto—our invention. Italian friends—who do not seem to be familiar with sorrel—are seduced by its subtly acrid taste, more mysterious than the taste of the classic green risotto made with spinach.

The natives of Brittany are especially fond of sorrel. In a Breton seaside restaurant we were served a delicately sautéed fish roe bathed in a creamy sorrel sauce that was as delightful as the wisteria-covered pergola we were dining under. And just as nothing is more refreshing on a hot summer evening than cold sorrel and potato soup, nothing is more comforting on a blustery winter night than a steaming bowl of sorrel and turnip soup à la bretonne.

There is no better soup than sorrel and potato soup if made with fresh sorrel from your garden. However, an acceptable version can be achieved by substituting a 13-ounce jar of Belgian sorrel, available at specialty shops. If you enjoy the sharp undiluted taste of sorrel, omit the cream.

6–8 SERVINGS

2 large onions, peeled and thinly sliced
1½ sticks (6 ounces) butter
2 medium-size potatoes, peeled and thinly sliced
8 cups fresh sorrel, washed and dried, or 1 13-ounce jar
   of sorrel
½ cup loosely packed fresh mint leaves
4 cups Chicken Broth (see page 48)
   Salt and pepper to taste
   Optional: ½ pint light or heavy cream

In a large pot over low heat, cook the onions in the butter for 5 minutes, stirring often. Add the potatoes and cook 10 minutes longer, stirring occasionally. Add the sorrel and mint and cook, stirring continuously, until the sorrel is wilted. Add the broth and cook until the potatoes and onions are soft. Season with salt and pepper. Remove from the heat and cool. Purée in a food processor in several batches. Stir in the cream if you like. Reheat just to the boiling point, correct the seasoning, and serve immediately. Or put the soup in a serving bowl and chill it for several hours. Then taste, correct the seasoning, and serve.

VARIATION: Turn this recipe into Sorrel and Turnip Soup à la bretonne (Brittany style) by substituting two or three small white turnips for the potatoes.

SQUASH SOUP IN SQUASH TUREENS

⌒⌒

An amusingly attractive presentation.

6 SERVINGS

6 butternut squashes, about 6–8 inches in diameter, or
   6 small pumpkins of the same size
3 cups milk
   A good pinch of saffron

> Salt and freshly ground pepper to taste
> About 2 tablespoons brown sugar
> A pinch of cinnamon
> A pinch of nutmeg

Preheat the oven to 450°.

Bake the squashes for 30–40 minutes, or until tender but still firm. With a strong sharp knife, cut a circular "lid" from the top of each squash and reserve. Cut a thin slice from the bottom of each squash to make it stand upright. Discard the seeds and stringy fibers. Scoop out most of the pulp, leaving a half-inch shell. Be careful not to pierce the skins. Cut the pulp into small cubes. Measure 3 cups of pulp and save the rest for another use. Boil the pulp in lightly salted water until tender. Drain and set aside.

Scald the milk, remove it from the heat and steep the saffron in it for 2 to 3 minutes. Mix the milk and squash together. Purée in a blender or food processor in two or three batches. Season with salt, pepper, sugar, cinnamon, and nutmeg. Bring the soup to a boil, ladle it into the squash shells, replace the lids and serve. The soup in the squash shells can be kept warm in a low oven until serving time.

SUSAN COSTNER'S PURÉE
OF FENNEL SOUP

❦

Our friend Susan is one of the best cooks we know.

6–8 SERVINGS

> 4 large fresh fennel bulbs
> 3 medium-size onions, chopped
> 4 tablespoons olive oil
> 4 tablespoons butter
> 1 tablespoon tomato paste
> 9 cups Chicken Broth (see page 48), skimmed of fat
>   Bouquet garni (made by tying together a bay leaf,
>   a few sprigs of parsley, and some sprigs of the
>   feathery part of the fennel)
>   Salt and pepper to taste

1–2 *tablespoons powdered fennel seed*
   Beurre manié: 2 tablespoons flour and 2 tablespoons
     cold butter rubbed together with your fingers
     and chilled until ready to use

Trim, peel, and wash the fennel. Discard the tough outer leaves. Cut the bulbs into quarters, then into thin slices. Reserve 2 cups for the garnish.

Sauté the onions in the olive oil and 2 tablespoons of the butter until soft but not browned. Add the fennel, tomato paste, and 2 cups of the chicken broth. Cover and simmer for 15 to 20 minutes, or until the vegetables are tender. Purée the vegetables and liquid through the medium sieve of a food mill. Pour the purée into a large pot. Add the remaining 7 cups of chicken broth and the bouquet garni. Cook, uncovered, over medium heat for about 30 minutes, or until the soup is reduced by a third. Stir occasionally.

Remove the bouquet garni. Season with salt and pepper and powdered fennel seed. Add the *beurre manié* in pea-size pieces, stirring vigorously with a whisk until the soup thickens. Taste and correct the seasoning.

Cut the reserved fennel slices in half and sauté them in the remaining 2 tablespoons of butter for 10 to 15 minutes. Serve the soup garnished with the sautéed fennel.

TOMATO AND OKRA SOUP, AUGUSTA MAYNARD

෴

Our friend Augusta Maynard, who has that special Maryland flair for good food, makes this exquisite soup with ripe tomatoes and small, young fresh okra. If only large okra is available, she uses frozen okra instead.

4 SERVINGS

1 *pound ripe tomatoes, peeled and coarsely chopped*
1 *pound small young okra, trimmed and sliced, or*
   1 10-ounce package frozen okra, defrosted

3½–4   cups Beef Broth (see page 47)
   1   teaspoon salt
   ½   teaspoon freshly ground pepper or more to taste
 2–3   teaspoons brown sugar or more to taste, depending
          on the acidity of the tomatoes
       Optimal garnish: 2 tablespoons butter, 1 cup hot
          boiled rice

Cover the bottom of a heavy pot with ½ inch of water. Add the tomatoes. Bring to a boil and add the okra. Simmer until the okra is tender.
Add all the remaining ingredients and simmer, covered, for 30 to 60
minutes. Taste and correct the seasoning. (If you are using frozen
okra, purée the soup in a blender.) If you like, add a lump of butter
and serve hot. Pass the rice separately for those who want it.

   The soup is also delicious cold, puréed in a blender. In that case,
omit the rice and butter garnishes.

TOMATO-SORREL SOUP, HOT OR COLD

⌢

8–10 SERVINGS

   ½   cup finely chopped onion
   ½   stick (4 tablespoons) butter
   2   pounds fresh sorrel, washed, trimmed of large stems,
          and coarsely chopped
   1   teaspoon salt
   1   teaspoon sugar
       Freshly ground pepper to taste
  10   plum tomatoes, peeled, seeded and coarsely chopped
          (or 1 35-ounce can of Italian peeled tomatoes,
          carefully drained)
   6   cups Chicken Broth (see page 48)
       Garnish (optional): 1 cup heavy cream and 16 large
          boiled shrimp, each cut into 2 or 3 pieces

Cook the onions in the butter over low heat in a heavy pot until translucent, stirring often. Add the sorrel. Cook, stirring, for 2 to 3 minutes,

or until the sorrel wilts. Add the salt, sugar, pepper, and tomatoes. Cook for 10 minutes, stirring occasionally. Add the broth and bring to a boil. Purée the soup in a blender or food processor, in several batches, until it is smooth, or pass it through a food mill. If you are using the garnish, stir in the cream and shrimp. Taste and correct the seasoning. Reheat the soup, but do not let it boil. Serve at once.

Tomato-sorrel soup is equally good served cold. Simply stir in the cream and shrimp, and refrigerate for a few hours. Then taste and correct the seasoning.

TURKISH TOMATO SOUP

❧

A quickly assembled, refreshing cold soup.

4–6 SERVINGS

2	cups V-8 juice
1	cup tomato juice
1	cup yogurt
1	tablespoon olive oil
2	tablespoons lemon juice
1½	tablespoons vinegar
½	tablespoon curry powder
2–3	dashes Tabasco sauce or a pinch of cayenne pepper
1	tablespoon chopped fresh mint or 1 teaspoon dried
1	tablespoon chopped fresh basil or 1 teaspoon dried
	Salt and freshly ground pepper to taste
2	tablespoons chopped Italian parsley
2	tablespoons chopped fresh basil
	Garnishes (optional): 1 cucumber, peeled and diced; 8 medium-size boiled shrimp, each cut into 2 or 3 pieces; 2 hard-boiled eggs, sliced

Blend all the ingredients except the parsley and basil in a blender or food processor until smooth. Chill for 4 hours or longer. Serve sprinkled with the chopped herbs.

Add cucumber, shrimp, and egg garnishes if you like.

VENETIAN FISH SOUP
(Zuppa di Pesce alla Veneziana)

6–8 SERVINGS

SOUP

2   ½-pound striped bass or other firm white-fleshed fish,
      cut into 2-inch slices (do not discard the heads and
      tails)
2   pounds fish bones and heads (gills removed)
2   cups clam juice
2   pounds onions, sliced
2   carrots, cut into pieces
1   stalk celery, sliced
2   tomatoes, peeled, seeded, and coarsely chopped
1   bay leaf
6   sprigs parsley
1   clove garlic, coarsely chopped
    Salt and pepper to taste
    A dash of cayenne pepper
1   teaspoon saffron
1   egg yolk, lightly beaten
1   cup of cream
    Optional: beurre manié (1 tablespoon each cold
         butter and flour, rubbed together with your fingers)

CROSTINI (Croutons)

4   slices Italian bread, trimmed of crust
2   tablespoons olive oil
2   tablespoons grated imported Parmesan cheese

Put all the soup ingredients except the egg yolk, cream, and *beurre
manié* in a large pot and cover them with cold water. Boil vigorously
for 7 to 10 minutes, or until the pieces of fish are cooked and flake
easily when tested with a fork. Remove the slices of fish and set them
aside. Discard the skin and bones. Leave the heads and tails in the pot.
Lower the heat to medium and cook the soup, covered, for 20 to 30
minutes.

Discard the fish heads, tails, and bones. Strain the soup through a sieve lined with cheesecloth into a large bowl, pressing down hard with the back of a spoon to extract all the juices. Discard what is left in the sieve. Rinse out the pot and put the broth back into it.

Beat the egg yolk and the cream together with a fork. Add some of the broth when it is warm but not hot, spoonful by spoonful, stirring constantly so that the egg-cream mixture does not curdle. Put this mixture into the pot and stir. Add the slices of fish. Reheat the soup very gently, gradually adding bits of *beurre manié* to thicken the broth if you like. Do not let it boil.

Meanwhile, make the *crostini.* Preheat the oven to 400°. Cut the bread into ½-inch cubes. Fry them in hot oil until lightly browned on both sides. Spread them on a cookie sheet and sprinkle them with grated cheese. Bake for 5 minutes, or until the cheese is golden brown. Put a few *crostini* in each portion of the soup.

EGG DISHES

*Yet, who can help loving the land that has taught us
Six hundred and eighty-five ways to dress eggs?*

THOMAS MOORE,
The Fudge Family in Paris

*"It's very easy to talk," said Mrs. Mantalini. "Not
so easy when one is eating a demnition egg," replied Mr. Mantalini; "for the yolk runs down the
waistcoat, and yolk of egg does not match any
waistcoat but a yellow waistcoat, demmit."*

CHARLES DICKENS,
Nicholas Nickleby

MAKING OMELETS
WITH PAUL BOCUSE

*W*hen we visited the great chef Paul Bocuse in his country restaurant near Lyons, he invited us into his kitchen to
watch him prepare the omelets that his grandmother used
to make for him. While he cooked he gave us some tips on
how to make an omelet:

- Do not use freshly laid eggs. The eggs should
  be at least two or three days old. (We assured
  Monsieur Bocuse that most of us in the United
  States would not have any problem with *that*.)
- Use two eggs per person for a plain omelet. For
  an omelet with a substantial garnish, three eggs
  are enough for two people.
- Never cook more than six eggs at a time. If you
  are making omelets for more than three people,
  make them in several batches.

- Use a well-cured iron or nonstick omelet pan with sloping sides and use it for omelets only. Never wash it. Scour it with coarse salt and paper towels after each use. (To cure a new pan, cover the bottom with a film of oil. Heat it until it bubbles. Tilt the pan to oil the sides. Turn off the heat and let the pan cure for an hour. Wipe it clean with a paper towel.)
- Never beat the eggs ahead of time. Just before cooking an omelet, beat the eggs lightly with a fork until the yolks and whites are combined but still viscous.

Bocuse's Method

Break the eggs into a bowl. Season them with salt and freshly ground pepper. Beat them lightly with a fork for 20 to 30 seconds.

For a 2- to 3-egg omelet, put a tablespoon of sweet butter in an 8- or 9-inch omelet pan over high heat. Tilt the pan so that the butter coats the sides and bottom. When the butter foams up, subsides, and begins to turn slightly dark, add the beaten eggs. As the omelet starts to thicken around the edges, scrape the edges toward the center with the flat side of a fork to ensure even cooking.

When the omelet is done to your taste (Bocuse, like most Frenchmen, feels it should be somewhat runny in the center), let it sit over the heat for 2 seconds to set. Then tilt the pan forward with your left hand and run the fork around the edges of the omelet to make sure it is not sticking. Still tilting the pan forward, tap the handle of the pan sharply a few times with your right hand to dislodge the omelet. It will slide down onto the lip of the pan. Fold the upper half down. Add another tablespoon of butter to the pan (the *dorure* or gilding). When the butter melts, roll the omelet out onto a warm platter. Adjust the shape if necessary. Rub a small piece of cold butter stuck onto the tip of a knife over the surface of the omelet. (This is called the *vernissage* or varnishing.)

"Like a painting in a gold frame, an omelet should be gilded and varnished. Practice makes perfect," said Bocuse. But even as he was telling us exactly how it should be done, the man considered by many to be the greatest chef in the world found his omelets stubbornly sticking to the pan. He had trouble turning them out, and when he did they were far from perfect. With an uneasy glance at his numerous *sous-chefs*, who had discreetly lowered their eyes, he muttered,

"*Merde alors!* I'm out of practice! It's been a long time since I've actu-
ally made an omelet." But then, miracle of miracles, Bocuse turned
disaster into triumph as only a truly great chef can. He quickly covered each misshapen omelet with a linen towel, patted it deftly, then
whipped off the towel to reveal the most perfectly shaped omelets
imaginable.

Here are recipes for four omelets that Bocuse gave us, one for each
season of the year.

BOCUSE'S SPRING OMELET
WITH ASPARAGUS TIPS
(Omelette du Printemps aux Pointes d'Asperges)

ᔆ~ᒍ

2 SERVINGS

GARNISH

12 *stalks asparagus (tips only)*
1   *tablespoon butter*
    Salt and freshly ground pepper to taste
    Juice of half a lemon

OMELET

1½ *tablespoons butter*
3–4 *eggs*
    Salt and pepper to taste

Plunge the asparagus tips into rapidly boiling water and cook, uncovered, for about 3 minutes, or until tender but still quite firm. Do
not overcook. Drain on paper towels. Place the asparagus tips in a
warm dish, smear them with 1 tablespoon of butter and season with
salt and pepper. Keep them warm while you make the omelet following the method described (on page 84).

Roll the omelet onto a warm oval platter. Brush the top with butter
and make an incision lengthwise down the center. Insert some of the
asparagus tips into this incision and arrange the rest around the omelet.
Squeeze the lemon juice over the asparagus tips and serve.

BOCUSE'S SUMMER OMELET
WITH HERBS AND
FRESH TOMATO SAUCE
(Omelette d'Été aux Fines Herbes, Sauce Tomate)

֍

2 SERVINGS

TOMATO SAUCE

1   strip bacon
1   medium-size onion, finely chopped
3   tablespoons butter
2   medium-size very ripe tomatoes
    Salt and freshly ground pepper to taste
    A pinch or two of sugar and nutmeg
1   tablespoon chopped fresh basil

OMELET

1½ tablespoons butter
2   tablespoons chopped mixed fresh herbs (chives and
        parsley or a mixture of chives, parsley, tarragon,
        and chervil)
4   eggs
    Salt and freshly ground pepper to taste

Blanch the bacon in boiling water for 1 minute, drain, and chop it fine. In a heavy saucepan with a tight-fitting cover, sauté the bacon and onion in 2 tablespoons of butter until the onion is translucent. Stir from time to time. Chop the tomatoes coarsely. Put them in the saucepan with the onion and bacon. Add salt, pepper, sugar, and nutmeg. Simmer, covered, over the lowest heat for 15 to 30 minutes, stirring occasionally. Add the basil, raise the heat, and cook, stirring frequently, until the sauce has the consistency of a fairly thick purée. Pass the sauce through a food mill or sieve, stir in the remaining tablespoon of butter, and keep it warm while you make the omelet.

In making the omelet, follow the method described on page 84, adding 1 tablespoon of the chopped herbs to the eggs before you beat them. Sprinkle the remaining herbs over the finished omelet, and transfer it to a warm platter. Pour the tomato sauce on and around the omelet and serve.

BOCUSE's TIP: Herbs have more taste if they are not chopped too fine. They should always be chopped just before using them. Cutting them with kitchen scissors is the best way to do it. "Nothing is more taste-less than a bowl of finely chopped parsley that has been standing around the kitchen all day," says the great chef.

BOCUSE'S AUTUMN OMELET, GRANDMOTHER'S STYLE

(Omelette d'Automne à la Façon de Ma Grand'mère)

2 SERVINGS

GARNISH

2 green apples or 1 apple and 1 pear, peeled, cored, and
    cut into ¾-inch cubes
2 tablespoons butter
    Salt and freshly ground pepper to taste
    Optional: A few thin slices of unpeeled apple or pear

OMELET

3–4 eggs
     Salt and freshly ground pepper to taste
2   tablespoons butter

Sauté the cubes of fruit in butter over medium heat. Season them with salt and a generous twist of pepper. Turn them occasionally and cook until tender but firm and golden brown on all sides. Keep them warm while you prepare the omelet, following the method described on page 84.

Turn the omelet out onto a warm platter (Bocuse likes to arrange this omelet in a square shape once it is on the platter), and place the cubes of sautéed fruit all around it.

A few thin slices of unpeeled apple or pear can be sautéed along with the apple or pear cubes for a minute or two and arranged in an overlapping row on top of the finished omelet.

BOCUSE'S WINTER OMELET
WITH ONIONS AND BACON
(Omelette d'Hiver aux Oignons et au Lard)

◆~ン

2 SERVINGS

GARNISH

4   slices bacon
1   medium-size onion, sliced, then separated into rings
2   tablespoons butter
    Salt and freshly ground pepper to taste
1   tablespoon chopped fresh parsley

OMELET

4   eggs
    Salt and pepper to taste
1   tablespoon butter

Blanch the bacon in boiling water for 1 minute. Drain and dry it on paper towels. Cut into ¼-inch strips. Sauté the onion rings in the butter. Season them lightly with salt and generously with pepper. After a minute or two, add the bacon. Sauté until the bacon is fairly crisp and the onion rings are translucent but not browned. Keep them warm while you prepare the omelet following the method described on page 84).

Instead of rolling the omelet, simply slide it onto a warm round serving platter. Arrange the onion rings and bacon strips on top of the omelet and garnish with chopped parsley.

PAUL BOCUSE'S MENU FOR FRIENDS

AN OMELET WITH THE SEASON'S GARNISH
(see pages 85–88)
SALAD WITH WALNUT-OIL DRESSING
FRESH FRUIT IN SEASON
wine: RIESLING

Bocuse's favorite menu for four is quickly prepared. Half an hour before eating, prepare the garnish for the omelet, then the salad, which, of course, should not be dressed until the moment before serving. Your guests for this informal meal should be at table, finishing the last drops of Bocuse's refreshing apéritif—chilled French champagne with a bit of raspberry syrup and a few drops of *eau de vie de framboise* (French raspberry brandy)—while the omelets are being prepared.

For the omelets, double Bocuse's recipe. Cook the omelets in two batches.

For the salad, 15 minutes before serving time, coarsely tear a mixture of washed and thoroughly dried salad greens, such as Bibb or Boston lettuce, curly escarole, romaine, etc. When ready to eat the salad, dress it with 1 tablespoon of French wine vinegar, 4 tablespoons of imported French walnut oil, a little salt, and a generous twist of freshly ground pepper.

There is no question in Bocuse's mind—or in ours—that this simple menu can only be enhanced by a resplendent and varied platter of French cheeses, accompanied by a crusty French bread, served between salad and dessert.

OMELET WITH CROUTONS
AND WALNUTS
(Omelette aux Croutons et aux Noix)

2 SERVINGS

2 slices French bread, trimmed of crust and cut into
    ½-inch cubes
3 tablespoons butter (more may be needed)
2 tablespoons coarsely broken walnut meats
4 eggs
    Salt and freshly ground pepper to taste
1 teaspoon finely chopped parsley
1 teaspoon finely chopped chives

Sauté the bread cubes in 2 tablespoons of the butter, turning them from time to time until golden brown on all sides. Add the walnuts and sauté them for 1 minute. Remove from heat.

Lightly beat together the eggs, salt, pepper, parsley, and chives. Heat 1 tablespoon of butter in an omelet pan over high heat. When the butter stops foaming, add the egg mixture. Cook, following the method described on page 84, until the omelet is set but still creamy. Put the croutons and nuts in the center, fold the omelet over the filling and turn out onto a warm dish.

A SUGGESTED MENU

(see Index for recipes)

RATATOUILLE

OMELET WITH CROUTONS AND WALNUTS

ROSAMOND RUSSELL'S STRAWBERRY-PAPAYA ICE

wine: JULIENAS

LOBSTER OMELET

❧

4 SERVINGS

1½ *pounds very ripe tomatoes, coarsely chopped*
2 *tablespoons heavy cream*
2 *tablespoons butter*
    Salt and freshly ground pepper to taste
1 *tablespoon chopped fresh herbs (tarragon, chervil,*
        parsley, chives, or any combination of these)
    Optional: 1 teaspoon Pernod
½ *pound cooked lobster meat, cut into ¾-inch pieces*
6 *eggs*
3 *tablespoons butter*

Cook the tomatoes in a heavy pan over fairly high heat, stirring frequently so that they do not stick. (No butter is needed.) After 7 to 8 minutes, remove them from the heat. Put them through a food mill.

You should have about 1½ cups of purée. Return the tomato purée to the pan over very low heat. Add all the remaining ingredients except the eggs and butter, and cook for a few minutes, stirring often, until the lobster pieces are heated through.

Make two omelets using 3 eggs and half the butter for each omelet and following the method described on page 84. Put some of the lobster-tomato sauce in the center of the omelets before folding them over. Turn them out onto a warm platter and pour the remaining sauce over them.

SCALLOP OMELET

2 SERVINGS

4 *shallots, coarsely chopped*
½ *cup coarsely chopped mushrooms*
3 *tablespoons butter*
½ *cup bay scallops*
Salt and pepper to taste
3–4 *eggs*
2 *tablespoons cream*
1½ *tablespoons butter*
2 *tablespoons finely chopped hazelnuts or almonds*

Sauté the shallots and mushrooms in the butter, at first over low heat and then, as the mushrooms begin to give off liquid, over higher heat until most of the liquid evaporates. Add the scallops, salt, and pepper. Sauté for a minute or two longer. Reserve in the pan in a warm place. Whisk the eggs and cream together lightly. Season with salt and pepper. Heat the butter in an omelet pan until it foams up and then subsides. Add the eggs and cook according to the method described on page 84. As soon as the omelet is set, and the top is still a bit runny, spoon the filling along the center of the omelet. Slide it out onto a warm dish folding the omelet over on itself to cover the filling.

Brown the hazelnuts or almonds in the omelet pan over high heat for a few seconds, adding a bit more butter if needed. Sprinkle the nuts on top of the omelet and serve at once.

MINI-FRITTATA

Excellent as part of a mixed antipasto or as a first course.

16 2-INCH MINIATURE ITALIAN OMELETS

1 *stick (¼ pound) butter, melted*
4 *eggs, lightly beaten with a fork*
   Salt and pepper to taste
   A dash of cayenne pepper
¾ *cup spinach, cooked, thoroughly drained, and chopped*
¼ *cup chopped green or red bell peppers, sautéed in oil*
1 *tablespoon finely grated onion*
1–2 *tablespoons freshly grated Parmesan cheese*

Preheat the oven to 400°.

With a pastry brush, coat the bottoms of a 16-cup muffin pan with melted butter. Put the pan in the oven to heat the butter. In a bowl, mix the eggs, seasonings, spinach, peppers, and onion. Remove the pan from the oven and spoon just enough of the mixture into each muffin cup so that it is about ¼ inch high. Return the pan to the oven for a few minutes until the mixture is set and begins to come away from the sides of the cups. Sprinkle the tops of the little omelets lightly with grated cheese and melted butter. Put them under the broiler for a few seconds until the cheese turns golden brown. Watch carefully so that they do not burn. Arrange on a platter and serve hot or at room temperature.

PASTA

Ticker tape ain't spaghetti.

MAYOR FIORELLO LA GUARDIA

*Spaghetti can be eaten successfully
if you inhale it like a vacuum cleaner.*

SOPHIA LOREN

*N*othing Italians make shows their inventive genius, their playful love of design, their endless ingenuity—and their love of food—more than the hundred ways they shape pasta. It is the only country whose basic food is as visually varied and fanciful as its baroque façades and chapels.

To dig into a delicious pasta or gaze into a clear golden consommé and find the shapes of butterflies, seashells, snails, cockscombs, thimbles, ribbons, and even cupids, is no small pleasure.

We prefer store-bought pasta imported from Italy for robust sauces, fresh-made pasta for delicate sauces like our saffron-cream or lemon spaghetti. With meat and other thick sauces, try *fusilli* (shaped like cockscrews) or those ridged tubes called *rigatoni*. The sauce will fill the crevices and adhere to the surfaces in a most satisfying way.

Ten Things to Remember About
Cooking Pasta

1. One pound will make 3 or 4 servings.
2. Use a large, inexpensive lightweight pot, which will bring water to a boil quickly.
3. You should have 4 quarts of water or more for 1 pound of pasta.
4. Add 2 tablespoons of salt and 1 tablespoon of oil or butter to the water for each pound of pasta to prevent sticking.
5. Bring the water to a rolling boil, add all the pasta gradually but quickly. If it is long pasta like spaghetti, stir and press it down with a wooden fork or spoon so that all the pasta is submerged.
6. Cover the pot but remove the cover as soon as the water comes back to a boil. Stir the pasta occasionally.
7. There are many tests for doneness. Some Italians throw a strand against the wall. If it sticks, it's done. A more practical method, and a necessary one, is to keep tasting after a few minutes. (With fresh pasta, after one minute!) Pasta *must* be cooked *al dente* ("to the tooth")—that is, resilient but certainly not hard, and above all, not too soft.
8. When the pasta is *al dente*, act quickly. Drain it through a colander placed in the sink. Many Italians do not drain pasta too thoroughly. They feel that a tablespoon or two of the cooking water lubricates the pasta and blends well with the sauce.
9. Put the drained pasta back into the pot or onto a warm platter to which you have added some butter. Quickly add more butter (an extravagant amount never hurts), grated imported Parmesan cheese, and the sauce. Toss the pasta rapidly with a large spoon and fork, lifting it from the bottom. Serve on warm (but not hot) soup dishes or other dishes with a raised rim. Pass additional grated cheese separately.
10. Do not add grated cheese to seafood pasta unless you want to be very *un*-Italian.

CAMILLA McGRATH'S
BAKED PASTA AND EGGPLANT

 ᗡᢞ

An Italian version of the Middle East's moussaka given to us by our Italian-food guru.

8–10 SERVINGS

2   cups *Meat Sauce, Bolognese Style (see page 42)*
3   *1-pound eggplants*
2–3 cups *Italian olive oil*
    Salt and freshly ground pepper to taste
1½ *pounds pasta (penne, ziti, or rigatoni)*
1   *stick (¼ pound) butter*
1   *cup freshly grated Parmesan cheese*
½   *pound mozzarella, thinly sliced*
3   *hard-boiled eggs, sliced in rounds*

Prepare the meat sauce well in advance. Trim the eggplants but do not peel them. Cut two of them lengthwise into thin slices. Cut the third eggplant into thin rounds. Fry them a few at a time in hot olive oil till browned on both sides. Season them with salt and pepper. Set them aside to drain in single layers on paper towels.

Bring a large pot of salted water to a rolling boil. Stir in a table-spoon of olive oil and add the pasta gradually. Stir from time to time to prevent sticking. Stop the cooking while the pasta is still quite firm, as you are going to bake it later. Drain it immediately and mix it well with the butter, the meat sauce, and ¼ cup of the grated cheese.

Preheat the oven to 375°.

Lightly butter a 3-quart baking dish. Line the bottom and sides with slightly overlapping eggplant strips. Fill the dish with the pasta–meat-sauce mixture. Sprinkle ½ cup of the grated cheese over the top. Arrange the eggplant rounds and the hard-boiled egg slices over all. Cover with the slices of mozzarella. Sprinkle with the remaining grated cheese and dot with butter. Bake for 30 to 40 minutes and serve. Superb!

A SUGGESTED LUNCH MENU
(see Index for recipes)

SLICED RIPE PEARS WITH PROSCIUTTO

BAKED PASTA AND EGGPLANT

FRENCH STRING BEAN SALAD

A RICOTTA PIE IN AN AMARETTO CRUST FOR ANNE

wine: BAROLO

PASTA BUTTERFLIES IN PESTO

∽

The pungent basil that grows along the Ligurian Coast near Genoa makes the best pesto sauce in Italy. In San Remo we enjoyed a combination of green farfalle (pasta butterflies), thinly sliced potatoes, and crisply cooked green beans, aromatically dressed in pesto sauce. Distinctly not for calorie counters but surprisingly light all the same.

4–6 SERVINGS

PESTO: (makes 1 cup)

1¼	*cups fresh basil leaves, washed and carefully dried*
6	*sprigs parsley*
½	*cup pine nuts (pignoli)*
2–3	*garlic cloves passed through a garlic press*
⅓	*cup freshly grated Parmesan cheese and ⅓ cup freshly grated Pecorino cheese or ⅔ cup freshly grated Parmesan cheese*
¼–½	*teaspoon salt*
6	*tablespoons olive oil*
2	*tablespoons softened butter*

2	*medium-size boiled potatoes, peeled and very thinly sliced*
½	*pound thin, young string beans, trimmed, cut in half, and cooked until tender but still crisp*
1	*pound farfalle or small shells*
2	*tablespoons olive oil*
	Salt and freshly ground pepper
1	*cup freshly grated Parmesan cheese*

Pound all the ingredients for the pesto except the oil and butter in a mortar. Gradually add the oil and butter and mix well. (Or work all the ingredients in a blender or food processor for a very short time until blended.) Place in a bowl or cup and cover with a film of oil until ready to use.

Boil 6 quarts of water in a large, lightweight pot. Place the cooked potatoes and beans with 1 tablespoon of the oil in an ovenproof serving platter large enough to hold the pasta when it is cooked. Season with salt and pepper to taste. Put in a low oven to keep warm while cooking the pasta.

When the water has come to a rolling boil, add 1 teaspoon of salt and 1 tablespoon of oil. Add the pasta gradually in order not to stop the boiling. Cook until *al dente.* Put 2 teaspoons of the pasta water into the pesto sauce and mix well. Drain the pasta. Remove the platter from the oven. Add the drained pasta and half of the pesto. Toss gently and serve. Pass the remaining sauce and the Parmesan cheese separately.

TIPS FOR MAKING AND USING PESTO: Pesto and freshly grated imported Parmesan cheese are, of course, wonderful over any pasta. They will immeasurably enhance a minestrone, a poached fish, and even a plain baked potato.

Pesto *must* be made with fresh basil. But nothing is easier than to make a large quantity in summer, when fresh basil is available. It freezes surprisingly well. If you plan to freeze it, reduce the amounts of grated cheese and oil. When ready to use, defrost and add the missing grated cheese and oil.

A traditional way to make pesto in winter is to use preserved fresh basil. In the summer, simply put spotless basil leaves sprinkled with salt in a clean screw-top jar. Fill the jar to the brim with good olive oil and store in a cool, dark place. Use the basil as you need it. When it is gone, you will be left with salted, basil-scented olive oil for salad dressing.

A SUGGESTED MENU

(*see Index for recipes*)

PASTA BUTTERFLIES IN PESTO

ARUGULA AND BEET SALAD

LEMON TART, LUTÈCE

wine: CORVO DI SALAPARUTA, RED OR WHITE

FETTUCCINE WITH LEMON CREAM

6–8 SERVINGS

2   pounds fettuccine (fresh if available)
    Salt
2   tablespoons olive oil
¾   cup heavy cream
1   teaspoon grated lemon rind
½   cup lemon juice
2   sticks (½ pound) butter, cut into pieces and softened
        to room temperature
    Salt and freshly ground pepper to taste
1   cup freshly grated imported Parmesan cheese

Bring a large pot of water to a rolling boil. Add 1 or 2 tablespoons each of salt and olive oil. Cover and keep at the boil till ready to cook the fettuccine.

Heat the cream with the lemon rind and juice. Do not let it boil.

Cook the fettuccine *al dente*, tender but decidedly firm. Warm a platter and put half the butter on it. Drain the fettuccine as soon as it is done and transfer it to the platter. Pour the lemon-cream sauce over it. Season with salt and pepper and add the remaining butter. Toss until well mixed. Pass the cheese separately, as there are those who prefer this delicate dish without cheese.

VARIATION: Begin by sautéing ¾ cup of finely chopped onions in 2 table-spoons of butter over low heat, stirring often, until the onions are limp and translucent. Stir the onions into the lemon-cream sauce along with ½ cup of chopped fresh parsley just before pouring it over the fettuccine.

LINGUINE WITH SCALLOPS
AND PEPPERS FOR BOB

⌒

3–4 SERVINGS

1 *pound bay scallops (whole) or sea scallops (quartered)*
4 *bell peppers (green, red, and yellow if possible)*
1 *clove garlic, finely chopped*
¼–⅓ *cup olive oil*
  Salt and pepper to taste
½–1 *teaspoon hot red pepper flakes (or more, to taste)*

ANCHOVY BUTTER

¼ *pound sweet butter and 4–5 anchovies with 1 teaspoon*
   of their oil, blended in a food processor until
   smooth, or pounded together in a mortar

1 *pound linguine or small pasta shells*

Bring a large pot of salted water to a boil for the pasta.

Pick over the scallops to remove any bits of foreign matter, but do not wash them. Char and peel the peppers following the directions for Roasted Peppers (see page 279). Discard the stems, seeds, and white membranes. Cut the peppers into 1-inch squares.

Sauté the peppers and garlic in half the oil in a heavy pan over medium heat for 3 to 4 minutes, stirring often. Season lightly with salt and pepper. Add the pepper flakes, scallops, and the remaining oil. Sauté for 2 to 3 minutes more over low heat. Remove the pan from the heat and set aside.

Prepare the anchovy butter.

Have a large platter for the pasta warmed and ready. Add the linguine or pasta shells to the boiling water and boil, uncovered, stirring from time to time so that the pasta does not stick together. (A little oil added to the water will help.) Cook for about 8 minutes, or until just *al dente*. Drain at once.

Reheat the scallop mixture for a few seconds. Place half the anchovy butter on the warm platter. Add the pasta. Top with the scallop mixture and the remaining anchovy butter. Mix well at the table and serve.

SPAGHETTI WITH GREEN SAUCE, FRANÇOISE DE LA RENTA

6 SERVINGS

SAUCE

5   cups chopped Italian parsley
½   cup mixed fresh herbs (basil, tarragon, oregano, etc.)
    Optional: 2 cloves garlic, peeled
1   green pepper, stemmed, seeded, and trimmed of white
    membrane
20 pitted green olives, rinsed and drained
2   tablespoons capers
    Freshly ground pepper to taste
1–2 cups green olive oil

1½–2 pounds spaghetti
    Optional: ½ stick (4 tablespoons) butter

Mix all the sauce ingredients except the oil and chop them fine. This can be done easily in a food processor with the metal blade. Add the oil. The sauce should be fairly thick.

Boil the spaghetti for about 8 minutes, or until cooked *al dente*, in a large pot of salted boiling water. Drain. Return it to the pot and add the butter, if you like, and the sauce. Toss well and serve. The lightest of light pastas.

SOME EASY PASTA DISHES

Here are some recipes (4 servings each) for easily prepared pasta dishes that we have enjoyed in our travels through Italy. See page 94 for things to remember about cooking pasta.

Spaghetti Ca' Norma

A specialty of Catania in Sicily honors its best-known citizen, Bellini, composer of the opera *Norma*, with a pungent spaghetti and eggplant.

Spaghetti cooked *al dente*, then dressed with a couple of small eggplants sliced unpeeled, fried in olive oil till golden brown and kept warm; 1½ cups of Tomato Sauce (see page 36) simmered for 10 minutes in a little olive oil with a large clove of garlic; chopped fresh basil, salt and pepper to taste, and a generous amount of grated cheese (hard ricotta if you can find it; otherwise Parmesan cheese does very nicely).

Spaghetti with Pesto alla Siciliana

A Sicilian version of Genoese pesto sauce. With a mortar and pestle, pound together 30 basil leaves trimmed of their stems, a handful of parsley, 3 cloves of garlic, a few fresh celery leaves, ½ cup of ripe tomatoes, peeled and seeded. Salt and pepper to taste. Add about ½ cup of olive oil, more if needed.

Serve over pasta (cooked *al dente*) with grated pecorino or Parmesan cheese.

Blender method: Place the oil in the blender first. Add all the remaining ingredients for the sauce. Blend until well mixed.

Food processor method: Place all the ingredients in a processor with the steel blade. Process the sauce until well mixed.

Spaghetti with Basil
(Spaghetti al Basilico)

Chop finely 30 fresh basil leaves together with 1 large clove of garlic. When your spaghetti is almost done, heat ¼ cup of olive oil in a large pan and lightly fry the basil-garlic mixture in it over low heat. Drain the spaghetti well, transfer it to the pan, sprinkle it with salt, a heady amount of freshly ground pepper, grated cheese (half pecorino, half Parmesan is traditional). Toss well and serve from the pan.

Spaghetti with Laurel

In a large heavy pan, cook 1 medium onion, finely chopped, in 2 tablespoons each of olive oil, butter, and water. Cook, covered, stirring from time to time till the onions are golden. Add ¾ pound of peeled, seeded, and chopped ripe tomatoes, 10 bay leaves, and ½ teaspoon each of salt, pepper, and cinnamon. Cook, covered, for 10 minutes while you boil the spaghetti. The bay leaves can be discarded, if you

like, before serving. When the spaghetti is cooked *al dente*, drain it
well. Add it to the sauce, mix well, sprinkle with grated Parmesan
cheese and serve.

Spaghetti with Uncooked Sauce

The uncooked sauce is made by beating 3 egg yolks in a bowl and
stirring in 4 to 6 chopped anchovies, ¼ pound of finely diced mozzarella, generous twists of pepper but little or no salt.

Drain 1 pound of spaghetti cooked *al dente* and return it *immediately* to the warm pot. Add the sauce and toss quickly but well over low
heat to melt the mozzarella and cook the eggs slightly.

A light but tasty dish with no butter or oil.

Fusilli alla Pizza

A nice change for pizza lovers. In an iron pan with a little olive oil,
heat ¾ pound of ripe tomatoes, peeled, seeded, and coarsely chopped
(or a 14-ounce can of imported Italian plum tomatoes, coarsely
chopped, with some of the juice) for 10 to 15 minutes with a peeled
and bruised garlic clove. Discard the garlic and season to taste with
salt, pepper, and oregano. Add 10 pitted black olives and 1 pound of
fusilli, cooked *al dente* and drained carefully. Sprinkle with grated
cheese. Transfer to a buttered baking dish. Decorate with 6 anchovies.
Cover with ¼ pound of thinly sliced mozzarella and bake in a hot oven
for about 10 minutes, or until the mozzarella melts.

SPAGHETTI À LA RUSSE

⌒

A Roman friend gave us this spaghetti with a Russian accent.

3–4 SERVINGS

1–2   *tablespoons olive oil*
1–2   *tablespoons salt*
   1   *pound angel hair spaghetti, capellini, or vermicelli*
2–3   *tablespoons butter, at room temperature*

½ cup sour cream, at room temperature
   Grated rind of half a lemon
1 teaspoon lemon juice
¼ pound red caviar, or black if you feel extravagant
   (separate the caviar into half-teaspoonfuls as
   carefully as possible)
1 tablespoon vodka
   Freshly ground pepper to taste
2–3 tablespoons chopped fresh dill
2–3 tablespoons chopped fresh chives

Bring a large pot of water to a rolling boil. Add the olive oil and salt.
Add the pasta and stir to separate the strands. Cook, uncovered, for
just a few minutes until *al dente*. Meanwhile, warm a platter with the
butter and the sour cream on it in a low oven.

Drain the pasta carefully. Transfer it to the warm platter. Add all
the remaining ingredients. Toss carefully in order not to bruise the
caviar and serve immediately. *No cheese with this one.*

RON LEHRMAN'S SEAFOOD
SPAGHETTI

෴

4–6 SERVINGS

2 dozen mussels, scrubbed, with beards removed
2 dozen small clams, scrubbed
1 cup white wine
1–1¼ pounds imported spaghetti
4 tablespoons sweet butter
6 tablespoons olive oil
3 cloves garlic, chopped
1½ pounds small squid, cleaned and cut into ½-inch
    slices
¾ pound shrimp, peeled, deveined, and cut in half
2 tablespoons lemon juice
   Freshly ground pepper
½–⅔ cup chopped parsley

Put the mussels and clams in a pot with a tight-fitting lid. Pour the wine over them, cover the pot and steam them open. As soon as they open, remove them from their shells and set them aside in a bowl with some of their broth. Strain the remaining broth through cheesecloth and set aside. If the clam-mussel broth is very salty, do not salt the spaghetti water or the spaghetti.

Cook the spaghetti for about 8 minutes, or until *al dente*. Stop the cooking a little sooner than usual, as the spaghetti will be cooked again when the ingredients are combined. Drain.

Reheat the broth. Put 2 tablespoons of the butter, the olive oil, and the garlic in a heavy-bottomed pot large enough to hold the finished dish. Cook until the garlic begins to brown. Add the squid and shrimp and cook for 1 to 2 minutes. Add half of the heated broth, the clams and mussels, the rest of the butter, and the spaghetti. Toss and stir quickly over high heat. Add more broth as it cooks away so that there is always some liquid at the bottom of the pot. The broth will absorb some starch from the spaghetti and thicken slightly.

Remove from heat, add the lemon juice, a generous amount of pepper, and all but 2 tablespoons of the parsley. Toss well and set aside for 3 to 4 minutes. Sprinkle with the remaining parsley and serve.

A SUGGESTED MENU

(*see Index for recipes*)

GRATIN OF TOMATOES AND ZUCCHINI

RON LEHRMAN'S SEAFOOD SPAGHETTI

GREEN SALAD

INSTANT PINEAPPLE ICE

wine: WHITE CHIANTI

SUSANNA AGNELLI'S SPAGHETTI IN SAFFRON CREAM

❧

12 SERVINGS

6   tablespoons salt
3   tablespoons olive oil
1½   cups heavy cream

1½   teaspoons saffron or more to taste, powdered if
        available
1   teaspoon lemon juice
1   stick (¼ pound) butter or more, cut into slices, softened
        to room temperature
3   pounds spaghetti, fresh if available
3   cups freshly grated imported Parmesan cheese
        Salt and freshly ground pepper to taste

Bring a 12-quart pot of water to a rolling boil. Add the salt and olive
oil. Cover and keep at the boil until ready to cook the spaghetti.

Scald the cream. Add the saffron and lemon juice. Cover and allow
the saffron to steep. Warm a platter and put half the butter on it.

Add the spaghetti to the boiling water and cook for about 10 minutes, or until *al dente*. If fresh, it will be ready in about 2 minutes.
Drain immediately, and transfer it to the platter. Pour the saffron-
cream sauce over the spaghetti. Sprinkle it with 1 cup of the grated
cheese. Add salt and pepper. Put the remaining butter on top and
toss thoroughly. Pass the remaining cheese separately.

TEN-MINUTE SPAGHETTI

What Harry of Harry's Bar in Venice likes to cook at home. The sauce
is made while the spaghetti cooks. Harry never adds grated cheese,
but he won't mind if you do.

4 SERVINGS

4   very ripe tomatoes
¼   cup chopped fresh basil
        Salt and freshly ground pepper
1   tablespoon olive oil
1   pound imported Italian spaghetti
2   tablespoons butter

Boil 4 quarts of water in a large pot. Score the tomatoes opposite the
stem ends and plunge them into the water for 30 seconds to loosen
the skins. Peel, seed, and chop them coarsely. Cook, with nothing
added, in a heavy saucepan, covered, for about 6 minutes over medium

heat, stirring often. Add the chopped basil with salt and pepper to taste. If the sauce is too thin, raise the heat to boil down the excess liquid and cook for a minute or two, stirring constantly.

Meanwhile, bring the water in the pot back to a rolling boil, add the oil and 2 tablespoons of salt. Add the spaghetti, separating the strands from time to time with a fork. Test the spaghetti after about 5 minutes. Do not overcook it; it should be *al dente*. Drain the spaghetti and return it to the pot. Add the tomato sauce and the butter. Mix together and serve.

VARIATION: Make an uncooked tomato sauce. Simply chop the tomatoes coarsely. Season to taste with salt and pepper. Add 6 tablespoons of olive oil and 1 tablespoon of vinegar. Set aside in a warm place while you cook the spaghetti. Small cubes of mozzarella can be added if you like.

RICE DISHES

And they brought an Owl, and a useful Cart,
And a pound of Rice, and a Cranberry Tart,
And a hive of silvery Bees.

EDWARD LEAR

Same old slippers,
Same old rice,
Same old glimpse of
Paradise.

WILLIAM JAMES LAMPTON,
June Weddings

*M*any people think that rice can be boiled only at the last minute. Not at all! Add 1 cup of rice to 1¾ cups of boiling salted water in a heavy pot with a tight-fitting lid. Bring it back to a boil, lower the heat, cover, and cook for 15 to 17 minutes, or until the water evaporates. Add 2 tablespoons of butter and ¼ cup of cold water. Toss well with a fork, and set the pot, tightly covered, on a flame tamer over low heat. It will keep for an hour.

Herbed Rice: Boil 1 cup of rice in the usual way. Put the cooked rice in a serving bowl with a generous amount of butter and a cup of chopped fresh parsley, dill, coriander, or mint. Salt, pepper, and mix well.

Armenian Rice: Use yogurt instead of butter. Light and delicious!

Crusty Persian Rice: Boil long-grain rice for 10 minutes in salted water. Drain well. Melt a stick (¼ pound) of butter. Pour half of it into the bottom of a lightweight pot with a tight-fitting lid. Add 2 tablespoons of water or yogurt. Pile the half-cooked rice into the pot, mounding it up in the center. Pour the rest of the melted butter over it. Cook over medium heat for 10 minutes, then cover it tightly with the lid wrapped in a clean dish towel to absorb the steam. Cook it for 30 minutes on a flame tamer over low heat. A golden crust will form at the bottom. Set the bottom of the pot in an inch of cold water for a minute or two, then set it on a table with a smart rap to loosen the crust. Serve each guest a portion of the rice with some of the crisp golden crust.

RICE SALADS

A fine way to use leftover rice (which should first be reheated in a steamer over boiling water) and a splendid addition to any buffet table.

Rice salads should not be refrigerated. Serve them cool or at room temperature. The basis for any rice salad is boiled rice mixed with French dressing while still warm. When cool, add a generous amount of chopped fresh herbs (chives, dill, chervil, tarragon, or basil). Among the possible additions are leftover cooked chicken or ham, or both; cooked shrimp, mussels, clams, lobster, or any of these combined.

Here are two possible ways of making rice salad:

Rice Salad I: Mix boiled rice with flaked tuna fish, capers, diced green peppers, celery, scallions, olives, radishes, and chopped parsley. Add three parts of olive oil to one part of tarragon vinegar, salt, and freshly ground pepper to taste and toss well.

Rice Salad II: Marinate ripe tomatoes, peeled, seeded, and coarsely chopped, and a teaspoon or two of finely sliced scallions in a vinaigrette dressing (three parts of olive oil to one part of wine vinegar, salt, and freshly ground pepper to taste) for 30 minutes. Add it to boiled rice at room temperature with an extravagant amount of chopped fresh basil. Toss well and serve.

RISOTTO, MILANESE STYLE
(Risotto alla Milanese)

⟨~⟩

We often use this recipe to serve three or four, reserving the leftover risotto to make crusty Risotto Pancake (see next page).

6–8 SERVINGS

5   *cups Beef Broth (see page 47) or Chicken Broth (see page 48)*
1   *teaspoon saffron*
2   *tablespoons olive oil*
5   *tablespoons butter*
1   *small onion, finely chopped*
2   *tablespoons diced beef marrow*
2   *cups imported Arborio rice*
1   *cup dry white wine*
    Salt and freshly ground pepper to taste
1   *cup freshly grated imported Parmesan cheese*

Bring the broth to a boil. Lower the heat and keep it simmering throughout the preparation of the risotto. Transfer ½ cup of the broth to a small pot over the lowest heat and steep the saffron in it.

In a heavy-bottomed pot, warm the oil and 3 tablespoons of the butter over medium heat. Add the chopped onion and the marrow and sauté them until the onion is translucent. Add the rice and cook, stirring until every grain is coated with fat (2 to 4 minutes). Add the wine and cook, stirring, until it has evaporated.

Add the simmering broth gradually—about ½ cup at a time—stirring and scraping the bottom of the pot with a wooden spoon. Wait until each addition is absorbed before adding more broth. After 15 minutes, add the saffron-infused broth to the rice. From now on, stir and scrape constantly and add broth as needed by quarter-cupfuls. The cooking will take about 30 minutes. The risotto is ready when the rice is *al dente*, cooked but still somewhat firm. Turn off the heat. Add salt and pepper to taste (salt may not be needed), the remaining 2 tablespoons of butter, and ¼ cup of the cheese. Let it rest, covered, for 2 minutes. Mix well and serve. Pass the remaining cheese separately.

VARIATIONS:

Risotto with White Truffles. Cover the risotto with finely sliced white truffles just before serving.

Risotto with Fennel. Add one diced fennel bulb to the chopped onion when you sauté it.

Risotto with Meat Sauce. Pack the cooked risotto tightly in a buttered ring mold. Invert it onto a platter and fill the center with 2 cups of hot Meat Sauce, Bolognese Style (see page 42).

Risotto with Chicken Livers. Sauté 4 chicken livers, coarsely cut up, in 2 tablespoons of butter for 2 or 3 minutes. Season them with salt and freshly ground pepper. Stir in 2 tablespoons of chopped fresh sage, parsley, or basil. Stir the livers into the risotto a few minutes before you stop cooking it. Or pack the cooked rice tightly in a buttered ring mold. Invert it onto a platter and fill the center with the cooked livers. Sprinkle generously wtih chopped parsley and chives.

RISOTTO PANCAKE
(Riso al Salto)

இ~ஃ

A great favorite in Milan is this crusty pancake made of leftover *risotto alla milanese.*

You will need an 8- or 9-inch nonstick pan with sloping sides, and a flexible spatula.

1–2 SERVINGS AS A FIRST COURSE;
3–4 SERVINGS A AS SIDE DISH

    1   *teaspoon olive oil*
    1   *tablespoon butter*
  1¼ *cups leftover Risotto, Milanese Style (see page 109)*
  ¼–½ *cup freshly grated imported Parmesan cheese*

Heat the oil and half the butter until sizzling. Turn the heat to low and and spoon the rice into the pan, pressing it down with the back of the spoon to form an even pancake about ½- to ¾-inch thick. Cook, shaking the pan often, over very low heat. Dribble a little more butter down the sides of the pan if needed, carefully prying up the edges of the pancake with the spatula to let the butter run under it. When the bottom is crusty and brown (after about 15 to 20 minutes), loosen it with the spatula and slide the pancake onto a dish. Protecting your hands with pot holders, invert the pan over it. Hold the pan and dish tightly together and turn them upside down so that the pancake falls back into the pan crusty side up. Do not be alarmed if it does not hold its shape. Just press it back into shape with the spatula. Cook for 5 to 10 minutes more over very low heat until the bottom is brown and crusty. Serve as a luncheon dish or as a first course. Pass the grated cheese separately.

NOTE: If you have a nonstick pan with an ovenproof handle, there is no need to invert the pancake. When the bottom is crusty, simply put the pan under the broiler until the top is browned.

RISOTTO WITH ASPARAGUS, MARIA-TERESA TRAIN

ᏏᏪ

4–6 SERVINGS

2 pounds asparagus
1 quart Chicken Broth (see page 48)
3 tablespoons olive oil
4–5 tablespoons sweet butter
½ cup finely chopped shallots or onions
Salt and freshly ground pepper to taste
1 pound imported Arborio rice
½ cup dry white wine
1 teaspoon saffron
1 cup grated imported Parmesan cheese

Break off and discard the tough ends of the asparagus. Wash the asparagus and cut off the tips in 3-inch lengths. Bring the chicken broth to a boil. Add the asparagus tips. Cook them until they are tender when pierced with the tip of a sharp knife but still crisp and bright green. Remove them from the broth with a slotted spoon and reserve. Put the asparagus stems into the broth, lower the heat and simmer, covered, to enrich the broth with the flavor of the asparagus.

Heat the oil and half the butter in a large heavy pan. Add the chopped shallots. Cook, stirring with a wooden spoon, for 3 to 4 minutes, or until translucent but not browned. Season lightly with salt and pepper. Add the rice and cook, stirring constantly, for 2 to 4 minutes, or until each grain is glistening with fat. Add the wine, raise the heat to medium and cook, stirring, until the wine has evaporated.

Remove the asparagus stems from the broth and discard them. Steep the saffron in the broth for 5 minutes. Add just enough hot broth to the rice to cover it and cook, stirring, until the broth is absorbed by the rice. Continue cooking and stirring, adding more broth a little at a time to keep the rice covered. After 10 minutes, begin to test the rice. It must be *al dente*. (You may not have to use all the broth to cook the rice to this point or you may have to use a little additional broth or hot water. Whatever you do, do not overcook the risotto.)

A couple of minutes before the risotto is ready, carefully stir in the reserved asparagus tips to heat them through. As soon as the risotto is *al dente*, remove the pan from the heat and stir in one third of the cheese and the remaining butter. Taste and correct the seasoning.

Let the risotto rest in the pan for 2 to 3 minutes. Serve it with the remaining grated cheese passed separately.

A SUGGESTED MENU

(see Index for recipes)

RISOTTO WITH ASPARAGUS, MARIA-TERESA TRAIN

CHICKEN BREASTS WITH MUSHROOMS

CHRISTOPHE DE MENIL'S PERNOD ICE CREAM

wine: LAMBRUSCO

RISOTTO WITH SAUSAGES
(Risotto con Salsiccie)

6–8 SERVINGS

12–16	*sweet Italian sausages (made with fennel if possible)*
10–12	*tablespoons butter*
2	*tablespoons olive oil*
1	*cup finely chopped onion*
1	*cup finely chopped celery*
½	*cup finely chopped green pepper*
2–3	*cups dry white wine*

3   cups imported Arborio rice
1   teaspoon dried sage or 1 tablespoon chopped fresh
       sage
   Salt and freshly ground pepper to taste
3–4 cups Chicken Broth (see page 48)
2   cups freshly grated imported Parmesan cheese

To prevent the sausages from splitting, prick them in several places on both sides with a small sharp knife or skewer, then soak them in lukewarm water for 2 minutes. Drain and dry on paper towels.

Heat 4 tablespoons of the butter in a heavy frying pan large enough to hold the sausages in a single layer. Sauté them over medium heat, turning them once to brown them well on both sides.

In another large heavy pan, heat 4 tablespoons of butter with the oil until the butter is melted. Add the onion, celery, and green pepper. Cook, stirring occasionally, until the vegetables are wilted. Do not brown them. Spoon 2 to 3 tablespoons of the fat from the sausages into the chopped vegetable mixture.

Add enough wine to the sausages to come halfway up their sides. (Reserve ½ cup wine for the rice.) Reduce the heat and cook slowly for 15 to 20 minutes, turning the sausages once.

Add the rice to the vegetables. Cook over low heat, stirring, till each grain of rice is glistening and coated with fat. Add ½ cup of wine; when it has evaporated, stir in the sage, salt, and pepper.

(The recipe can be prepared ahead of time up to this point. In that case, turn off the heat under both pans and let the sausages and rice rest uncovered. Reheat when ready to proceed.)

Heat the broth. Add just enough to cover the rice. Mix well with a wooden spoon and cook over low heat. As the liquid evaporates, add hot broth, a little at a time, so that the rice is always just covered. After 10 minutes, taste the rice. Do not overcook. If the broth is used up before the rice is cooked, a little hot water can be added. When the rice is *al dente*, remove the pan from the heat, stir in the remaining butter and 1 cup of the cheese. Taste and correct the seasoning. Mix well, then let it rest for 3 to 4 minutes.

Arrange the sausages like the spokes of a wheel on top of the rice in the pan. Reduce any liquid in the sausage pan over high heat until it is thick and syrupy and pour it over the sausages. Serve on warmed plates. Or if you prefer, transfer the rice to a heated platter, then top with the sausages and their sauce. Pass the remaining grated cheese separately.

GREEN RISOTTO WITH SORREL

⌒

6 SERVINGS

2   *tablespoons olive oil*
6   *tablespoons butter*
½   *cup finely chopped carrot*
1   *cup finely chopped onion*
1   *cup finely chopped fennel or celery*
4   *fully packed cups (about 1 pound) chopped sorrel*
2   *cups imported Arborio rice*
    Salt and freshly ground pepper to taste
4   *cups Chicken Broth (see page 48)*
1½ *cups freshly grated imported Parmesan cheese*

Melt the oil and 4 tablespoons of the butter in a large heavy frying pan over low heat. Add the chopped carrot, onion, and fennel to the pan. Cook for 10 minutes, stirring often.

Add all but 1 cup of the chopped sorrel. Cook, stirring, for 2 minutes. Add the rice and stir till all the grains are coated with the oil-butter mixture. Season to taste with salt and pepper. Add 3 cups of the chicken broth and bring to a boil, stirring occasionally. As the broth cooks away, gradually add just enough of the remaining broth to keep the rice covered. Simmer, uncovered, for about 15 minutes, or until the rice is cooked *al dente*, that is, still firm when you bite into it. About 2 minutes before you expect it to be ready, stir in the remaining cup of chopped sorrel.

Remove from the heat and stir in the remaining butter and ½ cup of the grated cheese. Let the risotto sit for 2 or 3 minutes before serving. Correct the seasoning. Pass the remaining cheese separately. Serve as a first course.

A SUGGESTED MENU

(see Index for recipes)

GREEN RISOTTO WITH SORREL

ZUCCHINI TOMATO SALAD

CAPUCCINO PARFAIT

wine: BIANCO TOSCANO (VILLA ANTINORI)

A SEAFOOD RISOTTO FOR SONO
(Risotto ai Frutti di Mare)

᠔

4–6 SERVINGS

2   pounds mussels
2   cups dry white wine
1   sprig thyme or 1 teaspoon dried
5   peppercorns
2   cloves or ½ teaspoon powdered
2   cloves garlic, peeled, halved, and bruised
1   small onion, coarsely chopped
12 shrimp, small to medium size
½   cup scallops
8   tablespoons butter
2   tablespoons olive oil
2   cloves garlic, peeled and bruised
1   cup chopped onion
½   cup finely chopped fennel or celery
2   cups imported Italian rice, such as Arborio rice
    Salt and freshly ground pepper to taste
    About 2 cups Fish Stock (see page 46) or clam broth
¼   cup chopped fresh parsley or chives

Scrub the mussels under cold water and remove the beards. Discard
any mussels that will not close; this means they have spoiled. Put an
inch of water in a pot large enough to hold all the mussels. Add the
wine, thyme, peppercorns, cloves, halved garlic cloves, and onion.
Bring to a boil, reduce the heat, and cook for 5 minutes. Add the
mussels. Cook over high heat till all the mussels open. (Discard any
that refuse to open.) Remove the mussels from their shells and reserve.
Strain the mussel broth into a bowl through a sieve lined with a triple
thickness of cheesecloth that has been wrung out in cold water. Reserve the broth.

Peel the shrimp and keep them in a cool place—but not in the refrigerator. Pick over the scallops, discarding any bits of foreign matter, *but do not wash them.* Set aside in a cool place.

Heat 4 tablespoons of the butter and the oil in a large heavy pan.

Add the garlic cloves, onion, and fennel. Cook, stirring often, over medium heat, until the onion is translucent but not browned. Discard the garlic as soon as it turns golden brown. (Garlic lovers may prefer to mince the garlic and add it when the onions are translucent. In that way it can be kept in the dish.)

Add the rice and cook, stirring, till each grain is coated with fat. Season lightly with salt and generously with pepper. Add enough of the reserved mussel broth to cover. Cook over medium heat, stirring often. As the liquid cooks away, add more mussel broth to cover. If you run out of mussel broth, add fish stock or clam broth as needed.

After 15 minutes, sauté the shrimp and scallops in 2 tablespoons of the butter, then push them down into the rice so that they are covered along with the mussels and cook the risotto for 2 minutes more.

Cut the remaining 2 tablespoons of butter into small bits and stir it into the rice. Taste and correct the seasoning. Sprinkle with parsley. Let the risotto rest for 2 minutes before serving it from the pan, or turning it out onto a heated platter. (Traditionally, grated cheese is not served with seafood risotto, but there are cheese-loving iconoclasts who prefer to have grated imported Parmesan cheese on everything. Pass it separately.)

FISH AND

SHELLFISH

'Tis the voice of the Lobster: I heard him declare
"You have baked me too brown, I must sugar my hair."

LEWIS CARROLL,
Alice's Adventures in Wonderland

In England it's fish, fish, fish!

LENA ROBBINS

Never flounder, never carp!

ARTHUR GOLD AND ROBERT FIZDALE

BAKED FISH WITH ASPARAGUS AND
ASPARAGUS PURÉE, FREDY GIRARDET

∾

Our version of an exquisite dish from the great Swiss chef.

4 SERVINGS

1   2- to 2½-pound red snapper or other firm-fleshed
       white fish
    Salt, freshly ground pepper, and cayenne pepper to
       taste
    Juice of 1 lemon
1   stick (¼ pound) butter, at room temperature
2½ pounds asparagus
½   cup Crème Fraîche (see page 151)
    Garnish: lemon slices

Preheat the oven to 350°.

Season the fish with salt, pepper, and a bit of cayenne. Sprinkle it with lemon juice and dot with 2 tablespoons of the butter. Bake in a buttered dish for 15 to 20 minutes, or until it flakes easily when tested with a fork.

Cut off and discard the tough ends of the asparagus. Peel the stems with a vegetable scraper. Tie the asparagus into bundles and cook them upright (and covered) in just enough boiling salted water so that the tips are steamed while the stems are boiled. Test with the tip of a knife and remove them as soon as they are tender. Important: Keep the liquid in the pot. Cut the asparagus one inch below the tips and drain on paper towels. Reserve.

Reduce the liquid by cooking it, uncovered, over high heat until only 3 to 4 tablespoons of concentrated essence remains. (This seemingly exaggerated procedure is essential to the recipe, as the essence of asparagus gives this dish its special flavor.)

Put the asparagus stems in the container of a food processor with the serrated knife attachment. Add the asparagus essence, 2 tablespoons of the butter, and the *crème fraîche*. Process till you have a very smooth purée. Taste and correct the seasoning. In a wide pan, heat the asparagus tips in the remaining butter. Remove the skin from the fish. Lay the fish on a heated platter, put the asparagus along one side, the tips pointing outward, and spoon the purée down the other side. Garnish with lemon slices and serve at once.

A SUGGESTED MENU

(see Index for recipes)

BRAISED LEEKS ON TOAST, FRED LAZARUS

BAKED FISH WITH ASPARAGUS AND ASPARAGUS PURÉE,

FREDY GIRARDET

ENDIVE SALAD WITH ALMOND DRESSING

STRAWBERRY MOUSSE, ALAIN CHAPEL

wine: WHITE CHASSAGNE-MONTRACHET

BAKED FISH, MOROCCAN STYLE

᠗

One of the world's great fish preparations. The fish is marinated in *chermoula*, the traditional Moroccan marinade, for several hours before it is cooked. *Chermoula* is a superb marinade for any fish, and for shad roe.

8–10 SERVINGS

CHERMOULA

1½ *cups (about 2 bunches) fresh coriander*
5 *cloves garlic, peeled*
1 *1-inch piece fresh ginger root, peeled, or 1 tablespoon*
    ground
2 *tablespoons paprika*
1 *tablespoon cumin*
½ *teaspoon cayenne pepper*
⅓ *cup water*
¼ *cup vinegar*
¼ *cup lemon juice*
¼ *cup peanut oil*

1 *6- to 7-pound whole striped bass, red snapper, tilefish,*
    whitefish, pike, or any other firm-fleshed fish
   Salt and freshly ground pepper to taste
4 *large potatoes*
3–4 *green peppers*
3–4 *small hot peppers (or 1–2 teaspoons hot red pepper*
    flakes)
8 *small ripe tomatoes or half the contents of a 2-pound*
    3-ounce can Italian plum tomatoes
3 *tablespoons peanut oil*

To make the chermoula: Chop the coriander, garlic, and ginger root, then mash them in a mortar with the paprika, cumin, and cayenne. Gradually add the water, vinegar, lemon juice, and oil. Mix till you have a smooth paste. Or put all the ingredients in a food processor with the knife blade and process until smooth.

Sprinkle the fish lightly inside and out with salt and pepper. Score it on both sides. Spoon a little of the *chermoula* marinade on the bottom of a platter. Lay the fish on top.

Spoon some of the marinade inside the fish and the remaining marinade over the top. Set the fish aside in a cool place for 4 hours or longer.

Preheat the oven to 450°.

Peel the potatoes and cut them into thin uniform slices. Parboil them for 3 to 4 minutes. Drain them well, dry them on paper towels and set them aside.

Char and skin the green peppers following the procedure for Roasted Peppers (see page 279). Discard the core, seeds, and white membrane, and cut the peppers into wide strips. Dice the hot peppers after removing the core and seeds.

Peel and seed the tomatoes and chop them coarsely. Reserve the juice. (If you are using canned tomatoes, drain them and reserve the juice, then chop them coarsely.)

Brush the oil over the bottom of a baking dish large enough to hold the fish. Arrange the potatoes on the bottom of the dish. Place the fish, with all the marinade that adheres to it, on top of the potatoes. Reserve the remaining marinade. Scatter the peppers and the tomatoes over and around the fish. Carefully spoon the reserved tomato juice and the remaining marinade over and around the fish. Bake for about 1 hour, or until the fish flakes easily and the potatoes are tender.

BRAISED SWORDFISH AND LETTUCE
(Chartreuse d'Espadon)

෴

The great French chef Carême called the *chartreuse* "the queen of entrées," and we heartily agree.

12 SERVINGS

> *Beurre manié: 3 tablespoons each chilled butter and*
>   *flour*
> 12 *heads Bibb lettuce*
> 4 *pounds fresh swordfish or tuna, sliced 1½ inches thick,*
>   *then cut into 12 portions*

12   *anchovies*
8–10   *tablespoons olive oil*
4   *large green peppers, trimmed and cut into strips*
2   *large onions, peeled and sliced*
4   *carrots, peeled and sliced*
     Salt and freshly ground pepper to taste
12   *bay leaves*
½   *cup chopped fresh basil or parsley*
4   *cups tightly packed sorrel, stemmed and coarsely*
        shredded
1   *cup tomato purée or 2 ripe tomatoes, skinned, seeded,*
        and chopped
2   *cups dry white wine*

Make a *beurre manié* by working the butter and flour together with your fingers until well combined. Refrigerate until ready to use.

Discard the outer leaves and rinse the lettuces well in several changes of water. Blanch them in boiling water for 1 to 2 minutes and drain them well. When they are cool enough to handle, squeeze out as much water as you can and set them aside.

Make an incision in each piece of fish and stuff an anchovy into it. In a very large casserole or two smaller ones, heat 4 tablespoons of the oil. Stirring constantly, sauté the green peppers over high heat. If the peppers become somewhat charred, so much the better. Lower the heat and add the remaining oil, the onions, and the carrots. Season with a little salt and a generous amount of pepper. Sauté the vegetables, stirring often, until they are almost tender. Lay the portions of swordfish on top of the vegetables in one or two layers. Season the fish lightly with salt and pepper, place a bay leaf on each piece of fish and sprinkle it with chopped basil.

Squeeze the heads of lettuce once more to drain them of as much water as possible and lay them over the fish. Season them with salt and pepper, cover them with the chopped sorrel and pour the tomato purée over them. Add the wine to the casserole and cover it. Simmer over medium heat for about 10 minutes, or until the fish flakes easily. Turn the lettuce once or twice during the cooking and baste with the juices in the casserole. Transfer the fish to a warmed platter and discard the bay leaves. Raise the heat under the casserole and cook for about 5 minutes, adding the *beurre manié* bit by bit to thicken the sauce. Arrange the lettuce over the fish and pour the sauce and vegetables over all.

A SUGGESTED MENU

(*see Index for recipes*)

OUR FAVORITE COLD MUSHROOM SOUP

BRAISED SWORDFISH AND LETTUCE

BLUEBERRY KUCHEN

wine: POUILLY-FUMÉ

COUSCOUS WITH FISH, TUNISIAN STYLE

❦

Couscous, a kind of semolina, is daily fare in North Africa, like pasta in Italy, or rice in the Orient.

In Morocco, couscous is usually prepared with lamb or chicken, but in Tunisia they make a fascinating light couscous with fish that is one of our favorite party dishes. It can be prepared a day ahead, for like many stews it tastes even better the following day.

An indispensable seasoning for couscous is *harissa*, a volcanically hot paste made of chili peppers. Although it is available in some specialty shops, it is easily made and keeps almost indefinitely in the refrigerator. Make it ahead of time. You will need only a spoonful or two for this recipe.

6–8 SERVINGS

HARISSA PASTE

4 *fresh chili peppers or 2 dried*
1 *clove garlic, diced or passed through a garlic press*
1 *teaspoon ground coriander seed*
1 *teaspoon ground caraway seed*
½ *teaspoon salt*
2 *tablespoons olive oil*

COURT BOUILLON

3 *pounds heads (gills discarded), bones, and tails from any white-fleshed fish*
2 *quarts water*

Couscous

2   *16-ounce boxes medium-grain* (grain moyen) *couscous*
¼   *cup vegetable oil*
1   *tablespoon salt*
1   *stick (¼ pound) butter, cut into 8 slices*

Stew

1   *cup vegetable oil*
4   *medium-size onions, sliced not too thin*
5   *green peppers, stemmed, seeded, and cut into 6 pieces
     each*
5   *zucchini, halved lengthwise, then cut into 1-inch pieces*
5   *ripe tomatoes, peeled and coarsely chopped
     Salt and freshly ground pepper to taste*
1   *4- to 6-pound striped bass, cut in half if necessary to
     fit your pot, or 2 3-pound mullets*
1½ *cups chopped parsley*
1   *cup coarsely chopped mint leaves*
1   *whole bulb garlic, each clove peeled and diced or put
     through a garlic press*

To prepare the harissa: Remove the stems and seeds and dice the peppers. If you are using dried peppers, soak them in water, then drain and dice them. In a mortar, mash all the ingredients into a thick paste.

To store the *harissa,* place it in a jar and cover it with a thin layer of olive oil, then cover the jar.

To prepare the court bouillon: Put the fish heads, bones, and tails into a pot with the water. Bring to a boil. Lower the heat and simmer for 30 minutes. Strain through a dampened cheesecloth-lined sieve into a large bowl. Return the liquid to the pot and cook, uncovered, over high heat until it is reduced by half. Set aside.

To prepare the couscous: Put the couscous in a large bowl. Add the oil and stir with a fork until it is well mixed. If you have a *couscoussière,* that special Moroccan double boiler, it is, of course, ideal. Otherwise you can improvise one easily enough. All you need is a large colander that fits tightly into the top of a pot. Add water to the pot, making certain that it will not touch the bottom of the colander, and bring it to a boil. Put the couscous in the colander. Steam the couscous, uncovered, for exactly 20 minutes from the time you see steam rising through the grains.

After the first steaming, return the couscous to the bowl. Stir 1 tablespoon of salt into 2 cups of cold water and pour it into the couscous. Stir gently with a fork or oiled hands until the couscous grains have absorbed the water. *Break up any lumps with your fingers.* Put the couscous back into the colander and steam it, uncovered, for another 20 minutes, again timing the process from the moment the steam becomes visible. Return it to the pot, and this time gently stir in 2 cups of water. As before, gently break up any lumps.

Return the couscous to the colander for the third and last time. By now the grains will have swelled so that you may have to steam it in two batches. Steam each batch, uncovered, for another 20 minutes from the time the steam becomes visible. Put the slices of butter in the bowl and add the couscous. Stir gently, pressing out the lumps with your fingers. Cover the bowl with a dish towel and keep it warm on the middle rack of the oven, set on low. Leave the oven door open. (If you prepare the couscous a day ahead of time, reheat it by steaming it again until it is hot.)

To prepare the stew: While the couscous is steaming, prepare the vegetables. Heat the oil in a heavy pot large enough to hold all the vegetables (and later, the fish). Add the onions and cook, stirring often, for 5 minutes. Add the green peppers. Cook, stirring occasionally, until tender but not too limp (about 10 minutes). Add the zucchini, mix well and cook for 5 minutes. Add the tomatoes, mix well and cook for 5 to 10 minutes, or until the tomatoes are falling apart. Season with 1 teaspoon of salt and 1 tablespoon or more of pepper. Add about 1 quart of the court bouillon. Simmer for 15 minutes.

Remove 2 cups of the liquid in the stew. Make harissa sauce by stirring 1 teaspoon of harissa paste (or more to taste) into the hot liquid. Pour ¼ cup of the sauce back into the stew and stir it in. Put the remaining sauce in a sauceboat and reserve.

Add the fish to the pot just before you steam the couscous for the last time. Simmer for about 15 minutes, or until the fish flakes easily. Five minutes before the fish is done, add the parsley, mint, and garlic to the pot and stir them in gently.

Transfer the fish to a platter. Remove the skin and bones and cut the fish into serving portions. Serve in dishes with rims (spaghetti dishes will do very nicely).

To follow the traditional presentation for this splendid-looking dish, heap the couscous on a large earthenware platter and distribute pieces of fish on top. Remove most of the vegetables from the stew with a slotted spoon and spread them over the couscous and fish. Put the remaining vegetables and some of the liquid in a serving bowl for those who prefer a more liquid couscous. Pass the harissa sauce separately. Be sure to remind your friends that it is very, very hot.

A SUGGESTED MENU

(see Index for recipes)

COUSCOUS WITH FISH, TUNISIAN STYLE

GREEN SALAD

PEARS IN WINE

wine: MÂCON BLANC (WHITE) OR CÔTE DU RHÔNE (RED)

POACHED FISH WITH VEGETABLES AND GARLIC MAYONNAISE

(Pot-au-Feu de Poissons à l'Aïoli)

ᕦᕤ

Use saltwater fish, such as striped bass, sea bass, bluefish, tilefish, or a combination. Or freshwater fish, such as perch, pike, or whitefish.

6–8 SERVINGS

1 *4- to 5-pound fish or 2 2½-pound fish*
Fish Stock (see page 46)

GARLIC MAYONNAISE (Aïoli)
10–12 *cloves garlic, peeled and put through a garlic press*
½ *teaspoon Dijon mustard*
Salt
4 *large egg yolks*
3 *cups olive oil*
Juice of 1 lemon
¼ *cup lukewarm fish stock or water*

1   *pound each: snow peas, ends trimmed and strings*
      removed; baby carrots, peeled, trimmed, and left
      whole; zucchini, unpeeled and cut into strips;
      scallions, with a little of their green (or almost any
      vegetable you like—green beans, peas, lima beans,
      potatoes, cauliflower or broccoli florets)
    Garnish: 4–6 hard-boiled eggs, halved; several sprigs
      of parsley or watercress

Remove the fish from the refrigerator while you prepare the fish stock and the garlic mayonnaise.

Garlic mayonnaise: Place the garlic in a mortar with the mustard and a pinch of salt. Pound it to a smooth paste. Add the egg yolks. Stir and pound until the mixture is thick and creamy. Add 1 cup of oil, a teaspoon at a time, pounding and stirring it in as you go until you have a thick sauce.

With a whisk, beat in some of the lemon juice and fish stock or water. Add the remaining oil gradually, whisking constantly. Thin as you go, if necessary, with more lemon juice and fish stock or water. The sauce should have the consistency of a heavy mayonnaise. Taste and correct the seasoning by adding more salt or lemon juice. Set aside.

Put the fish (wrapped in cheesecloth for easy removal) in a fish poacher and add enough fish stock to cover. Simmer for about 20 minutes, or until the fish flakes easily when tested with a fork.

Remove the fish to a large platter. Carefully peel off the skin, remove the fins, but leave the head and tail intact. Turn the fish and remove the skin from the other side. Cover it with plastic wrap and keep it in a cool place.

Boil each vegetable separately in lightly salted boiling water until it is tender but still crisp. (Snow peas, for example, will be ready in a minute or two.) Rinse the vegetables immediately in cold water to stop the cooking process and drain them well. Cover with plastic wrap and keep them in a cool place.

Arrange the vegetables in decorative clusters around the fish and garnish with hard-boiled eggs and sprigs of parsley or watercress. Serve the fish accompanied by garlic mayonnaise. Equally good served hot.

NOTE: For those who find a rich garlic mayonnaise too challenging, try Green Sauce (see page 219).

FISH ROE WITH SORREL SAUCE

❦

Shad roe is a highly prized delicacy. But do not overlook the roe of less glamorous fish. You will find them subtly intriguing, and much less expensive.

4 SERVINGS

1½ *pounds fish roe (roe of weakfish, bluefish, herring, cod*
       —or, of course, shad)
     Salt and freshly ground pepper to taste
     Flour for dredging
4   *tablespoons butter*

SAUCE

4   *tablespoons butter*
2–4 *tablespoons minced scallions*
2   *tablespoons chopped mint (or tarragon)*
1   *pound sorrel leaves, shredded*
1   *cup heavy cream*
2   *egg yolks*
     A pinch of sugar

Have the roe at room temperature. Wash and pat it dry. Season with salt and pepper. Dredge with flour on both sides. Melt the butter over low heat in a skillet just large enough to hold the roe in a single layer. Cook the roe, turning it once, for 5 to 10 minutes, or until tender. Do not overcook it.

Make the sauce: Heat the butter in another skillet. Sauté the scallions till wilted. Add the mint and sorrel and cook, stirring, for 2 or 3 minutes. Remove from the heat. Whisk the cream and egg yolks together. Whisking constantly, add this mixture to the saucepan. Return to low heat and continue whisking until the sauce thickens slightly. Add a pinch of sugar. Salt and pepper to taste. Pour the sauce over the roe and serve at once.

STRIPED BASS WITH ANISE, VIRGIL THOMSON

෧෴

4–6 SERVINGS

1   *4-pound striped bass or other firm white-fleshed fish,*
       cleaned and boned
2   *teaspoons ground anise*
     Salt and freshly ground pepper to taste
     Béarnaise Sauce (see below)

Preheat the oven to 350°. Sprinkle the fish inside and out with the anise, salt, and pepper. Wrap the fish tightly in heavy-duty aluminum foil, and bake it for 40 minutes, or until it flakes easily.

Make a heavy Béarnaise sauce by using 4 egg yolks instead of 3. When the fish is done, remove it from the oven, open one end of the foil and drain the fish juice into a cup. Very gradually stir 3 to 4 tablespoons of the fish juice into the Béarnaise. Open the foil at the table and serve the fish along with boiled potatoes. Pass the sauce separately.

BÉARNAISE SAUCE

෧෴

1   *tablespoon tarragon vinegar*
2   *tablespoons dry white wine*
1   *tablespoon fresh tarragon, chopped, or 1 teaspoon*
       dried
¼   *cup chopped shallots*
½   *teaspoon freshly ground pepper*
1   *stick (¼ pound) butter*
3   *egg yolks*
¼   *teaspoon each of salt and freshly ground pepper*
     Optional: a dash of cayenne pepper

Simmer the first 5 ingredients in a small saucepan until the liquid is reduced to about 1 tablespoon. Remove it from the heat, strain it and reserve. Melt the butter in a small saucepan. Do not allow it to brown. Put the egg yolks and the remaining ingredients in a blender. Cover and blend at high speed, flicking the motor on and off for a few seconds. Remove the cover and, with the motor still on high, blend, pouring in the melted butter very slowly in a thin steady stream. Stop the motor. Add the strained wine-vinegar mixture, cover and blend for 5 seconds longer. Set the blender container in lukewarm water until ready to use.

STUFFED FISH SCHEHERAZADE

෨

A distinguished publisher once told us that if one great recipe can be found in a cookbook, it is well worth its price. This, we like to think, is one of those recipes.

8 SERVINGS

STUFFING

½ pound onions, peeled, halved, and sliced very thin
3 tablespoons olive oil
½ cup dried currants
2–3 dried apricots, coarsely chopped
½ cup lemon juice
½ cup coarsely chopped walnuts
    Salt and freshly ground pepper
½ teaspoon each cinnamon, turmeric, and saffron
1 tablespoon powdered coriander
4 tablespoons chopped fresh coriander (if unavailable,
    use 4 tablespoons chopped fresh parsley and
    increase the powdered coriander to 2–3
    tablespoons)
1 4- to 5-pound striped bass or any other firm-fleshed
    fish, cleaned and with bones removed but left
    whole
3–4 lemons, thinly sliced
½ cup Tomato Sauce (see page 36)

Preheat the oven to 350°.

In a heavy skillet over low heat, sauté the onions in the oil until translucent but not browned. In a small bowl, soak the currants and apricots in the lemon juice. When the onions are ready, add the currants and apricots, draining off and reserving the lemon juice. Add the walnuts, salt and pepper to taste, cinnamon, turmeric, saffron, and powdered and fresh coriander. Cook, stirring, for 2 to 3 minutes. Remove from the heat and stir in half the lemon juice.

Oil a baking dish. Lightly salt and pepper the fish, inside and out, and lay it in the baking dish on a row of half the lemon slices. Open the fish and fill it with the stuffing. (Any stuffing that does not fit easily into the fish can be baked wrapped in foil or in a small buttered baking dish at the same time as the fish, and served along with it.) Close the fish and fasten it with toothpicks or small skewers. Mix the remaining lemon juice with the tomato sauce and pour it over the fish. Lay a row of overlapping lemon slices along the top. Bake for 45 minutes, or until the fish flakes easily when tested with a fork. Serve hot, with parsleyed potatoes, or—equally good—at room temperature, with a rice salad.

Excellent served with Stuffed Mushrooms (see page 274). A chilled Muscadet or Sancerre would be a fine accompaniment.

MACKEREL MARSEILLAISE

෬෴ා

One of the joys of spring when fresh mackerel and herring are available is this incomparable yet simple dish.

2–4 SERVINGS

4   *fillets fresh mackerel or fresh herring*
    Flour for dredging (about ⅓ cup)
    Salt and freshly ground pepper to taste
6   *tablespoons olive oil*
4   *cloves garlic, slightly crushed*
1   *bay leaf*
1   *tablespoon vinegar*
8   *slices lemon*

Dredge the fish fillets lightly on both sides with flour and season them with salt and pepper. Put 4 tablespoons of the oil in a pan and heat it till very hot. Sauté the fillets for 1 to 2 minutes on each side, or until golden brown. Remove them to a warm platter.

Add the remaining oil and the garlic to the pan. Sauté till the garlic is browned, then discard it. Add the bay leaf and vinegar. Add the lemon slices and press down on them with the back of a spoon to extract their juice. Cook a few seconds till the liquid boils up. Pour it over the fish fillets and serve.

A SUGGESTED MENU

(see Index for recipes)

BOUILLABAISSE OF SPINACH

MACKEREL MARSEILLAISE

ARUGULA AND BEET SALAD

OUR FAVORITE STRAWBERRY TART

wine: ROSÉ DE PROVENCE

POACHED SALMON, DOROTHY LICHTENSTEIN

ᔓ

The beautiful wife of the painter Roy Lichtenstein makes a classic poached salmon artistically decorated with cucumber "fish scales."

10–12 SERVINGS

1 *5-to-6-pound fresh salmon, cleaned, wrapped in cheesecloth, with the head and tail intact*

COURT BOUILLON

1 *quart water*
1 *quart dry white wine*
12 *peppercorns*
1 *tablespoon salt*
1 *bay leaf*

1   onion, peeled and quartered
3   stalks celery with green leaves attached, coarsely
        chopped
    A few sprigs of parsley

GARNISH

2–3 cucumbers
     A bunch of watercress
2   lemons, cut into quarters
     Optional: 1 carrot curl, 1 radish, 1 caper

1   cup Green Mayonnaise (see below)

Keep the salmon at room temperature while preparing the court
bouillon. Place all the court bouillon ingredients in a fish poacher
large enough to hold the salmon. Bring to a boil, then cover, reduce
the heat, and simmer for 20 minutes.

Add the salmon and more water if necessary to cover the fish. Bring
to a boil, then lower the heat and poach the fish at the slowest simmer
for about 40 minutes, or until the fish flakes easily when tested with
a fork. Do not overcook, or the fish will break when transferred to a
platter.

Let the salmon cool in the poacher. Drain, discard the cheesecloth,
then pat the salmon with paper towels. Carefully remove the skin.
Transfer the fish to a serving platter, skinned side down, and remove
the remaining skin. Wash the cucumbers, but do not peel them. Slice
them as thin as possible. Decorate the salmon with overlapping rows
of cucumber slices arranged to look like fish scales. Remove any
liquid that accumulates in the platter with a bulb baster.

Surround the fish with watercress and lemons. If you like, outline
the head with a carrot curl, pop a radish into the mouth, and place a
caper over the eye. Serve cold with green mayonnaise.

GREEN MAYONNAISE, OLIVIA MOTCH

ⱳ

ABOUT 1 CUP

2   tablespoons chopped fresh chives
2   tablespoons chopped fresh basil

2   tablespoons tarragon vinegar (or 2 tablespoons
    chopped fresh tarragon and 2 tablespoons plain
    vinegar)
   A pinch of dry mustard
½   teaspoon salt
¼   teaspoon freshly ground white pepper
1   egg
1   cup vegetable or safflower oil

Put all the ingredients except the oil in the blender. Blend on low speed for 30 seconds. Immediately remove the cover or inner cap of the cover and, with the blender running, pour the oil in gradually but not too slowly—it should all be poured in 20 seconds. Should the sauce fail to thicken, transfer it to a small pitcher. Put another egg in the blender and blend on low speed for 30 seconds. Then, with the blender running, pour the failed mayonnaise in gradually and watch it turn into a success.

COULIBIACA
(Russian Salmon Pie)

ᠻᢂ

A recipe from Robert Fizdale's Russian mother.

ABOUT 16 SERVINGS

PASTRY

2   batches Sour Cream Pastry (see page 372) or
    Cream Cheese Pastry (see page 155)

FILLING

1   2½-pound piece fresh salmon
   Court Bouillon (see page 131)
   Juice of 2 lemons
3   tablespoons capers
   Salt and freshly ground pepper to taste
1½ cups rice
1   stick (¼ pound) sweet butter
1   cup finely chopped fresh dill
3   cups finely chopped onions

 2   *teaspoons sugar*
 4   *carrots, boiled and finely chopped*
 3   *hard-boiled eggs, finely chopped*
 2   *egg yolks, lightly beaten with 1 tablespoon water*
 2   *tablespoons melted butter mixed with ½ teaspoon*
        curry powder

SAUCE

 1   *pint sour cream*
 ½   *pint heavy cream, whipped until stiff*
 ¼   *cup finely chopped fresh dill*

Pastry dough: Make two batches of dough, omitting the sugar and using the full amount of the other ingredients each time. (Leftover dough, if any, can be frozen.) Gather the batches of dough together, then divide them into 2 balls, one somewhat larger than the other. Roll the balls of dough lightly in flour, wrap them in foil or plastic and refrigerate them for at least 1 hour before rolling them out.

Filling: Cook the salmon following the procedure for Poached Salmon (see page 131). Reduce the amounts of water and wine so that you have just enough to cover the salmon in the fish poacher. After the fish is cooked and skinned, carefully remove all the bones. Break the fish into small pieces. Mix with the lemon juice and capers. Season with salt and pepper.

Boil the rice *al dente*, about 15 minutes, in a generous amount of salted water. Drain it well. While it is still hot, stir in 2 tablespoons of butter. Add the chopped dill when the rice has cooled a little. Mix thoroughly. Season with salt and pepper. Set aside.

In a heavy pan, heat the remaining butter and sauté the onions until they are wilted but not browned. Just before they are ready, stir in the sugar. Season with salt and pepper. Set aside.

Season the chopped carrots and chopped eggs with salt and pepper, and set them aside.

Preheat the oven to 400°. On a floured board, roll out the smaller ball of dough ⅛ inch thick in a round or an oval to fit the size and shape of your serving platter. Transfer the dough to a baking sheet. Spread the rice-dill mixture to within an inch of the pastry's edge. Cover the rice with layers of salmon, onions, carrots, and chopped eggs, always leaving a 1 inch border of dough. Brush the border with water.

Roll out the larger ball of dough to cover the filling. Carefully place the dough on the filling. Pinch the edges of the upper and lower pastry layers together. Cut off any excess dough. Use a pastry brush to paint the dough with the beaten-egg mixture. Slash the upper crust in several places. Bake for 20 to 25 minutes, or until the pastry is golden brown. Remove the fish from the oven. Pour the melted butter-curry mixture into the slashes in the crust.

Make the sauce by combining the 3 ingredients. Transfer the *coulibiaca* carefully to a serving platter. Serve hot. Pass the sauce separately.

A SUGGESTED MENU FOR GALA OCCASIONS

(see Index for recipes)

BORSCHOK (*a double recipe*)

COULIBIACA

GREEN SALAD

MERINGUE SHELL WITH LEMON FILLING

wine: MEURSAULT

SALMON AND SHRIMP STEW, FREDY GIRARDET

(Blanquette de Saumon, Girardet)

❧

Our adaptation of a recipe given to us by Fredy Girardet, whose restaurant near Lausanne is one of the greatest in the world.

8 SERVINGS

½ pound (16 tablespoons) butter, at room temperature
8 tablespoons finely chopped fresh chives
4 carrots, peeled and cut into ¾-inch lengths
½ pound string beans, trimmed and cut into ¾-inch lengths
16 pearl onions, peeled
1½ cups fresh young peas, shelled
   Salt, pepper, and cayenne pepper to taste

1½ pounds salmon, cut from the tail, filleted and cut into
       1-inch cubes
1½ pounds shrimp, peeled
 1   cup Fish Stock (see page 46) or clam juice
 ¾   cup Crème Fraîche (see page 151)
 2   ripe tomatoes, peeled, seeded, and coarsely chopped

Cream together 6 tablespoons of the butter with 6 tablespoons of the chopped chives until well combined. Cook the carrots, string beans, onions, and peas separately in boiling salted water to cover, with 1 tablespoon of butter in each pot. Drain each vegetable as soon as it is tender and reserve. Season the vegetables with salt, pepper, and cayenne.

In a wide heavy pan, such as a metal paella pan, sauté the salmon cubes (from which you have extracted any remaining bones) and the shrimp in the remaining 6 tablespoons of the butter over medium heat. Stir and turn the salmon and shrimp for 3 minutes, or until they change color on all sides.

Remove the fish to a platter and season with salt, pepper, and a bit of cayenne. Deglaze the pan by adding the fish stock and then stirring and scraping over the heat for a minute or two. Pour the liquid into a large saucepan. Cook it over high heat until it is reduced by half.

Add the crème fraîche and cook, stirring, till it has dissolved. Add the chive butter, cook and stir until it melts. Taste and correct the seasoning. Arrange the salmon and shrimp in a single layer on the bottom of a large buttered paella pan or other large baking dish. Arrange the cooked vegetables and the tomatoes on top, distributing them so that each portion includes some of the vegetables. Pour the sauce over all. Heat in a low oven for 5 to 10 minutes. Sprinkle with the remaining chopped chives, and serve.

RUSSIAN SALMON CUTLETS

ᕲᕽ

You who disdain canned salmon, pass on! We find it—along with canned tuna and canned sardines—as useful and delicious as it is convenient.

4–6 SERVINGS

2   *7¾-ounce cans salmon*
1   *stick (¼ pound) butter*
4   *tablespoons finely chopped onion*
1   *cup minced celery and celery leaves*
½   *cup minced green pepper*
½   *cup finely chopped fresh dill*
2   *eggs, lightly beaten*
1   *cup bread crumbs*
    Salt and freshly ground pepper to taste
    About ⅔ cup bread crumbs for breading

SAUCE

2   *cups sour cream*
¼–½   *cup capers, carefully drained*
    Salt and freshly ground pepper to taste

Drain the salmon thoroughly. Without removing the skin and bones, place it in a bowl and mash it well. Heat 2 tablespoons of the butter in a small heavy frying pan and sauté the onions, celery, and green pepper over low heat until tender but not browned. Add the dill and cook, stirring, for a minute or two. Add this mixture to the salmon. Add the eggs, bread crumbs, salt, and pepper. Mix well.

Rinse your hands in cold water and shape the salmon mixture into 8 or 12 cutlets. Coat the cutlets well on all sides with bread crumbs. Set them on a dish lined with waxed paper and refrigerate them for at least 30 minutes. Sauté them over medium heat in the remaining butter for 8 to 10 minutes, or until they are browned and crusty on both sides. Transfer to a platter and keep warm.

To make the sauce, spoon the sour cream into the same pan. Add the capers. Stir the mixture over low heat, scraping the brown bits from the bottom of the pan into the sauce. Season to taste, pour over the cutlets, and serve.

A SUGGESTED MENU

(see Index for recipes)

TOMATOES PROVENÇALE

RUSSIAN SALMON CUTLETS

RON LEHRMAN'S CUCUMBER SALAD

RHUBARB FOOL

wine: WHITE HERMITAGE

DOUBLE SALMON MOUSSE

❧

You will need a food processor or blender and a 4-cup mold or bowl.
With all the ingredients ready, the mousse can be made in minutes.

6–8 SERVINGS

1   *7¾-ounce can salmon*
½   *pound smoked salmon, sliced and cut into pieces*
3   *tablespoons lemon juice*
¼   *cup firmly packed fresh dill sprigs*
2   *large shallots, peeled and halved*
1   *envelope unflavored gelatin*
½   *cup mayonnaise*
3   *dashes Tabasco sauce*
1   *cup light cream*
    Garnish: 1 bunch watercress

Drain the salmon over a small bowl to collect the juice. Mix the
drained salmon, bones and all, with the smoked salmon and reserve.
Pour the salmon juice into a measuring cup. Add water if needed to
bring the juice to the half-cup mark. Pour it back into the bowl, add
the lemon juice, and reserve.

Process the dill and shallots for 20 seconds in a food processor,
using the steel-knife attachment. Stop the machine and add the
gelatin.

Bring the mixture of salmon juice and lemon juice to a boil. Add
it to the processor immediately and blend for 20 seconds. Add the
canned and smoked salmon, mayonnaise, and Tabasco. Process for
60 seconds.

With the machine running, pour the cream gradually through the
feed tube. Stop the machine. If the mousse is not blended, run it
again for a few seconds until it is smooth. Taste, add more Tabasco
if you like, and blend 1 or 2 seconds longer. Pour into a 4-cup mold
rinsed in cold water but not dried. Refrigerate 4 hours or overnight.

To unmold, run a knife point around the edge of the mold. Dip the mold in hot water for a few seconds, wipe it dry immediately, cover it with an inverted serving platter and turn it upside down, giving the platter and mold, held tightly together, a sharp tap. Serve the mousse garnished with sprigs of fresh watercress.

BAKED MOROCCAN SHAD ROE

6~

4 SERVINGS

4   *pairs shad roe*
    Chermoula *(use one-half the amount in the recipe*
        given in Baked Fish, Moroccan Style (see page
        119)
8–10   *tablespoons butter*
    Salt

Marinate the shad roe in the *chermoula* in a cool place for 2 to 3 hours.

When ready to cook, preheat the broiler. Carefully scrape off and reserve most of the *chermoula* marinade. Melt the butter and put a quarter of it in the bottom of a baking pan large enough to hold the shad roe in a single layer. Place the roe in the pan and brush a little more butter over them. Season lightly with salt. Place 3 to 4 inches from the broiler and cook for 3 minutes. Turn the heat down to 400° and bake the roe in the oven for 12 minutes more, or until they are cooked through, basting often with the remaining butter.

Serve with the remaining *chermoula*, passed separately as a sauce.

A SUGGESTED MENU

(see Index for recipes)

BAKED MOROCCAN SHAD ROE

ALGERIAN CAULIFLOWER AND OLIVE SALAD

ANISE-FLAVORED MELON BALLS

wine: ROSÉ

SAUTÉED SMELTS

❧

Smelts, the freshest possible (allow 4 per person)
Freshly squeezed lemon juice to cover the smelts
Flour for dredging
Butter or vegetable oil
Salt and pepper to taste
Lemon wedges

Marinate the smelts in lemon juice for 1 hour. Dry them on paper towels. Dredge them with flour, coating both sides lightly. Sauté them in butter or oil for 5 minutes, or until they are golden brown, turning them several times to be sure they do not stick. Season with salt and pepper. Serve with lemon wedges.

NOTE: Excellent served cold with vinaigrette sauce. In that case, cook them in oil rather than butter.

FILLETS OF SOLE WITH FRESH NOODLES, LÉON DE LYON
(Filets de Sole aux Nouilles Fraîches)

❧

There is a restaurant tucked away in a small street in Lyons. Called Léon de Lyon, it is one of the most appealing places we know. Jean-Paul Lacombe, the endlessly inventive young chef, was generous enough to give us this exquisite recipe. Do try it.

6 SERVINGS

Fish Fumet (see page 47)
Béarnaise Sauce (see page 128)
3   *tablespoons finely chopped shallots*
3   *tablespoons finely chopped parsley leaves*

3   tablespoons chopped fresh ripe tomatoes (or Italian-
       style canned tomatoes, drained and chopped)
       Salt and freshly ground pepper to taste
6   fillets of sole or flounder
1   stick (¼ pound) butter
3–4 tablespoons heavy cream
3–4 tablespoons Crème Fraîche (see page 151)
1½   pounds egg noodles, freshly made if possible
6   sprigs fresh tarragon or parsley

Prepare the fish *fumet*. Make the Béarnaise sauce and set it in a pan of tepid water until you are ready to use it.

Preheat the oven to 350°.

Butter the bottom of a flameproof baking dish large enough to hold the fish fillets. Sprinkle the dish with half of the shallots, parsley, and tomatoes. Salt and pepper the fillets lightly on both sides, and lay them in the baking dish, overlapping them if necessary. Pour in just enough *fumet* to cover the fish. If necessary, add a bit of white wine or water. Sprinkle the sole with the remaining shallots, parsley, and tomatoes. Bring to a simmer on top of the stove, then dot with about 2 tablespoons of the butter, and cover it with a buttered sheet of waxed or brown paper, cut to fit the dish, buttered side down. Bake just until the fish can be easily pierced with a fork. With a slotted spatula, transfer the fish to a warmed platter. Cover with the paper and keep it warm.

Reduce the liquid in the baking dish over high heat to about ⅔ cup. Remove from heat and stir in the cream, the *crème fraîche*, and 3 tablespoons of the Béarnaise sauce. Season with salt and pepper. Keep the sauce warm, whisking it occasionally.

Cook the noodles in a large pot of boiling salted water (add a bit of oil to prevent sticking). Do not overcook. Fresh noodles are ready after 2 to 3 minutes. Drain them well. Put them on a warm serving platter and toss them with 3 to 4 tablespoons of the butter. Season with salt and pepper. Spoon half of the sauce over the noodles, and arrange the fillets of sole on top. Pour the remaining sauce over all. Put about a tablespoon of Béarnaise sauce on each fillet, decorate with a sprig of tarragon or parsley, and serve.

FISH FRICASSEE

❦

You will need 3 small saucepans, each with a tight-fitting cover and
1 large heavy skillet.

4 SERVINGS

2 *large or 4 small fillets of sole or flounder, cut into
       strips 2½ inches by ½ inch*
   Salt and white pepper to taste
3 *carrots*
½–⅔ *pound string beans*
3–4 *leeks (or 2 bunches scallions)*
   About 1 stick (¼ pound) sweet butter
¼ *cup dry white wine or vermouth*
½ *cup heavy cream*
½ *cup chopped fresh chives*

Season the fish with salt and pepper and reserve.

Peel and trim the carrots. Cut them into 2½-inch lengths, then cut
each piece into vertical strips as close in size and shape to the fish
strips as possible. Trim the beans, cut them in half vertically unless
they are very small, and cut them into 2½-inch lengths. Use only the
white part of the leeks. Wash them carefully and cut them into strips
the length of the fish.

Cook the vegetables separately, each in its own saucepan with
about 1 tablespoon of butter and just enough lightly salted water to
cover. Boil each vegetable, covered, over medium heat until the
vegetables are cooked but still quite crisp. Drain.

Heat 4 tablespoons of the butter in a heavy skillet large enough to
hold all the fish strips in one layer. Sauté for 1 minute, turn the strips
over and cook 1 minute longer, or just until the fish is firm and white.
Remove the fish to a warm platter and arrange the vegetable strips
decoratively around it. Keep it warm in a very low oven while you
prepare the sauce.

Put the remaining butter into the skillet in which the fish was
sautéed. Add the wine and cook over high heat, scraping the sides

and bottom of the pan to incorporate any brown bits. Cook until the wine has almost evaporated. Stir in the cream and cook until it is hot and somewhat thickened. Correct the seasoning. Pour the sauce over the fish and vegetables, sprinkle with chives and serve.

SOLE OR FLOUNDER
WITH SORREL SAUCE

That great invention of the Troisgros brothers, salmon with sorrel sauce, has become a standard dish in many French restaurants. Sole and flounder are also enhanced by the taste of sorrel and are much more easily prepared.

4 SERVINGS

2   large or 4 small fillets of sole or flounder
    Flour for dredging
    Salt, pepper, and cayenne pepper to taste
    About ¼ pound sweet butter
1½ cups fresh spinach, trimmed of stems, and coarsely
      chopped
1½ cups fresh sorrel, trimmed of stems and coarsely
      chopped
1–2 teaspoons finely chopped shallots or scallions
½   cup dry white wine or vermouth
⅓–½ cup Crème Fraîche (see page 151), heavy cream, or
      sour cream, at room temperature

Dredge the fish fillets lightly with flour on both sides, and season them with salt, pepper, and a pinch of cayenne.

Melt 2 tablespoons of the butter in a saucepan and cook the spinach and sorrel together until wilted. Reserve. In a small frying pan, sauté the chopped shallots in 1 tablespoon of the butter for a minute or two. Do not let them brown. Reserve.

Heat 3 tablespoons of butter in a frying pan large enough to hold the fish in a single layer. When the butter is sizzling, add the fish fillets. Sauté them 2 to 4 minutes or until golden brown, shaking the pan often so that they do not stick. Turn them over, and cook the other side until golden brown. Add a bit more butter if needed. Remove them to a heated platter and keep them warm.

Add the shallots and the wine to the fish pan. Cook over high heat, stirring and scraping up all the brown bits till the sauce is reduced to a syrupy consistency. Stir in the cream. Add the spinach and sorrel mixture and stir until the sauce is well combined. Swirl in 1 tablespoon of butter. Taste and correct the seasoning, adding salt, pepper, and a bit of cayenne as desired.

Pour the sauce over the fish. Serve with tiny boiled potatoes.

WHITEBAIT PROVENÇALE
(Sartagnade)

For those who like whitebait but do not enjoy deep-fat frying, the Provençal method of sautéing them *en galette* (in large flat cakes) provides the perfect solution. You will need two 8-inch omelet pans with sloping sides (nonstick pans are ideal) and two round platters with 8-inch flat centers.

8 SERVINGS

> 1   *quart (1½ pounds) whitebait*
> 1   *teaspoon each salt and freshly ground pepper*
> ¼–⅓   *cup flour*
> *About ½ cup olive oil or peanut oil*
> *About ½ cup white wine vinegar or tarragon vinegar*
> *Garnish: ½ cup chopped fresh parsley and chives*
> *mixed together*

If whitebait is truly fresh, and *it must be, to be worth eating*, it is better not to wash it. Just pick over and discard any bits of foreign matter: seaweed, etc. If you feel compelled to wash it, drain and dry it *very* carefully. Season to taste with salt and pepper.

Place the whitebait and flour in a large paper bag and shake it vigorously to coat the fish lightly with flour.

Pour ⅛ inch of oil in each of two 8-inch pans. Warm over medium heat until a few bubbles appear. Put half the whitebait in each pan, spreading and flattening them with the back of a spatula to make flat, even, tightly packed cakes. Continue to press down on the fish cakes as they cook so that they stick together. When the edges begin to brown, carefully lift each cake with the tip of a spatula and dribble a little more oil down the sides of the pan to brown the bottom of the cake. When nicely browned, cover with an inverted platter. Using pads to protect your hands, firmly grasp the pan and platter together, then turn them upside down quickly (over the sink in case any oil runs out) so that the cake falls onto the platter. Add more oil to the pan, heat it until sizzling, then slide the cake back into the pan to brown the other side. Season with more salt and pepper to taste. When both sides of each cake are well browned, slide the cake onto a warm platter. Add a generous splash (2–4 tablespoons) of vinegar to each hot pan, let it sizzle, then pour it over each fish cake. Cut into wedges, sprinkle with parsley and chives, and serve hot. Delicious!

VARIATION: Ovenproof pans, such as cast-iron omelet pans, are essential for this variation. Turn the *provençale sartagnade* into an Italian *frittata* by adding 3 to 4 lightly beaten eggs to the floured whitebait as soon as you put them into the pan. Season to taste with salt and freshly ground pepper. Then fry them, following the recipe, except that when the eggs are set and browned on the bottom, place the pans under the broiler until the tops are set and nicely browned.

ANGELO TORRICINI'S
MARYLAND CRAB CAKES

༄

4–8 SERVINGS

1	pound lump crab meat
2	tablespoons mayonnaise
6	tablespoons finely chopped parsley
1	egg, lightly beaten
8–10	saltine crackers, coarsely crushed

Salt and freshly ground pepper to taste
1 teaspoon Old Bay Seasoning (available at fish stores)
8 saltine crackers, very finely crushed
Vegetable oil for sautéing
4 tablespoons butter
Juice of 1 lemon

Carefully pick over the crab meat. Chop it coarsely. Combine it with
the mayonnaise, 2 tablespoons of the parsley, the egg, the coarsely
crushed crackers, salt, pepper, and Old Bay Seasoning. Mix well.
Rinse your hands in cold water, then mold the mixture into 8 round
cakes.

Roll the cakes in the fine cracker crumbs, then flatten them slightly
with a spatula so that they are about an inch thick. Transfer them to
a platter lined with waxed paper and refrigerate them for 1 hour.

Heat just enough vegetable oil to coat the pan. Sauté the crab
cakes for about 10 minutes, or until golden brown on both sides.
Drain them on paper towels. They can be served immediately or
kept warm in a low oven. Just before serving, heat the butter, lemon
juice, and the remaining 4 tablespoons of the parsley, stirring until
the butter is melted. Pour over the cakes and serve.

CRAB MEAT THOMSON

Virgil Thomson is not only one of America's greatest composers and
music critics, but an extraordinary cook as well. He described this
dish as "a period piece from Prohibition days when everything was
served on toast—chicken à la king, lobster Newburg, and other
goodies."

6–8 SERVINGS

1½ cups heavy cream
2 teaspoons arrowroot
1 pound fresh crab meat, carefully picked over
Salt, white pepper, cayenne pepper to taste
3 tablespoons brandy

In a double boiler, heat the cream with the arrowroot, stirring until it thickens. Add the crab meat and seasonings. Heat through. Stir in the brandy and serve piping hot on buttered white toast.

LOBSTER STEW PIERRE AMORY
(Blanquette de Langoustines)

∽

A complicated, sumptuously festive dish, as prepared by one of France's great private chefs.

6 SERVINGS

6 1¼-pound lobsters, the tails only (the rest can be
        reserved for a lobster salad)
6 medium cucumbers
    Salt and freshly ground white (or black) pepper
¾ pound firm white mushrooms
1½ sticks (12 tablespoons) sweet butter
½ pound bay scallops (or sea scallops, quartered), picked
        over but not washed
4 shallots, minced
2 cups loosely packed fresh sorrel, washed, stemmed,
        patted dry, coarsely shredded, and refrigerated
        until ready to use
1½ cups Crème Fraîche (see page 151)
    A few pinches of saffron
    Nutmeg, freshly ground if possible
    Cayenne pepper to taste
1 tablespoon Pernod
    Beurre manié (2 tablespoons flour and 3 tablespoons
    butter rubbed together with your fingers)
¼ cup finely chopped parsley

Preheat the oven to 275°.
  Steam the lobsters for 5 minutes and drain them. When cool enough to handle, remove the tail meat in one piece from each lobster.

Peel the cucumbers, cut them in half lengthwise and remove the seeds (a melon-ball cutter or serrated grapefruit spoon is good for this purpose). Cut the cucumbers into ¾-inch slices. Steam them over boiling water in a covered pot just until tender. Drain at once and pat them dry. Season them to taste with salt and pepper and reserve.

Remove the stems from the mushrooms and reserve them for another use. Wipe the caps clean with a damp cloth. Sauté them in 2 tablespoons of the butter over medium heat for 3 minutes. Season with salt and pepper. Remove with a slotted spoon to a bowl. Reduce any liquid in the pan to 1 or 2 tablespoons and pour it over the mushrooms in the bowl. Reserve.

Add 2 tablespoons of the butter to the same pan and sauté the scallops for 2 minutes over medium heat, turning and stirring occasionally. Season lightly with salt and pepper. Remove from heat.

Pat the lobster tails dry. Butter a large baking dish. Place the lobster tails and the scallops in it, cover them tightly with foil and bake for 10 minutes.

In a large heavy pan, sauté the shallots in 4 tablespoons of the butter over medium heat, stirring constantly for 2 to 3 minutes. Add the shredded sorrel. Cook, stirring, for 1 to 2 minutes, or until the sorrel wilts. Stir in the *crème fraîche*, add the saffron, a generous squeeze of nutmeg and a pinch or two of cayenne pepper. Cook over low heat, stirring often, for 5 minutes. Add the reserved cucumbers and mushrooms. Cook for another 5 minutes.

Remove the lobsters and scallops from the oven. Arrange the lobster tails in a line down the center of a warm platter with a row of scallops on either side.

Add the Pernod to the pan of cucumbers and mushrooms, raise the heat and cook for 1 minute. If the sauce is thin, add the *beurre manié*, a bit at a time, and cook, stirring, for 2 to 3 minutes, or until the sauce has the desired consistency. With a slotted spoon, remove the mushrooms and cucumbers and any of the sauce that clings to them and arrange them alongside the scallops.

Taste and correct the seasoning of the sauce remaining in the pan. Pour it over all, sprinkle with parsley, and serve at once, accompanied by rice mixed with butter and chopped chives.

BRUSSELS MUSSELS
(Moules Bruxelloise)

6~ɔ

Mussels with celery are to Belgians what hamburgers and onions are to Americans.

4–6 SERVINGS

8 *quarts mussels*
5 *cups celery, cut into ½-inch slices*
2 *cups thinly sliced onions*
2 *shallots, finely chopped*
8 *sprigs parsley, chopped*
1 *clove garlic, finely chopped*
1 *lemon, sliced but not peeled*
  Generous amounts of freshly ground pepper
  Small amount of salt
1 *cup dry white wine*

Scrub the mussels well with a hard brush, remove their beards, and wash them thoroughly in cold water.

Place everything except the mussels in a pot large enough to hold all the ingredients. Add water just to cover. Cover and cook till the vegetables are tender. Add the mussels, cover and cook till all of them open, shaking the pot from time to time. Serve with the broth and vegetables accompanied by French-fried potatoes, the way Belgians do.

MUSSELS WITH BASIL
(Cozze al Basilico)

6~ɔ

You will need one or perhaps two large pots with covers.

4–6 SERVINGS

6 *quarts fresh mussels*
¾ *cup olive oil*
4 *cloves garlic, finely chopped*
1 *hot red pepper, thinly sliced, or about 2 teaspoons*
  hot red pepper flakes

1½ *cups dry white wine*
4 *sprigs fresh oregano or 2 teaspoons dried*
    Salt and pepper to taste
20–30 *fresh basil leaves, coarsely chopped, or 4–5 teaspoons*
      dried
3 *tablespoons butter*

Clean the mussels under cold running water, scrubbing them and removing their beards. Put the oil, garlic, and pepper in a very large pot, uncovered. If necessary, use two pots. When the garlic begins to color, add the mussels. Cook over medium heat, scooping the mussels up from the bottom and removing the opened ones to a platter. In about 10 minutes all the mussels should be open. Discard any that refuse to open. Keep the mussels warm in a very low oven.

To the pot in which the mussels were cooked, add all the remaining ingredients except the butter. Simmer this sauce, covered, for 10 minutes. Stir in the butter.

Put the mussels, in their shells, in individual bowls. Pour some sauce over each portion, and serve with crusty Italian bread.

STEAMED MUSSELS IN CREAM
(Moules à la Crème)

☙

4–6 SERVINGS

6 *quarts mussels*
4 *shallots, chopped*
½ *cup mixed chopped fresh herbs: parsley, chives,*
    tarragon, chervil
1 *cup dry white wine*
¼–½ *cup Crème Fraîche (see next page)*
    Salt and freshly ground pepper
1–2 *teaspoons curry powder*

Scrub the mussels well and remove the beards under cold running water. Put the shallots, herbs, and wine in a large pot. Bring to a boil. Add the mussels. Cover and cook over low heat for a few minutes.

As soon as the shells open, remove the mussels with a slotted spoon to a large serving bowl. Discard any mussels that do not open. Stir the *crème fraîche* into the liquid in the pot. Season to taste with salt, pepper, and curry. Pour over the mussels and serve with warm French bread.

CRÈME FRAÎCHE

1 CUP

1   *cup heavy cream, at room temperature*
1   *tablespoon yogurt or buttermilk, at room temperature*

Put the cream and yogurt in a screw-top jar. Cover the jar and shake it well. Store in a warm place until the cream thickens. In a sunny window on a hot day it may be ready in 3 to 4 hours; in winter it may not be ready for 2 to 3 days. Once the *crème fraîche* has thickened, it will keep in the refrigerator for 2 to 3 weeks.

BAY SCALLOPS À LA NAGE, LA GRENOUILLE
(Coquilles Saint-Jacques à la Nage)

A superb dish from one of our favorite New York restaurants. The recipe was given to us by La Grenouille's great chef André Joanlanne with the blessing of the charming *patronne* Gisèle Masson.

6 SERVINGS

2   *pounds bay scallops*

COURT BOUILLON

1   *cup water*
2   *cups dry white wine*

2   *small carrots, sliced*
2   *small onions, sliced*
½   *cup sliced celery*
4   *sprigs parsley*
1   *bay leaf*
6   *whole peppercorns*
1   *sprig fresh thyme or ½ teaspoon dried*
½   *teaspoon salt*

BEURRE BLANC

2   *tablespoons white wine*
¼   *cup white wine vinegar*
2   *shallots, finely chopped*
¼   *teaspoon salt*
¼   *teaspoon freshly ground pepper or more to taste*
12–16 *tablespoons chilled butter (1½–2 sticks cut into 12*
       slices)

Pick over the scallops to remove any black particles or bits of shell but do not wash them. Keep them in a cool place.

Combine all the court bouillon ingredients in a pot large enough to hold the scallops (which will be added later). Bring to a boil, then cook over low heat for 15 to 20 minutes.

Add the scallops, cover the pot, and cook for 2 to 3 minutes. Do not overcook, or the scallops will be tough.

Prepare the *beurre blanc* (which must be used as soon as it is ready). Place all the ingredients except the butter in a small heavy-bottomed saucepan. Boil until reduced to a very small amount, about 1½ to 2 tablespoons. Remove from the heat. Pass through a fine strainer and return to the saucepan. Add 2 slices of cold butter, one slice at a time, whipping constantly with a wire whisk. Place the pan over the lowest possible heat. Whisking constantly, add each slice of the remaining butter as soon as the previous one is almost dissolved, removing the pan from the heat from time to time. When all the butter is incorporated, pour the sauce into a warm serving bowl. Taste, and if desired, whisk in additional seasoning. The sauce should have the consistency of a light hollandaise.

To serve, put the scallops and some of the vegetables on each plate with a little of the cooking liquid. Pass the *beurre blanc* sauce separately.

CHINESE SEA SCALLOPS
IN GARLIC SAUCE

❧

You will need a wok. All the Chinese ingredients are available at Oriental groceries and specialty food shops, and in many supermarkets as well.

2–3 SERVINGS

3   *cups vegetable or corn oil*
1   *tablespoon each chopped garlic and chopped fresh ginger*
1   *pound sea scallops, cut in halves horizontally (do not wash them)*
8–10   *pieces tree ear mushrooms, shredded*
½   *cup water chestnuts, cut into thin strips*
1   *cup chicken broth*
1   *tablespoon white wine*
1   *teaspoon Szechuan paste (chili paste with garlic)*
1   *tablespoon rice vinegar (or plain white vinegar)*
1   *tablespoon soy sauce*
1   *tablespoon sugar*
2   *tablespoons cornstarch mixed with a little water until smooth*

Mix 1 or 2 tablespoons of the oil with the chopped garlic and ginger. Reserve. Heat the wok. Put the remaining oil in it and heat it until it is very hot but not smoking. Add the scallops and deep-fry them for 30 seconds, stirring constantly to keep the pieces separate. Add the tree ear mushrooms and water chestnuts and fry for another 30 seconds. Drain at once through a sieve into a bowl. (Discard the oil or strain it and reserve for future use.)

Return the wok to the heat. Add the garlic-ginger mixture, chicken broth, wine, Szechuan paste, vinegar, soy sauce, and sugar. Stir over the heat until the liquid boils. Stir in the cornstarch mixture until it dissolves. Add the pre-fried scallops, tree ear mushrooms and water chestnuts. Cook, stirring, for about 15 seconds. Serve at once with boiled rice.

GINGERED SCALLOPS FOR LEE

⌒

An instant recipe.

4–5 SERVINGS

6   *tablespoons butter*
1   *pound bay scallops (remove any black particles or*
      bits of shell but do not wash)
2   *tablespoons thinly sliced fresh ginger*
      Salt and freshly ground pepper to taste
2   *tablespoons finely chopped parsley or coriander*

Heat the butter till it sizzles. Sauté the scallops and the ginger for 1
to 2 minutes, just long enough to heat the scallops through and brown
them lightly. Season, sprinkle with parsley, and serve.

SCALLOPS CROMWELL

⌒

We have adapted or, rather, usurped this very old English treatment
of scallops from Elizabeth, wife of "the usurper" Oliver Cromwell. A
very quick preparation for two, and a surprisingly sybaritic dish from
so puritan a lady.

2 SERVINGS

3   *tablespoons butter*
2½   *tablespoons finely chopped shallots or onions*
½   *pound (1 cup) scallops: whole bay scallops or quartered*
       sea scallops (remove any black particles or bits of
       shell but do not wash)
1–2 *tablespoons lemon juice*
¼   *pint (½ cup) shucked oysters with their juice*
1   *tablespoon chopped fresh thyme or 1 teaspoon dried*

1 teaspoon anchovy paste
¾ cup fresh bread crumbs (can be made in a blender or
    food processor)
¼ cup chopped fresh parsley
A pinch of salt
A few generous dashes of pepper
Optional: 1–2 tablespoons more lemon juice and 1–2
    tablespoons butter

Heat the butter in a large pan and sauté the shallots over medium heat, stirring often until they are translucent. Push them to one side of the pan and add the scallops. Cook for 1 minute. Add the lemon juice, 2 to 3 tablespoons of the oyster juice, the thyme, and anchovy paste. Cook, stirring, till the anchovy paste has dissolved. Add the oysters and cook for 1 minute. Add the bread crumbs and parsley. Cook, stirring, for another minute. Taste and correct the seasoning, adding more lemon juice if you like, and swirl in 1 to 2 tablespoons butter. Serve the scallops with rice or small boiled potatoes.

SCALLOPS IN PASTRY-TOPPED
SCALLOP SHELLS

A playful party dish for those who like to fuss. The pastry initials serve as edible place cards.

4 SERVINGS USING 5-INCH SCALLOP SHELLS
6 SERVINGS USING 4-INCH SCALLOP SHELLS

CREAM CHEESE PASTRY
1 8-ounce package of cream cheese
2 sticks (½ pound) sweet butter
2 cups flour
½ teaspoon salt
1 large or 2 small egg yolks

Beat the cream cheese and butter together in an electric mixer until blended. Beat in the egg yolk. Mix the flour and salt and add to the bowl. Beat until no lumps are visible. Refrigerate until ready to use, as the dough must be very cold when you roll it out.

Cream Cheese Pastry dough must be prepared at least 2 hours before you plan to use it. It should be refrigerated until the last minute. Keeps well in the freezer. Defrost when ready to use.

FILLING

1	*pound bay or sea scallops*
	Salt and freshly ground pepper to taste
3–4	*tablespoons butter*
½	*pound mushrooms, coarsely chopped*
2	*tablespoons finely chopped shallots*
¼	*cup cream*
⅔	*cup cooked peas, at room temperature*
	Curry powder
1	*egg, lightly beaten*

Pick over the scallops but do not wash them. Discard any black bits or pieces of shell. If bay scallops are used, leave the smallest ones whole and cut the others in half. If sea scallops are used, cut them into ⅓-inch cubes. Season them lightly with salt and pepper. Sauté them in 2 tablespoons of the butter over medium heat for 1 to 2 minutes, stirring often. Transfer the scallops to a bowl. To the same pan, add another 1 to 2 tablespoons of butter, the chopped mushrooms and shallots. Season with salt and pepper and cook over medium heat for 1 to 2 minutes, stirring often. Add to the scallops in the bowl. Stir in the cream.

Drain the peas well. Add a pinch or two of curry and a bit of salt and pepper. Purée in a food processor or food mill. Stir the purée into the scallop mixture gradually, adding just enough to make it fairly thick.

Butter the scallop shells lightly but not quite to the edges. Fill them with the scallop mixture, making mounds that do not quite touch the edges of the shells.

Roll out the pastry dough to ¼-inch thickness. Using an inverted shell as a model, cut it into pieces slightly larger than the scallop shells. (The scraps of dough will be used for the pastry initials.) Lightly moisten the edges of each piece of rolled dough with a bit of water. Lay each piece over the filling and pinch it tightly to the edges of the shell.

Knead the remaining scraps of dough together, roll them out thin and cut them into your guests' initials. Set the initials on top of the pastry crusts. Place the filled shells in the refrigerator until you are ready to bake them.

Preheat the oven to 400°. Arrange the filled shells on a jelly-roll pan. (An extra scallop shell or two inverted on the baking sheet will help to balance and prop up the filled shells. Balls of crumpled foil can be used for the same purpose.) Use a pastry brush to coat the crusts lightly with beaten egg. Bake for about 15 minutes, or until the crusts are golden brown. Serve at once, then summon your guests to the table to find their baked "place cards."

Of course, these scallops baked with pastry crusts taste just as good without the initials.

SCALLOPS WITH PEPPERS

〜

3–4 SERVINGS

1½ *pounds bay scallops (whole) or sea scallops (quartered)*
   Flour
   Salt and freshly ground pepper to taste
3 *green peppers (or a combination of green, red, and*
     yellow peppers)
2 *tablespoons olive oil*
2 *tablespoons butter*
1 *teaspoon hot red pepper flakes*

Pick over the scallops, discarding any black bits or pieces of shell, but do not wash them. Roll them lightly in flour, season them with salt and very little pepper, and reserve in a cool place.

Skin the peppers following the procedure for Roasted Peppers (see page 279). Discard the stems, seeds, and white membranes. Cut the peppers into 1-inch squares.

Heat the oil and butter in a wide heavy pan. Add the scallops, peppers, and pepper flakes. Cook, stirring often, over medium heat for 2 to 3 minutes. Taste and correct the seasoning. Serve at once.

Subtle and colorful! If you like this dish as much as we do, try our Linguine with Scallops and Peppers for Bob as well (see page 99).

SCALLOPS PROVENÇALE
(Coquilles Saint-Jacques à la Provençale)

❧

You will need four 5-inch scallop shells.

4 SERVINGS

2   *large cloves garlic, minced*
2   *large shallots, minced*
¼   *cup chopped fresh parsley*
1   *fresh sprig thyme, finely chopped, or 1 teaspoon dried*
2   *tablespoons olive oil*
6   *tablespoons butter*
½   *cup dry vermouth or dry white wine*
    Salt and freshly ground pepper
1   *pound bay scallops, whole, or sea scallops, quartered*
    (remove any black particles or bits of shell but do
    not wash them)
8   *cherry tomatoes, halved*

Preheat the oven to 350°.

Place the garlic, shallots, parsley, and thyme in a small heavy pan with the oil and 3 tablespoons of the butter. Sauté over medium heat for 2 minutes, stirring. Add the vermouth and raise the heat. Cook, stirring, for 1 to 2 minutes until the liquid reduces by half. Add salt and pepper to taste.

Coat the scallop shells with butter. Place the scallops in the buttered shells and season them lightly with salt and pepper. Put 2 tomato halves on top of each filled shell and spoon the mixture from the pan over all. Dot with butter. Set the shells on the baking sheet and bake for 5 to 6 minutes. If the scallops are not browned, set them under the broiler for a few seconds.

SEAFOOD CHOWDER PIE

⁓

6 SERVINGS

PASTRY

2 cups flour
½ teaspoon salt
A pinch of sugar
¼ pound (8 tablespoons) cold butter, cut into slices
3 tablespoons cold vegetable shortening
4–5 tablespoons ice water

FILLING

1 stalk celery, diced
4 tablespoons butter
3 tablespoons scallions or onions
½ cup peeled and diced shrimp
⅔ cup fresh crab meat, carefully picked over and coarsely
   chopped
Salt and freshly ground pepper to taste
3 tablespoons dry white wine or Pernod
2 thick slices bacon, fried till crisp, drained, and broken
   into bits
1 medium-size potato, boiled, peeled, and diced
3 eggs
1 cup heavy cream
1 tablespoon tomato paste
½ teaspoon salt
½ teaspoon freshly ground pepper
⅓ cup grated imported Swiss or Parmesan cheese, or a
   combination of both
1–2 tablespoons butter

Make the pastry the day before you plan to serve the chowder pie
or at least a few hours in advance. Mix all the pastry ingredients
except the water in a large bowl. Work with a pastry cutter or your
fingers until the mixture resembles coarse meal. Add most of the
water. Work the dough with your hands until it holds together. Add

more water only if needed. Gather the dough into a ball, roll it lightly in flour, wrap in foil, and chill in the refrigerator for 2 or 3 hours or overnight. If you are in a hurry, 30 minutes in the freezer will do. Defrost before using.

Preheat the oven to 400°.

Roll out the dough to ⅛-inch thickness. Line a 10- or 11-inch pie plate with it. Prick in several places with a fork. Cover the dough with foil, pressing it against the sides and bottom of the pie plate. Fill with rice, beans, or metal pie weights to help the dough hold its shape. Bake for 8 to 9 minutes. Remove the rice and foil, prick the bottom of the crust with a fork in several places to prevent it from "bubbling," and return it to the oven for a few minutes, or until it begins to shrink from the sides of the pie plate. Let the crust cool while you prepare the filling.

Sauté the celery in the butter for 3 to 4 minutes. Add the scallions and sauté for 2 to 3 minutes more, or until tender but not brown. Add the shrimp and crab and cook, stirring, for 1 to 2 minutes. Season with salt and pepper. Add the wine and raise the heat until it begins to bubble. Remove from the heat, stir in the bacon and potato, and let the mixture cool. In a large bowl, beat together all the remaining ingredients except the cheese and butter. Stir in the seafood mixture. Taste and correct the seasoning.

Spoon the mixture into the pie crust, sprinkle with cheese, then dot with bits of butter and bake for about 30 minutes, or until the filling is well browned. Delicious hot or at room temperature.

ALGERIAN SHRIMP

c⁓ɔ

In some parts of Algiers, shrimp in their shells are prepared in the quickest way imaginable. Amusingly enough, they take longer to eat than to cook.

4 SERVINGS

2   *tablespoons coarse salt*
2   *dozen shrimp, unshelled*
2   *lemons, cut in halves*
    Salt and freshly ground pepper

Sprinkle a large cast-iron frying pan with coarse salt. Place over high heat for 5 to 10 minutes. (Be sure not to touch the handle without a protective pad.) Spread the shrimp in the pan. Cook for 3 to 5 minutes, turning occasionally. Serve them in their shells with lemon halves, salt and pepper, and plenty of paper napkins.

VARIATION: Marinate the shrimp for 1 hour in lemon juice, olive oil, a clove of crushed garlic, and a few slices of onion. Drain and dry the shrimp thoroughly before cooking them. Thinly sliced cucumbers simmered in the marinade till tender make an ideal accompaniment.

PICKLED SHRIMP IN LEMON ASPIC

ᔕᕽ

4–6 SERVINGS

1   *pound shrimp*
½   *cup lemon juice*
1   *tablespoon vinegar*
1   *medium-size onion, sliced very thin*
4   *teaspoons mixed pickling spices*
1   *bay leaf*
4   *teaspoons sugar*
3   *sprigs parsley*
1½ *packages unflavored gelatin*
    Garnish: lemon slices
    Horseradish Sauce: 3 teaspoons grated fresh horseradish
        or carefully drained bottled horseradish mixed
        thoroughly with 1½ cups sour cream or
        whipped cream and chilled

Peel the shrimp and put their shells in a pot with 1 cup of water. Add all the other ingredients except the shrimp, gelatin, lemon slices, and horseradish sauce. Simmer, covered, for 20 minutes. Add the shrimp and simmer for 2 to 3 minutes more.

Put a sieve lined with a triple layer of moistened cheesecloth over a large bowl and pour the contents of the pot through the sieve. Remove the shrimp and about half the onions, making certain that none of the pickling spices cling to them, and arrange them in a decorative pattern in a deep bowl. Discard the contents of the sieve.

Let the strained liquid cool. Remove ½ cup of this liquid, sprinkle the gelatin over it and stir to let it soften. Put the rest of the liquid in a pot over low heat. Pour the ½ cup of liquid and gelatin into the pot and cook for 3 to 4 minutes, stirring constantly until the gelatin is completely dissolved. Pour it over the shrimp slowly in order not to disturb them. When cool, put the bowl into the refrigerator for at least 2 hours or until the aspic is set.

When ready to serve, carefully run a knife around the edges of the bowl to loosen the aspic. Wrap a dish cloth wrung out in very hot water around the bowl for a few seconds. Cover with a round serving dish and invert to unmold. Garnish with lemon slices and serve with the horseradish sauce.

SKEWERED SHRIMP WITH BASIL
(Spiedini di Scampi con Basilìco)

6~9

4 SERVINGS

20	(about 2 pounds) large shrimp
1	cup dry white wine
¾	cup olive oil
1	teaspoon salt
1	teaspoon freshly ground pepper
	A sprinkling of hot red pepper flakes
2	cloves garlic, minced or passed through a press
¼	cup finely chopped parsley
¼	cup finely chopped chives
20	large basil leaves or 3–4 teaspoons dried

About 1 hour before serving, rinse the shrimp in cold water without shelling them. Put the wine and 1 cup of water in a pot and bring to a boil. Add the shrimp. When the water boils again, remove the shrimp and set them aside.

Make a marinade by combining all the other ingredients except the basil leaves. (If dried basil is used, however, stir it into the marinade.)

Shell the shrimp and marinate them for 1 hour, stirring frequently. Remove them, but reserve the marinade. Press a fresh basil leaf onto each one and thread them close together on 4 metal skewers. Lay the skewered shrimp in a broiling pan. Pour half the marinade over them. Broil 3 to 4 inches from the heat for 3 to 4 minutes. Turn them, pour the marinade over them and broil for 2 minutes.

Place the skewered shrimp on the serving platter and pour the hot marinade over them. Use a fork to slide the shrimp off the skewers onto each plate.

Serve with buttered rice.

POULTRY

Never quail, never grouse!

ARTHUR GOLD AND ROBERT FIZDALE

i have often noticed that when chickens quit
quarreling over their food they often find
that there is enough for all of them i wonder
if it might not be the same with the human race.

DON MARQUIS,
archy's life of mehitabel

*C*hickens must be well bred to be worth eating—not man-
nerly, for chickens by nature have bad manners. They wake
up too early in the morning, they run away when we try
to catch them, and their voices leave everything to be
desired. All this can easily be forgiven when, properly fed
and allowed to run free, they are served up at table. If
good country air, jogging, and a good feed make us feel
better, think of what they do for the motherly hen or the
jaunty rooster. Then and only then are they worthy of
William Blake's "wondrous, wondrous, still, the cock and
hen." A few inquiries and most of us can find a good source
for the real article, which is meatier, more tender and
relatively free of fat. Then roast, fry, poach or stew and
you will find that fresh chicken—and all other fresh poultry,
for that matter—make noble eating.

CHICKEN BREASTS WITH LEEKS
AND TRUFFLES, GIRARDET
(Aile de Volaille aux Poireaux et aux Truffes)

❧

Our adaptation of an exquisite creation by Fredy Girardet, one of
the world's greatest innovative chefs.

4 SERVINGS

2	*whole chicken breasts, boned and halved,*
	but not skinned
	Salt and freshly ground pepper to taste
1	*¾-ounce can black truffles (or fresh, if available)*
2	*cups Chicken Broth (see page 48)*
12	*leeks, white part with a little of the green,*
	enough to make about 4 cups chopped leeks
8	*shallots, peeled and halved*
1	*stick (¼ pound) butter*
2	*tablespoons oil*
⅔	*cup Crème Fraîche (see page 151)*

Make horizontal incisions in the chicken breasts to form pockets.
Season the chicken, inside and out, with salt and pepper. Drain the
truffles, reserving the juice. Slide a very thin slice or two of truffle
into the pocket of each breast. Fasten with toothpicks. Chop the
remaining truffles very fine, and reserve.

Boil the broth over high heat until reduced to about one-third of
its volume. Set aside.

Trim the leeks and cut them into 1-inch lengths. Put them in the
container of a food processor along with the shallots. Using the knife
blade, process till very finely chopped. Stop the motor once or twice
to scrape down the sides of the container with a rubber spatula, then
process again. (Of course, the shallots and leeks can also be finely
chopped by hand.) Cook the leek-shallot mixture in a heavy pot over
low heat with 4 tablespoons of the butter, stirring often, till you have
a soft purée. The leeks should not brown. Let them cool, then add half
the chopped truffles and half of the *crème fraîche*. Season with salt,
pepper, and cayenne.

Sauté the chicken breasts in a heavy frying pan in 2 tablespoons of the butter and 2 tablespoons of oil over very low heat for 10 minutes, or until tender but not browned. Sprinkle them on both sides with salt and pepper. When the chicken is tender, spread the leek purée on a warm serving platter and arrange the chicken breasts on top. Keep the chicken warm in a low oven while preparing the sauce.

Put 1 cup of the reduced broth into the pan in which you cooked the chicken. Over high heat, reduce the broth a bit more, stirring and scraping the browned bits from the pan into the sauce. After 2 to 3 minutes, reduce the heat, add the chopped truffles and the truffle juice. Stir in the remaining *créme fraîche*. Correct the seasoning, pour over the chicken breasts, and serve.

CHICKEN BREASTS WITH MUSHROOMS

୧‿୬

4 SERVINGS

½   ounce dried mushrooms (chanterelles or cèpes)
2   whole chicken breasts, skinned, boned, separated into
        4 portions, and flattened with a cleaver
¼   cup flour for dredging
        Salt and pepper (freshly ground white or black) to taste
4   tablespoons olive oil
4   tablespoons butter
¾   pound fresh mushrooms, thinly sliced
2   ¼-inch-thick slices prosciutto, cut into julienne
        strips
3   tablespoons cognac
⅔   cup heavy cream, Crème Fraîche (see page 151) or
        sour cream, at room temperature

Soak the dried mushrooms in warm water for about 20 minutes. Drain, rinse and dry them on paper towels. Chop them fine. Dip each piece of chicken lightly in flour on both sides and season with salt and pepper.

Cook the mushrooms and chicken in separate frying pans. The pan for the chicken must be large enough to hold the pieces in a single layer. Heat 2 tablespoons of the oil and 2 tablespoons of the butter in each pan. Sauté the dried and fresh mushrooms together over medium heat for a few minutes. Salt and pepper them to taste. Sauté the pieces of chicken for 3 to 4 minutes on each side, until they are lightly browned. Add the prosciutto and cognac. Heat the cognac for a minute, and light it. When the flames die down, add the mushrooms and cream. Cook, stirring, until the cream thickens. Correct the seasoning and serve.

CHICKEN BREASTS, PERSIAN STYLE

4 SERVINGS

2   *whole chicken breasts*
    Juice of 1 lemon
4   *large seedless oranges*
    Seasonings: ½ teaspoon salt, ¼ teaspoon freshly ground
        pepper, ¼ teaspoon turmeric
½   *cup chopped onions*
5   *tablespoons butter*
¼   *cup vinegar*
6   *tablespoons sugar*

Skin and bone the chicken breasts and cut them into ¾-inch cubes. Marinate them in the lemon juice for about 1 hour. Stir occasionally. With a vegetable peeler, make thin, short strips of orange peel (about 2 tablespoons), carefully avoiding the bitter white pith. Set them aside. Peel the oranges, removing the white pith, and divide them into sections. Put them in a pot. Add the seasonings. (More seasoning can be used if you like.)

In a small heavy frying pan, sauté the onions in 1 tablespoon of the butter for about 10 minutes, or until browned. Add the orange peel. Cook, stirring, 1 to 2 minutes. Add this mixture to the orange sections in the pot. Add the vinegar and sugar. Cook for 15 minutes, stirring gently so that the orange sections remain intact.

Just before serving, remove the chicken cubes from the marinade with a slotted spoon. Sauté them in the remaining butter for 2 to 3 minutes. Spoon the hot oranges and their sauce onto a serving platter. Arrange the chicken cubes on top. Season the chicken lightly with salt and pepper and serve with rice.

A SUGGESTED MENU

(see Index for recipes)

CAIRO CHEESE AND CUCUMBER SALAD

CHICKEN BREASTS, PERSIAN STYLE

COLD SAUTÉED CELERY ROOT

QUICK GRAPE DESSERT

wine: PIESPORTER

NADIA GARDINER'S
CHICKEN CUTLETS À LA RUSSE

5–6 SERVINGS

3 *whole chicken breasts, skinned and boned (ask the butcher to give you the bones and to put the chicken breasts through the grinder twice using the fine disk)*

BROTH

The breast bones and trimmings
1 *bay leaf*
1 *small onion, quartered*
   Salt and freshly ground white pepper to taste

4 *thin slices white bread, trimmed of crust*
½ *cup minced shallots*
1 *stick (¼ pound) butter*
1 *egg, lightly beaten*

2-4 tablespoons finely chopped fresh dill
     Salt and freshly ground white pepper
     Bread crumbs for breading
     A bowl of cold water with a few ice cubes in it
1   stick (¼ pound) butter for sautéing

MUSHROOM SAUCE

1½ pounds mushrooms
     Salt and freshly ground white pepper
4   tablespoons sweet butter
3   shallots, minced
¾   cup heavy cream
¾   cup sour cream
½   cup finely chopped fresh dill

If your butcher has not ground the chicken breasts, cut them into 1-inch cubes and put them through a meat grinder twice, using the fine disk. Transfer to a large bowl.

To make the broth, simmer the bones, the bay leaf, onion, and a little salt and pepper in water to cover for 30 minutes. (Instead of making it, you can use ready-made chicken broth.)

Strain the broth and soak the bread in it for a few minutes. Squeeze the bread dry and reserve.

Cook the shallots in a stick of butter in a small saucepan over very low heat for 3 to 4 minutes. Do not let them brown. Remove from heat to cool.

Add the bread with 1 tablespoon of the broth, the shallots with all their butter, the egg and the dill to the ground chicken. (The mixture should be moist but not liquid.) Season to taste with salt and pepper and work the mixture with your fingers until it is well combined. Refrigerate for 1 hour or more.

Spread the bread crumbs on a large dish. Have the bowl of ice water at hand. Moisten your hands before you shape each cutlet. Scoop out a rounded tablespoon (no more) of the chicken mixture, then lightly toss the mixture from one hand to the other to form smooth oval patties. Roll them lightly in bread crumbs to coat them on all sides. Transfer them to a large platter. Flatten them slightly with the side of a knife, then score them with the dull edge of the knife, making two horizontal and two vertical lines on each one. Refrigerate for at least 30 minutes before sautéing them.

Heat the butter in a heavy frying pan until sizzling. Sauté the cutlets without crowding them until they are lightly browned on both sides. Lower the heat and cook for a few minutes longer. They should not cook for more than 8 minutes in all. Transfer to a platter, cover loosely with foil, and keep warm in a low oven.

Make the mushroom sauce. Wipe the mushrooms clean with a damp cloth. Cut them into thin slices. Season them with salt and pepper to taste. Heat the butter in a large enamel-lined pan. Sauté the shallots, stirring for 2 to 3 minutes. Add the mushrooms and cook for 6 to 7 minutes. Mix the two kinds of cream together and stir them into the mushrooms. Season to taste with salt and pepper, pour over the cutlets, sprinkle with dill, and serve.

TIP: Cold or frozen leftover chicken cutlets can be reheated if sprinkled with a few drops of Maggi sauce and a little fresh cream, covered with foil, and warmed in a moderate oven. They are also delicious eaten cold.

VARIATION: Cutlets *à la Russe* are sometimes made with equal amounts of chicken and veal ground together.

A SUGGESTED MENU

(see Index for recipes)

SLAVIC SUMMER SOUP

NADIA GARDINER'S CHICKEN CUTLETS À LA RUSSE

GREEN SALAD

OLD-FASIONED ORANGE JELLY WITH LEMON TILES

wine: RIESLING

CHICKEN EN COCOTTE

When made with the freshest possible ingredients, this preparation epitomizes the best of French bourgeois cooking. We serve it time and again to friends who savor simplicity. Followed by a green salad, an assortment of cheeses, a crusty French loaf, and a fruit tart, it makes a perfect centerpiece for a perfect meal. Best when cooked in a *cocotte*, an oval casserole with a tight-fitting lid.

    1   *3-pound roasting chicken*
         Salt and freshly ground pepper to taste
    1   *medium-size onion, finely chopped*
         About 1½ sticks (12 tablespoons) butter
   ⅛   *pound piece of salt pork, cut into very small cubes*
         Bouquet garni: a bay leaf and a few sprigs each of
              parsley, thyme, and tarragon tied together
12–16   *small white onions, peeled*
  12   *small carrots, peeled and cut into 2-inch strips*
         About 2 cups Chicken Broth (see page 48)
    1   *tablespoon sugar*
   ½   *cup dry white wine*
   ¼   *cup Madeira or sherry*
    2   *tablespoons glace de viande (or beef extract), available*
              in specialty shops
         Beurre manié (made by rubbing together with your
              fingers 2 tablespoons each of chilled butter and
              flour)
    1   *clove garlic, cut in half*
    6   *tablespoons olive oil*
  12   *small new potatoes, peeled*
   ½   *cup chopped parsley*

Preheat the oven to 350°.

Season the chicken inside and out with salt and pepper. Put the chopped onion with 1 tablespoon of butter inside the chicken and tie it with string as if for roasting. In a heavy pan, brown the chicken on all sides in 2 tablespoons of butter.

Put 3 tablespoons of butter and the salt pork in a casserole with a tight-fitting lid. Place it in the oven to melt the butter. Put the bouquet garni and the chicken, breast side up, in the casserole. Lay a large piece of buttered paper over it and cover it tightly. Bake for 30 minutes.

Put the onions and carrots in the same pan used to brown the chicken. (If the fat in the pan has burned, remove it with a paper towel and add more butter.) Add enough chicken broth to barely cover the vegetables, 2 tablespoons of butter, salt, pepper, and 1 tablespoon sugar. Cook over moderate heat until the broth cooks away. Add a little more butter and broth if needed. Turn the vegetables from time to time until the broth has reduced to a syrupy glaze.

Remove the chicken from the casserole and discard the strings. Strain the juice in the casserole through a fine sieve into a bowl. Discard the salt pork. Return the bouquet garni and the chicken to the casserole and pour the strained juice over them. Add the onions, carrots, the scrapings from the pan, the white wine, Madeira, and *glace de viande*. Taste and correct the seasoning. Return the casserole to the oven for 30 minutes, or until a leg moves easily and a second joint, when pierced with a sharp knife, gives off a clear juice. If the gravy is too thin, simmer it with bits of *beurre manié*, added gradually.

While the chicken is cooking, rub a large heavy pan with garlic, heat the oil and sauté the potatoes, turning them often, until they are tender and browned on all sides. Season them with salt and pepper. Carve the chicken at the table. Serve with the potatoes sprinkled with parsley.

A SUGGESTED MENU

(*see Index for recipes*)

CHICKEN EN COCOTTE

GREEN SALAD

PEAR TART

wine: SANCERRE OR CÔTE DE BEAUNE

PERSIAN CURRIED CHICKEN
AND CUCUMBERS

༽

4 SERVINGS

1   *medium-size onion, finely chopped*
4   *tablespoons butter*
3   *tablespoons curry powder*

1   cucumber
2   *whole chicken breasts, skinned, boned, and cut into*
       ½-inch cubes
½   *teaspoon salt*
1   *cup yogurt, at room temperature*

In a heavy pot, sauté the onion in 1 tablespoon of the butter over low heat for about 10 minutes, or until they are translucent but not browned. Add the curry powder and 1 inch of water. Cook, stirring constantly, till most of the water has evaporated, leaving a thick sauce. Pour most of this sauce into a bowl, leaving 2 tablespoonfuls in the pot.

Peel the cucumber with a vegetable peeler. Still using the peeler, cut 12 long, thin strips of cucumber and add them to the pot. Cook over low heat till the cucumber strips are tender but still firm. Return the curry sauce to the pot and keep it warm over low heat.

Sauté the cubes of chicken in the remaining 3 tablespoons of butter in a wide pan for 2 to 3 minutes, or until they are white and tender. Sprinkle with salt and add them to the curry sauce. Raise the heat to high, mix well, and cook for 1 minute. Remove the pot from the heat for 2 to 3 minutes. Stir in the yogurt and serve immediately.

VARIATION: Substitute sour cream for the yogurt. Untraditional but delicious.

BRAISED CAPON
WITH WILD RICE STUFFING

ᕤᕽ

6–8 SERVINGS

1   *5-pound capon or roasting chicken*
    Salt and freshly ground pepper to taste
1   *cup wild rice*
¼   *pound chicken livers*
3   *tablespoons finely chopped scallions*
4   *tablespoons butter*
2   *tablespoons chopped fennel or celery*

1 carrot, chopped
1 leek, white part only, chopped
½ cup chopped parsley (or ¼ cup each chopped parsley
    and tarragon)
1 egg, lightly beaten
6 carrots, peeled and cut into 1-inch lengths
12 small white onions, each peeled and studded with a
    clove
1 bottle champagne (or dry white wine)
    Grated rind and juice of 1 lemon
3 egg yolks
2 cups sour cream

Wipe the capon with a damp cloth and season it inside and out with salt and pepper. Cook the wild rice in 2 cups of salted boiling water for about 50 minutes, or until the grains of rice split open. Drain. Fry the chicken livers and scallions in 2 tablespoons of the butter over medium heat for 3 to 4 minutes. Chop the livers and the scallions together in a large wooden bowl. Sauté the fennel, carrot, leek, and parsley in the remaining 2 tablespoons of butter for 10 minutes, stirring occasionally. Add to the liver-scallion mixture along with the wild rice and egg. Mix thoroughly and season with salt and pepper. Stuff the capon with this mixture, but not too full. Truss it or seal the opening with a crumpled ball of aluminum foil. (Any excess stuffing can be baked in a buttered dish for 45 minutes at 350° and served along with the capon.

Put the capon, breast side up, in a heavy casserole (with a tight-fitting lid) large enough to hold all the vegetables. Surround it with the carrots and onions. Pour the champagne or wine into the casserole and cover it. Cook over medium heat on top of the stove until it begins to boil, then reduce the heat to low, and simmer, covered, for about 1½ hours, or until the drumstick can be moved easily. Remove the capon, carve it, and put it, surrounded by the vegetables, on a large ovenproof platter. Moisten with 1 cup of liquid from the casserole and keep it warm in a low oven while you prepare the sauce that gives this recipe such distinction.

Add the lemon rind and juice to the casserole, raise the heat to high, and cook, uncovered, till the liquid is reduced by half. Remove from the fire and let it cool a bit. In a fairly large bowl, beat the egg yolks and sour cream together. Season with salt and pepper. Beat in a cup of the warm liquid from the casserole, a tablespoon at a time, then pour it all back into the casserole and cook over the lowest possible heat, stirring constantly, until the sauce thickens. Do not boil, or it will curdle. Serve the capon and vegetables with a little of the sauce poured over them and the rest passed separately.

ROAST CHICKEN WITH STRING BEANS

Do not be alarmed by the large amount of garlic. A suave, surprisingly mild dish.

4–6 SERVINGS

1 *3½-pound roasting chicken, with its liver and 1 extra chicken liver*
1 *stick (¼ pound) sweet butter, at room temperature*
 Coarse salt and freshly ground pepper to taste
 Several sprigs of thyme or rosemary, or 1 tablespoon dried
1 *cup dry white wine or vermouth*
1 *large bulb (about 10 cloves), garlic, unpeeled*
1 *pound string beans, trimmed*

Remove the chicken from the refrigerator at least 2 hours before cooking it. Preheat the oven to 475°.

Rub the chicken generously with butter. Salt and pepper it well, inside and out. Place the chicken livers in the cavity of the chicken along with half the thyme. Put the remaining thyme in the bottom of a roasting pan with the wine and ½ cup of water. Place a roasting rack in the pan and lay the chicken, on its side, on the rack. Roast, uncovered, in the oven. Baste every 7 or 8 minutes throughout the roasting time. After 15 minutes, turn the chicken on its other side. Continue basting.

After 30 minutes, turn the chicken breast side up. From now on, baste even more frequently so that the breast does not dry out. The chicken is ready when the leg can be moved easily and the juice from the second joint runs clear when pierced with the point of a knife. Total roasting time: 45 to 60 minutes.

While the chicken is roasting, separate the garlic bulb into cloves *but do not peel them.* Cook the garlic in boiling water for 5 minutes. Drain completely, cover again with boiling water and cook for another 5 minutes. Drain. When cool enough to handle, cut the skin off the stem end of each garlic clove. Pinch the other end and the garlic will slip out of its skin. Just before the chicken is ready, sauté the peeled garlic in 2 tablespoons of butter for 2 to 3 minutes. Season with salt and pepper. Set aside.

Boil the beans in a large amount of salted water till tender but still crisp and bright green. Drain them at once, rinse them in cold water, and drain again. When the chicken is almost ready, sauté the beans for 2 to 3 minutes in 2 tablespoons of butter. Season to taste with salt and pepper.

When the chicken is well roasted, place it on a heated serving platter. Remove the livers from the cavity and reserve them for the chicory salad, which follows this dish so nicely. Surround the chicken with the garlic. Scatter the beans over and around the chicken and serve. Pass the pan juices in a sauceboat.

CHICORY SALAD: Make a vinaigrette dressing by mixing together 1 part wine vinegar to 3 or 4 parts olive oil, salt and pepper to taste, and a little Dijon mustard. Pour it over chicory (or watercress) and toss. Cut the roasted chicken livers into thin slices and scatter them over the salad.

PERSIAN ROAST CHICKEN

The traditional Persian way of cooking chicken combines fowl, fruit, and spices in imaginative ways.

6–8 SERVINGS

1 3½- to 4-pound roasting chicken
   Salt to taste
6 tablespoons butter, softened at room temperature
1 onion, finely chopped
6 prunes, pitted and chopped

10 *dried apricots, chopped*
¼ *cup each raisins and dried currants*
2 *apples, peeled, cored, and coarsely chopped*
Seasonings: 1 teaspoon each salt, pepper, cinnamon,
saffron, and tarragon

Preheat the oven to 375°.

Wipe the chicken with a damp cloth, salt it inside and out, and rub half the butter on it.

Sauté the onion over low heat in a large frying pan in the remaining butter, stirring often, until the onion is translucent. Add the remaining ingredients and sauté for 2 to 3 minutes, mixing well. Let the mixture cool somewhat and stuff the chicken with it. Set the chicken on a rack in a roasting pan with ¼ cup of water at the bottom of the pan. Roast the chicken for about 1½ hours, or until the juice runs clear when the second joint is pricked with a fork. Be sure to baste frequently during the roasting. Serve with rice.

ROAST CHICKEN, BERCY
(Poulet Rôti Bercy)

❧

4–6 SERVINGS

2 *sticks (½ pound) sweet butter*
1 *3½-pound chicken*
Salt and freshly ground pepper to taste
1 *bay leaf*
1 *sprig fresh thyme or ½ teaspoon dried*

CHICKEN STOCK

The giblets and neck of the chicken
A few sprigs of parsley
1 *small onion, cut into quarters*
2 *cups sliced mushrooms*
2 *tablespoons finely chopped shallots*
1 *cup dry white wine*
3 *tablespoons chopped fresh parsley*

Preheat the oven to 375°.

Clarify the butter: Cut the butter into pieces and put them in a heavy saucepan in a moderate oven. When the butter has melted, skim off the foam, and pour the butter into a bowl, discarding the milky white residue in the saucepan. (This can be done ahead of time and stored in the refrigerator until ready to use.)

Pull out and discard any excess fat on the chicken. Sprinkle the bird inside and out with salt and pepper. Put the bay leaf and thyme inside the cavity and brush the skin with clarified butter. Roast the chicken on its side in a metal or flameproof baking pan for about 1 hour, turning it from one side to the other after 20 minutes to ensure even browning. Baste it frequently with the butter. Roast the bird breast side up for the last 20 minutes. To test for doneness, prick the second joint with a sharp fork. When the chicken is ready, the juices will be transparent.

While the chicken is roasting, prepare the chicken stock. Put the giblets and neck in a small pot with the parsley and onion. Add a little salt and pepper with just enough water to cover. Simmer, covered.

When the chicken is done, transfer it to a pan with a cover to keep it warm and juicy while you prepare the sauce. Or cover it loosely with foil.

Pour off the excess fat from the roasting pan. Add the mushrooms and shallots. Cook on top of the stove over medium heat for 5 minutes, stirring often. Add the white wine and ½ cup of the chicken stock. Raise the heat and reduce the sauce by half. Taste and correct the seasoning. Pour the sauce over the chicken and sprinkle it with the chopped parsley. Carve at the table and spoon the sauce over each portion.

ARMENIAN LEMON CHICKEN, ANYA KAYALOFF

᷍

A subtle dish with a mysterious, refreshing flavor.

4 SERVINGS

1   2½-*pound chicken, cut into 8 pieces*
    Salt and freshly ground pepper
2   *tablespoons sweet butter*

5   carrots, cut into paper-thin slices
4   small white turnips, quartered and sliced paper-thin
4   lemons
2   tablespoons confectioners' sugar
4   tablespoons finely chopped fresh dill or coriander

Season the chicken lightly with salt and pepper. Melt the butter in a heavy casserole, with a tight-fitting lid, over the lowest heat. Put the pieces of chicken into the casserole, turning them to coat them with butter. Do not let them brown. Add the carrots and turnips. Sprinkle them lightly with salt and pepper. Cover and cook over low heat for 20 minutes.

Meanwhile, cut the lemons in half horizontally. Using a curved grapefruit knife, scoop out all the pulp, but none of the membrane, into a bowl. Add the sugar and mix well. Stir the mixture into the casserole. Cook over low heat for 10 to 20 minutes more, or until the chicken is tender. Correct the seasoning, sprinkle with dill, and serve with rice.

CHICKEN CACCIATORA WITH PESTICINO

The addition of *pesticino* (the chopped lemon rind, basil, and garlic garnish) makes this recipe for chicken *alla cacciatora* an unusually good one.

8 SERVINGS

¼   cup dried mushrooms
2   2½-pound chickens, cut into eighths
     Flour for dredging
     Salt and freshly ground pepper to taste
2   tablespoons oil
6   tablespoons butter
1   onion, finely chopped
2   green peppers, seeded and cut into thin strips
1   stalk celery, finely chopped

2   bay leaves
2   tablespoons chopped fresh basil or 2 teaspoons dried
1   clove garlic, peeled and bruised
1   pound ripe tomatoes, peeled, seeded, and chopped, or
        1½ cups drained canned Italian-style tomatoes
1   teaspoon sugar
¾   cup dry white wine
1   cup Chicken Broth (see page 48)
½   pound mushrooms, sliced
    Optional: beurre manié (made by rubbing together with
        your fingers 2 tablespoons each of butter and flour)

PESTICINO

2   lemons
3   cloves garlic
¾   cup coarsely chopped fresh basil leaves
½   cup coarsely chopped fresh parsley
    Salt to taste

Soak the dried mushrooms in warm water for 20 minutes. Drain them
and slice them. Dip the pieces of chicken in flour, coating them lightly
on both sides. Season with salt and pepper. Heat the oil and butter in
a heavy pan and fry the chicken, a few pieces at a time, until golden
brown on both sides. Transfer the pieces as they are done to a large
heavy casserole. Reserve the chicken breasts, which will be added
later. Add the onion, green pepper, celery, bay leaves, basil, garlic,
and tomatoes. Cook over medium heat for 10 minutes.

Meanwhile, add the sugar, wine, and broth to the pan in which you
browned the chicken and bring them just to the simmer, scraping the
brown bits in the pan into the mixture. When it is hot, pour it into
the casserole. Add the chicken breasts. Cover and cook for 20 minutes. Add the fresh and the dried mushrooms and cook for 10 minutes
more, or until the chicken is tender. If the sauce is too liquid, thicken
it, while simmering, by adding *beurre manié*, a bit at a time, until
the desired consistency is reached.

Make the *pesticino*. With a vegetable peeler, peel the lemons, avoiding the white pith. Dice the rind as finely as possible with a sharp
knife. Chop the garlic very fine. Mash the lemon rind, garlic, basil,
parsley, and salt in a mortar.

Correct the seasoning for the chicken, stir in the *pesticino* and serve
with polenta.

POLENTA

⟋⟍

1   *teaspoon salt*
1½ *cups polenta (yellow cornmeal)*
    Salt and freshly ground pepper to taste
2   *tablespoons butter*

Bring 3 cups of water and the salt to a rolling boil. Add the polenta
in a thin stream, stirring with a wooden spoon so that the water does
not stop boiling. Cook for 20 to 25 minutes, stirring often until the
mixture has the consistency of cooked cereal. Press out any lumps
against the sides of the pot with the back of the spoon. Add salt and
pepper and stir in the butter.

A SUGGESTED MENU

(see Index for recipes)

ZUCCHINI AND ANCHOVIES

CHICKEN CACCIATORA WITH PESTICINO

ARUGULA AND ROMAINE SALAD

PRUNES IN PORT WINE

wine: BARDOLINO

MOROCCAN CHICKEN
WITH PRESERVED LEMONS

⟋⟍

Preserved lemons are an important ingredient in many Moroccan
dishes. Very simple to prepare, they should be made 3 weeks in advance and will keep indefinitely. (They are also available in some
specialty shops.)

4 SERVINGS

1   *3½-pound chicken, cut into 8 pieces*
½   *cup olive oil*
1   *teaspoon salt*
1   *teaspoon freshly ground pepper*

1   *large onion, peeled and chopped*
¾   *cup Italian-style canned tomatoes, drained and coarsely*
       chopped
2   *cloves garlic, crushed*
       Seasonings: 1 teaspoon each sugar, ginger, and
       coriander; 1 teaspoon saffron; ½ teaspoon pepper
       but no salt
12 *green olives, halved and pitted*
       The diced rind of 1 or 2 Moroccan Preserved Lemons
       (see below) (or ¼ cup of lemon juice and ½
       teaspoon salt)
1½ *cups Chicken Broth (see page 48)*
¼   *cup slivered, blanched almonds*
¼   *cup currants*

Preheat the oven to 350°.

Sauté the chicken in ¼ cup of the olive oil in a heavy cast-iron frying pan large enough to hold all the pieces in one layer. Brown them on both sides, transfer to a warm platter, and season with the salt and pepper. Add the remaining oil to the pan and sauté the onion over low heat till translucent but not browned.

Add the tomatoes, garlic, seasonings, olives, lemon rind and broth. Mix well. Put the pieces of chicken back in the pan. Spoon some of the sauce over them, leaving the lemon rind immersed in the sauce as much as possible. Simmer gently over low heat for about 20 minutes.

Add the almonds and currants and cover the pan with foil pierced in several places. Bake for 25 minutes. Cover each portion of chicken with a generous amount of the sauce and serve with Herbed Rice (see page 107). Drink Spanish Marques de Riscal red wine with this splendid dish.

MOROCCAN PRESERVED LEMONS

ᕣᕩ

You will need a 1-quart canning jar with a wide mouth, 10 to 12 small lemons, and about 1 cup of coarse salt. Rinse the jar and its lid in boiling water. Cut the lemons into quarters lengthwise to within half an inch of the bottom so that the sections are still attached. Open them up and sprinkle them heavily with coarse salt.

Pour a ¼-inch layer of salt into the bottom of the jar. Stuff the salted lemons into the jar as close together as possible. Press them down to release some of their juice. Sprinkle salt generously over them as you go. Boil 2 cups of water. Let it cool to lukewarm, then pour it over the lemons to fill the jar completely. Wait till the air bubbles stop rising to the surface before sealing the jar. Store in a cool dry place for 3 weeks or longer. When ready to use, rinse the lemons in cold water to wash off the salt. Dice the rind. (Discard the pulp.)

MOROCCAN CHICKEN
WITH PRUNES AND HONEY

6∼2

8–10 SERVINGS

2 *2½- to 3-pound chickens, cut into eighths, with the
     giblets (gizzards, hearts, and livers)*
1 *cup Chicken Broth (see page 48)*
1 *teaspoon saffron*
1 *stick (¼ pound) butter*
2 *cups chopped onions*
   Salt and freshly ground pepper to taste

MOROCCAN SEASONINGS (mixed together)
1½ *tablespoons cumin*
1½ *tablespoons powdered coriander*
1½ *tablespoons cardamom*
1 *tablespoon powdered ginger or a 1-inch-thick slice fresh
     ginger root put through a garlic press*
   A pinch of hot red pepper flakes

1 *cinnamon stick*
   Juice of half a lemon
4 *tablespoons honey*
1 *teaspoon powdered cinnamon*
   About ½ pound pitted prunes
   *Optional: 2 tablespoons finely diced rind of Moroccan
     Preserved Lemons (see preceding page)*
2 *tablespoons vegetable oil*
1 *cup whole blanched almonds*
¼ *cup sesame seeds*
   Optional: ½ cup chopped fresh coriander

Trim, wash, and chop the giblets. Heat the chicken broth and steep the saffron in it over low heat while you prepare the chicken.

Sauté the chicken in butter, a few pieces at a time, in a large casserole till golden brown on both sides. Remove the pieces to a platter as they are done so that the next pieces can be sautéed without crowding. Then sauté the chopped giblets along with the onions in the same casserole, adding more butter only if needed. Stir often. Cook until the onions and the giblets have browned. Remove them with a slotted spoon and set aside.

Return the dark meat of the chicken to the casserole, then half the onions and giblets, seasoning as you go with salt, pepper, and half the mixed Moroccan seasonings. Add the cinnamon stick, then the chicken breasts and wings and the rest of the onions and giblets, seasoning as you go with salt and pepper and the remaining mixed Moroccan seasonings. Pour in the warm, saffron-flavored chicken broth.

Cover the casserole and cook over medium heat till the chicken is tender. About 15 minutes before it is ready, add the lemon juice, honey, and powdered cinnamon, stirring them into the liquid at the bottom of the casserole. Add the prunes 5 minutes later and, if you like, the diced preserved lemon. When ready, transfer the chicken, giblets, onions, and prunes to a large platter and keep warm in a low oven.

Taste the sauce and correct the seasoning. Cook the sauce in the casserole, uncovered, stirring often, until it is reduced and syrupy.

Meanwhile, heat the oil in a heavy frying pan and sauté the almonds till golden, turning them often, as they burn easily. Remove them with a slotted spoon and drain on paper towels. Heat the sesame seeds in an ungreased pan in a moderate oven for a few minutes. Remove them as soon as they are lightly toasted.

Pour the contents of the casserole over the prunes and chicken. Scatter the almonds, the sesame seeds, and the chopped fresh coriander over all and serve with rice.

A SUGGESTED MENU

(see Index for recipes)

INSTANT ICED PEA SOUP

MOROCCAN CHICKEN WITH PRUNES AND HONEY

GREEN SALAD

BAKED MELON

wine: RIOJA, RED OR WHITE

MUSTARD CHICKEN

༄

Nothing could be simpler than this dish, and yet the marriage, or rather the *ménage à trois,* of three simple ingredients—broth, mustard, and cream—produces a sauce that is subtle and sophisticated.

4 SERVINGS

1　2½- to 3-pound chicken, cut into quarters
1　3½-ounce jar Gulden's mustard
　　Freshly ground pepper to taste
1½　cups Chicken Broth (see page 48)
1　cup sour cream, at room temperature
1　cup orzo (Italian pasta shaped like rice)
　　Salt and pepper to taste

Preheat the oven to 350°.

Coat the chicken on all sides with the mustard and let it stand for 1 hour. Season it with pepper only and put it in a heavy casserole with a tight-fitting lid. Add ½ cup of the broth. Bake, covered, for 45 minutes, or until the chicken is tender. Remove it from the oven. Reduce the heat to low.

Scrape the mustard clinging to the chicken down into the broth and stir it in. Add the sour cream and stir it in. Baste the chicken with this sauce. Reheat in the oven for a few minutes.

Prepare the *orzo* by cooking it for about 5 minutes in the remaining broth till it is just *al dente.* Drain it. Taste and correct the seasoning. Serve the chicken and sauce on a bed of *orzo.*

CHICKEN SAULIEU

 ᕲᕰ

4 SERVINGS

1   2½- to 3-pound chicken, cut into eight pieces
    Salt and freshly ground pepper, preferably white
        pepper, to taste
5   tablespoons sweet butter
1   clove garlic
    Bouquet garni (1 bay leaf and 2–3 sprigs each thyme
        and parsley, tied together with string or sewn
        into a cheesecloth bag)
1   cup Meursault or other dry white wine
5   egg yolks
1   cup heavy cream
    Juice of half a lemon
    Garnish: ½ cup minced chives

Season the chicken with salt and pepper. In a large heavy frying pan with a tight-fitting cover, melt 4 tablespoons of the butter over moderately low heat. Add the chicken and cook, covered, for 15 minutes. (The chicken should not brown.) Add the garlic, the bouquet garni, and the wine. Simmer, covered, over low heat for 20 minutes, or until the chicken is tender. Discard the garlic and the bouquet garni. Transfer the chicken to a platter, cover it loosely with foil, and keep it warm in a low oven.

Lightly beat together the egg yolks and the cream. Add them to the pan off the heat. Cook the sauce over the lowest possible heat, stirring constantly, until it thickens slightly. Do not let it boil. Stir in the lemon juice and the remaining butter. Add more salt and pepper to taste. Pour the sauce over the chicken, and garnish with the chives. Serve with rice and a chilled Meursault.

A PASTILLA FOR JERRY
(Moroccan Chicken Pie)

❧

One of the marvels of Moroccan cuisine and well worth the effort. Traditionally made with pigeons, *pastilla* is equally delicious when made with the more easily obtained chickens. You will need a 12-inch cast-iron pan or a 10-cup cake pan and a pastry brush.

12–16 SERVINGS

2   3- to 3½-pound chickens, cut in quarters, with giblets, trimmed and chopped
¾   cup French peanut oil
      Seasoning: 2 teaspoons each ginger, paprika, cumin, coriander, turmeric, salt, and pepper or more to taste
1   cinnamon stick
1   quart Chicken Broth (see page 48)
1   teaspoon powdered saffron
4   cups finely chopped onions
1½   cups currants
¼   cup sesame seeds, toasted in the oven for a few minutes
1½   cups whole blanched almonds
½   cup confectioners' sugar
2   teaspoons ground cinnamon
      Salt and freshly ground pepper to taste
¼   cup lemon juice
10   eggs
12   leaves from a box of filo pastry leaves (available in specialty shops and supermarkets), refrigerated until ready to use
1   cup melted butter

Preheat the oven to 400°.

Wipe the pieces of chicken with a damp cloth. Remove the excess fat.

In a large casserole, heat ½ cup of the oil. Add the dark meat of the chicken. Sprinkle it with half the seasoning mixture. Place the white meat and giblets on top. Sprinkle with the rest of the seasoning mixture. Add the cinnamon stick. Cover and cook over medium heat for 15 minutes, stirring occasionally.

Heat the broth to a simmer. Turn off the heat, add the saffron and let it steep in the broth for 10 minutes. Add the broth to the chicken, cover, and cook for 1 hour, or until the chicken begins to fall off the bones.

While the chicken is cooking, heat 3 tablespoons of the oil in a large frying pan. Add the onions, and cook them, covered, over medium heat for 10 to 15 minutes, or until they are translucent but not browned. Stir in the currants and 1 tablespoon of the sesame seeds. Cook, stirring, for 1 to 2 minutes. Set aside.

Heat the remaining tablespoon of oil in a small pan. Add the almonds and fry until they are golden. Remove with a slotted spoon and dry them on paper towels. When they are cool, grind them coarsely. Mix them with ¼ cup of the confectioners' sugar and 1 teaspoon of the ground cinnamon. Set aside.

When the chicken is cooked, use a slotted spoon to remove all the solid material. Discard the cinnamon stick and the skin, bones, and gristle.

Shred the chicken with your fingers and put it in a large bowl. Add 1 cup of the broth and mix well. Salt and pepper to taste. Set aside. Reduce the remaining broth over high heat to 1¾ cups. Add the lemon juice. Beat the eggs lightly with a whisk. Pour them into the broth and cook, whisking frequently, for 15 to 20 minutes, or until the eggs are a fairly solid mass with the consistency of curd. Most of the broth should be absorbed. Drain off any excess liquid in a colander. The eggs must be dry.

Preheat the oven to 400°.

Brush the bottom and sides of a 12-inch cast-iron pan with melted butter. Carefully unwrap the *filo* leaves, unfold them, lay twelve of them on a damp dish towel and cover them with another. Remove one leaf at a time and immediately cover the others, or they will dry out and break. Arrange six of the *filo* leaves on the bottom of the pan and up and over the sides. Brush each one with melted butter as you go. Turn the pan a little each time you add a *filo* leaf so that the overhanging leaves are evenly distributed around and over the edges.

Spread the almond mixture over the *filo* pastry, and then add in layers the chicken, onion-currant mixture, and drained eggs. Bring the overhanging ends of the *filo* leaves up and over to cover the top as much as possible, brushing them with some melted butter.

Brush the remaining six *filo* leaves with melted butter—one at a
time and keeping the others covered—and arrange them to cover the
top of the pie. Tuck the overhanging edges down inside the pan.

Bake the *pastilla* for about 20 minutes, or until the pastry is golden
brown. Remove it from the oven, loosen the edges with a spatula and
pour off the excess butter. (Or remove it with a bulb baster.) Invert
the *pastilla* onto a lightly buttered baking sheet or large pizza pan.
(*Pastilla* can be prepared up to this point in advance and set aside for
several hours.)

Bake the inverted *pastilla* for 10 to 20 minutes more, or until it is
nicely browned. Slide it onto a large round platter. Let it rest for 10
to 15 minutes. Sprinkle it with the remaining confectioners' sugar, cinnamon, and sesame seeds in a decorative pattern and serve.

A SIMPLER PROCEDURE: Do not unmold. Bake for 30 minutes. With a
bulb baster, remove as much butter from the pan as possible. Decorate
and serve from the pan.

PASTILLA PASTRIES: Prepare the pastilla filling with three chickens instead of two, increasing the other ingredients in proportion. When
you make the pastilla, reserve a third of each layer of filling: almonds,
chicken, onions, and eggs. Chop them all together. Use them to fill
small pastries of sour cream dough, following the procedure for
Russian Cheese Pastries (see page 372). The chopped filling can be
frozen until you are ready to make the pastries, or the pastries can
be baked, frozen, and reheated. Serve with chicken broth.

A *SUGGESTED MENU*

(*see Index for recipes*)

A PASTILLA FOR JERRY

GREEN SALAD

ANISE-FLAVORED MELON BALLS

wine: BEAUMES-DE-VENISE

ROAST DUCK WITH GINGER MARMALADE

❧

The duck is roasted twice to ensure a bird that is greaseless and crisp. The first roasting should be done the day before or several hours ahead of time.

3–4 SERVINGS

1   5- to 6-pound duck
1   lemon, cut in half
    Soy sauce and freshly ground pepper
1   onion, peeled
2   cups cooked Kasha (see page 8)
½   cup ginger marmalade

Preheat the oven to 375°.

Remove as much fat as possible from the inside of the duck. Rub it with lemon and soy sauce and sprinkle it with pepper both inside and out. Place the lemon halves and the onion in the cavity. Fold the wings under the body and tie them and the legs close to the body. Place the duck, breast side down, on a V-shaped rack set in a roasting pan. Prick the bird all over to allow the fat to run out. Put about 1½ cups of water at the bottom of the pan to prevent the fat from burning. Place the duck in the oven for 15 minutes. Lower the heat to 350° and roast for 45 minutes without basting. Remove from the oven and let the duck cool at room temperature. (Refrigerate the pan juices. When the fat congeals, discard it. Later the pan juices can be reheated for basting and to serve with the bird.)

Let the duck rest for a day or at least for several hours before proceeding with the recipe.

Stuff the duck either with cooked *kasha* or with any stuffing you prefer. For other ideas, see the suggestions for stuffing Roast Turkey (page 197) and reduce the amounts of the ingredients in proportion.

Preheat the oven to 350°. Coat the duck with ginger marmalade. Sew up the openings and tie the wings and legs close to the body again.

Roast the duck again for 1 hour, or until the leg moves easily and the juice runs clear when the second joint is pierced with a fork. Baste often with the pan juices. Excellent served hot or cold.

NOTE: If you are able to find a Muscovy duck, a much leaner bird than those normally available, preroasting is unnecessary. Stuff the duck as soon as you have seasoned it. Preheat the oven to 450°. Roast the bird for 2 hours, reducing the heat to 350° after the first 20 minutes. Baste often.

SQUABS ON CANAPÉS

6~~)

4 SERVINGS

4   *squabs with their livers and hearts*
4   *shallots, finely chopped*
1½   *sticks (12 tablespoons) butter*
½   *cup Madeira*
     Salt and freshly ground pepper to taste
4   *slices firm white bread*
1   *carrot, finely chopped*
     Garnish: watercress

Preheat the oven to 350°.

Trim and coarsely chop the livers and hearts of the squabs. Sauté half of the shallots in 2 tablespoons of the butter over medium heat for 1 minute, stirring, then add the hearts and livers. Cook for 3 to 4 minutes. Add ¼ cup of the Madeira and season with salt and pepper. Raise the heat for a few seconds until the Madeira has reduced a little. Purée the mixture in a blender or food processor. If the purée is very liquid, let it thicken over low heat in a saucepan.

Prepare the canapés: Leave the crusts of the bread untrimmed and cut each slice into 2 triangles. Sauté them lightly on each side in 4 tablespoons of the butter.

Prepare the squabs: Melt the remaining butter in a casserole just large enough to hold the four squabs comfortably. Brown the squabs on both sides in the hot butter. Remove them and set them aside. Add the remaining chopped shallots and the carrots to the casserole, season them with salt and pepper, and sauté till the shallots are translucent. Add the remaining Madeira and a little water and return the squabs to the casserole. Bake for about 20 minutes, or until they are tender.

Remove the squabs to a warm platter. If the sauce is not thick enough, put the uncovered casserole over low heat. If it becomes too thick, it can be deglazed with additional Madeira.

Meanwhile, spread the liver purée on the sautéed bread and put the canapés in the oven to heat. Put two of the canapés under each squab on the platter and pour the sauce from the casserole over the squabs. Garnish with sprigs of watercress and serve.

BREADED TURKEY SCALLOPS
(Turkey Scaloppine alla Milanese)

Once, in a restaurant in Milan, we complimented the chef on his veal scaloppine. "What a pity we can't get such tender young veal in America," we said regretfully. His response was a smile so inscrutable, it made the Mona Lisa's seem like a broad grin.

When pressed for his recipe, he leaned forward, to be sure that no one was within earshot, and whispered dramatically, "Signori, I have a dark confession to make. I will tell you my secret. I make my veal out of turkey!"

Since that momentous revelation, which we call the Great Turkey Breakthrough, we have often followed suit. As it is difficult to find that exquisite delicacy, young milk-fed veal, we use in its place breast of turkey sliced into thin fillets—delicious, white, tender, easy to find, and infinitely less expensive.

4–6 SERVINGS

1   *breast of turkey*
2   *eggs, lightly beaten*
¼   *cup flour*
¾   *cup fine bread crumbs*
1   *teaspoon salt*
½   *teaspoon freshly ground pepper*
½   *teaspoon paprika*
4   *tablespoons butter*
2   *tablespoons oil*
6   *lemon slices*
6   *rolled anchovies*
1   *tablespoon capers*

Have your butcher cut the turkey breast into 6 thin fillets, removing the skin, tendons, and fat, and pound the fillets as thin as possible. Or buy a fresh (not "fresh-frozen") turkey breast, available in supermarkets, and slice it yourself with a sharp knife. Put the fillets between sheets of waxed paper and pound each one with a heavy frying pan or wooden mallet.

Put the beaten eggs on a large flat plate. Combine the flour, bread crumbs, salt, pepper, and paprika and spread this mixture on a large platter. Dip each turkey fillet lightly, on both sides, first in the egg, then in the breading mixture. Heat some of the butter and oil in a heavy skillet until it is very hot. Sauté the fillets until they are golden brown on both sides (2 to 4 minutes, depending on the thickness of the fillets). Add more butter and oil as needed. Transfer the fillets to a warm serving platter. Place a lemon slice with a rolled anchovy on each fillet, and sprinkle it with capers. Serve with buttery mashed potatoes to which you have added chopped chives and a squeeze of lemon.

TURKEY FILLETS
WITH HAM AND CHEESE
(Turkey Saltimbocca alla Romana)

ᗧ〜ᗧ

Saltimbocca is so delicious, it will "jump into your mouth," as the name implies.

4–6 SERVINGS

6   *thin fillets of turkey breast, prepared as for Breaded
        Turkey Scallops (see preceding page)*
6   *thin slices prosciutto (or smoked ham)*
6   *thin slices mozzarella cheese
        Salt and freshly ground pepper*
4   *tablespoons butter*
2   *tablespoons oil*

Cover each turkey fillet with a slice of prosciutto, then a slice of mozzarella, both trimmed to follow the shape of the turkey fillet but a little smaller all around. Roll them up and fasten with toothpicks. Season them with very little salt and a generous amount of pepper. Sauté in very hot butter and oil in a heavy skillet for 3 to 5 minutes, or until they are golden brown. The mozzarella should become soft and slightly runny. Remove the toothpicks and serve.

TURKEY FILLETS
IN LEMON SAUCE
(Piccata di Tacchino)

⌒〜⌒

A quick, light, fresh-tasting treatment of turkey fillets.

4–6 SERVINGS

6   *thin fillets of turkey breast, prepared as for Breaded*
    Turkey Scallops (see page 193)
    Salt and freshly ground pepper to taste
¼   *cup flour*
2   *tablespoons olive oil*
4   *tablespoons butter*
2   *tablespoons lemon juice*
6   *tablespoons finely chopped parsley or basil*
2   *lemons, thinly sliced*

Cut the fillets into 2½-inch squares. Season with salt and pepper. Coat them on both sides very lightly with flour. Heat the oil and 2 tablespoons of the butter in a large heavy frying pan until bubbling hot. Sauté the turkey for 2 to 4 minutes, or until golden brown on both sides. Remove them to a warm serving platter. Pour the fat out of the pan. Add the remaining butter, lemon juice, and half the parsley. Heat thoroughly.

Arrange the turkey squares and lemon slices in an alternating pattern, pour the pan juices over all, and garnish with the remaining parsley.

TURKEY FILLETS
WITH TUNA MAYONNAISE
(Turkey Tonnato)

෪

Vitello tonnato, the well-known Italian cold veal with tuna mayonnaise, is equally appealing when turned into turkey tonnato.

6 SERVINGS

6   *thin fillets of turkey breast, prepared as for Breaded*
         Turkey Scallops (see page 193)
     Salt and freshly ground pepper to taste
6   *tablespoons olive oil*

     TONNATO SAUCE (Tuna Mayonnaise)
2   *egg yolks, at room temperature*
3   *tablespoons lemon juice*
½   *teaspoon dry mustard*
½   *teaspoon salt*
¼   *teaspoon freshly ground pepper*
1   *cup olive oil*
3½ *ounces canned tuna fish, drained and mashed*
2–3 *anchovies, mashed (or 1½ teaspoons anchovy paste)*
1   *tablespoon capers*

Season the turkey fillets lightly with salt and pepper. Sauté them in the olive oil for 2 to 5 minutes, or until tender. Do not brown. Put them in one layer on a large serving platter. Cool to room temperature.

Prepare the sauce. Beat the egg yolks until thick and lemony in color. Add half the lemon juice, the mustard, salt, and pepper. Mix well. Add the oil drop by drop, stirring continuously. As it thickens, add the remaining oil a little more quickly. Add the tuna and the remaining lemon juice. Stir in the mashed anchovies. Spread the sauce on the turkey fillets to cover them completely. Sprinkle them with capers. Set aside in a cool place for at least 3 to 4 hours before serving. An excellent dish for lunch with a rice salad or as a first course at dinner.

BAKED TURKEY FILLETS

ᖇᗝ

A delightful French dish.

6 SERVINGS

4–6 *tablespoons butter*
  6 *fillets of turkey breast, ½ inch thick*
      Salt and freshly ground pepper to taste
 1½ *cups finely chopped onion*
  ½ *cup finely chopped fresh tarragon (or parsley)*
  1 *clove garlic, put through a garlic press*
  ½ *cup dry white wine*

Preheat the oven to 350°.

Grease a baking dish with half the butter. Place the turkey fillets in the dish, overlapping them slightly. Season them with salt and pepper. Sprinkle them with the onion, tarragon, and garlic. Dot with the remaining butter. Add the wine and bake for 20 to 25 minutes. Baste frequently. Serve with a purée of potatoes and carrots.

ROAST TURKEY

ᖇᗝ

For roast turkey, experiment with stuffings and basting liquids. You will need approximately 2 cups of stuffing to stuff a 6- to 8-pound turkey, 3 cups for a 12-pound bird. The mixture should be moist, as it dries a little in the roasting. Bread crumbs or cubes will stretch it; an egg or two will hold it together. And immense amounts of basting will do it a world of good.

One of our favorite simple stuffings is made with French blood sausage, *boudin noir*, available at French butchers. For a 6-pound turkey, buy a pound of sausage. Discard the casing and chop the sausage coarsely. Sauté it in butter for 10 minutes, mix it with ½ cup of coarsely broken walnut meats and stuff the bird. *Et voilà!*

Even simpler: As they sometimes do in Brittany, put one or two unpeeled pears in the cavity of a small turkey. Sprinkle the cavity with some pear brandy (*eau de vie de poire*) and roast. Serve surrounded by sliced pears sautéed in butter.

You can make a luxurious French *farce* by stuffing a turkey with a combination of sautéed chicken livers, boiled rice, *pâté de foie gras*, and truffles.

A rich Italian stuffing consists of giblets, chopped beef, sausage, bacon, and chestnuts, chopped together and sautéed, then mixed with egg and grated Parmesan cheese.

In Sicily we were given turkey inexpensively stuffed with bread, cooked pasta, sautéed chopped meat and onion, and in Verona we ate an exquisite young, unstuffed turkey, basted in pomegranate juice and roasted on a spit.

A fine French marinade for basting is made of beef broth, Madeira, lemon juice and rind, and raspberry jelly, all heated together till the jelly melts.

The combinations are endless. In fact, at a country Thanksgiving weekend, one of our guests—after one martini too many—basted our turkey (which we had stuffed with saffron rice, currants, and almonds) with Pernod. Unexpectedly delicious!

ROAST TURKEY
WITH CHESTNUT-FRUIT STUFFING

༂

12–16 SERVINGS

1   12- to 15-*pound fresh (not "fresh-frozen") turkey*
    Salt and pepper to taste
1   *stick (¼ pound) butter, at room temperature*

STUFFING

1   *1-pound can (about 2 cups) whole chestnuts,*
        unsweetened
3   *cups mixed dried fruits (prunes, apricots, peaches,*
        apples, currants, etc.)

3   *cups hot tea*
½   *pound sausage meat*
2   *tablespoons brandy (or rum)*
    Salt and pepper to taste
1   *tablespoon each dried sage and thyme*
2   *tablespoons chopped parsley*

Juice of 2 oranges
3   *tablespoons honey*

Preheat the oven to 450°.

Prepare the turkey for roasting by wiping it inside and out with a damp cloth. Season it inside and out with salt and pepper. Rub half the butter all over the bird.

Prepare the stuffing. Drain the chestnuts and break them into large pieces. Soak the dried fruits for 30 minutes in the hot tea. Drain and chop them coarsely. Fry the sausage meat and drain off all the fat. In a large bowl, chop the chestnuts, dried fruit, and sausage with the remaining ingredients. Mix well.

Stuff the turkey with the mixture. Do not pack it too tightly. Crumple a ball of foil and seal the opening with it. Fasten the wings behind the back and place the turkey, breast side up, on a rack in a buttered broiler pan. Spread a doubled piece of cheesecloth dipped in melted butter over the turkey. Roast for 30 minutes. Reduce the heat to 350° and roast for 3½ hours. (The cooking time is approximately 20 minutes per pound.) Remove the cheesecloth for the last 30 minutes of roasting and baste the turkey frequently with a mixture of orange juice and honey.

If you care to, cut potatoes, sweet potatoes, and zucchini into matchstick-size strips. French-fry them, put them around the turkey on a serving platter, and call it Turkey in the Straw.

ROAST TURKEY,
NORMANDY STYLE

ᖶᖶ

Novel and delicious at Thanksgiving—or at any other time, for that
matter.

8–10 SERVINGS

1   *8- to 10-pound turkey, wiped inside and out with a*
          damp cloth
1   *lemon*
    About 2 sticks (½ pound) butter
    Salt and freshly ground pepper to taste
12–14 *apples*
¼   *cup Calvados*
    Thin strips of salt pork
24 *boudins blancs (French white sausages available at*
          French butchers) or other mild sausage links

Preheat the oven to 425°.

Rub the turkey inside and out with half the lemon, then with a generous amount of butter. Salt and pepper the turkey lightly inside and
out. Peel and core four of the apples, moisten them with the Calvados,
and stuff the turkey with them. Truss it with a trussing needle or
with skewers and string. Fasten the neck skin to the back. Tie the
legs together, then tie them to the tail. Butter a roasting pan and place
the turkey, breast side up, on a rack in the pan. Cover the turkey with
the salt pork and put it in the oven. After 30 minutes, reduce the heat
to 375° and roast for 2 to 2½ hours.

Peel and core the remaining apples, sprinkle them with lemon juice,
and dot with butter. Set aside.

Baste the turkey frequently throughout the cooking, adding butter
as needed. Add a few tablespoons of water to the pan if the fat looks
as though it might burn. An hour before the turkey is done, add the
apples to the pan. Half an hour before it is done, discard the salt pork
so that the bird will brown. Prick the *boudin blanc* sausages and add
them to the pan. Continue to baste often with the fat in the pan. Test
the turkey by pricking the thigh with a sharp knife. When the juice
runs clear, the bird is ready. Allow it to rest in a warm place for 15
minutes before carving. Arrange it on a warm platter with the baked
apples and sausages around it.

MEAT

*L*ong ago, Homer tells us, oxen roasted and crackled and the divine Helen dined on the crisp fat of mutton chops. Later, Emma Bovary, looking at her wedding feast through her bridal veil, saw "four sirloins, six fricassees of chicken, a veal casserole, three legs of mutton, an appetizing roast suckling-pig flanked by four sorrel-sausages."

We are not, nowadays, as heroic as those legendary figures. Many of us, in fact, eat less meat for fear of cholesterol and calories. Or because we prefer vegetables, fish and fowl. Yet America, we find as we travel, is still quite a meat-and-potato country. Perhaps we are not as far from Homer as we imagine.

ROASTS

RECOMMENDATIONS FOR ROASTING

1. Always remove the meat from the refrigerator 2 hours before roasting.
2. Except for veal, all roasts should be placed on a V-shaped or flat rack set in a shallow pan, such as the oven broiler pan. Never put the roast directly in the pan or in a "roaster" with high sides, or it will be soggy.
3. A rack or leg of lamb does not need basting, but a shoulder of lamb or a roast beef or veal will benefit immeasurably from frequent basting. Veal is even better braised in a covered casserole.
4. If you want a roast that is crisp on the outside, the oven temperature should be 450° to 500° for the first 20 to 30 minutes. Lower the heat to 325° to 350° to finish the cooking. Otherwise roast the meat at moderate heat throughout.
5. If you have no time to thaw a frozen piece of meat, roast it slowly at 325°.
6. If you do not have a meat thermometer, test the meat for doneness with your fingers. It is ready when it feels firm yet resilient.
7. If you want large roasted potatoes or onions with your roast, parboil them for 15 minutes before placing them in the pan with the meat.
8. After removing a roast from the oven, let it rest for 15 minutes in a warm place before carving it.

ROAST FILLET OF BEEF, PROVENÇALE

᪥

8–10 SERVINGS

MARINADE
1 cup olive oil
1 teaspoon freshly ground pepper
   A few sprigs thyme
   A few sprigs parsley
1 bay leaf
1 small onion, sliced
1 tablespoon vinegar

1 5-pound fillet of beef, trimmed of all fat and tendons
   Pork fat, cut into thin sheets, enough to wrap the fillet
4 tablespoons each melted butter and olive oil mixed
      together

In a large bowl, combine all the ingredients for the marinade. Add the beef and let it marinate for 4 to 5 hours.

Preheat the oven to 500°.

Remove the beef from the marinade. Dry it carefully, wrap it with the sheets of pork fat and tie it securely. Roast for 20 minutes, basting frequently with the mixture of butter and olive oil. Remove the pork fat and roast for 5 minutes more, or just until the meat thermometer registers 120°, for a rare roast.

Loosely cover the roast with foil and let it rest for 5 minutes before carving into ½-inch slices. Serve with Béarnaise Sauce (see page 128). A Sformato of Broccoli (see page 37) makes a splendid accompaniment.

VEAL ROAST WITH KIDNEYS
(Rognonnade de Veau)

6–8 SERVINGS

1   3-pound loin of veal
1   veal kidney
    Salt and freshly ground pepper
½   cup Dijon mustard
3   strips bacon
    Bouquet garni (1 bay leaf, 1 sprig of thyme, and 1 clove
       of garlic tied in cheesecloth)
2   medium-size onions, sliced
4   carrots, sliced
1   cup white wine

Have your butcher bone the loin of veal, stuff it with the kidney, and tie it securely.

Preheat the oven to 325°.

Rub the veal generously with salt and pepper. Sear it on all sides in hot oil in a casserole with a cover. Coat the veal with the mustard. Blanch the bacon strips and lay them over the veal. Add the bouquet garni, the onions, carrots, and wine. Roast, tightly covered, for about 1½ hours, basting frequently with the pan juices, until the meat thermometer registers 175°. Let the meat rest for 15 minutes before carving.

Serve each guest a slice of veal, a slice of kidney, and some of the onions and carrots. Excellent accompanied by Stuffed Mushrooms (see page 274).

ROAST LEG OF LAMB

8–10 SERVINGS

1   6-pound leg of lamb
1–2   cloves garlic, peeled and slivered
⅓   cup oil

1   tablespoon dried thyme
    Salt and freshly ground pepper to taste
    Freshly grated nutmeg to taste

Preheat the oven to 450°.

Remove the fell (the thin, transparent membrane) and some of the fat from the leg of lamb. Make incisions in the meat and insert the slivers of garlic. Rub the lamb with the oil, thyme, salt, and pepper. Put it on a rack set in the broiler pan and roast for 20 minutes. Reduce the heat to 350° and roast for about 40 minutes more, or until the meat thermometer registers 135°. The meat should be pink and tender. Let it rest for 15 minutes lightly covered with foil before carving.

Pass a nutmeg grater or fill individual butter dishes with freshly grated nutmeg to season the lamb.

VARIATION: Have your butcher bone the lamb and stuff it with the lamb kidney. Follow the procedure above but coat the meat liberally with Dijon mustard. The roast will be medium rare after about 1½ hours, or when the meat thermometer registers 147° to 150°. In place of the nutmeg, pass hot pepper jelly.

ROAST LEG OF LAMB, BOULANGÈRE

An old-fashioned French country recipe. The lamb is set on a rack over a gratin dish of partially baked potatoes so that they are flavored by the drippings from the meat. Loin of pork can be cooked in the same way.

8–10 SERVINGS

1   5- to 6-pound leg of lamb
    Lemon Potatoes Saint-Tropez (see page 284), with an
        extra pound of potatoes and 1–2 cups chopped
        tomato pulp added to the recipe

Have the butcher trim the lamb and cut off the bone at the knuckle. Remove the fell (the thin, transparent membrane) and most of the fat from the leg of lamb.

Preheat the oven to 375°.

Assemble the ingredients (including the extra potatoes and the chopped tomato) for the lemon potatoes Saint-Tropez. Arrange the vegetables in a 12- by 8-inch ovenproof baking pan. Set the pan in a larger baking pan (with an inch of water) to catch any excess drippings. Bake for 1 hour

Set a cake rack over the potatoes, and lay the lamb on it fat side up. Lower the heat to 350° and roast for 1 hour, or until the meat thermometer reads 135° and the juice of the roast runs pink. Remove the roast and let it rest, lightly covered with foil, for 15 minutes in a warm place before carving. If the potatoes are still not tender, leave them, lightly covered with foil, in the 350° oven while the meat rests.

ROAST PORK WITH APRICOTS

ᐧᐧᐧ

4 SERVINGS

1	2½-pound loin of pork
10	dried apricots, soaked in apricot brandy, Grand Marnier, or cognac for 30 minutes
4	tablespoons butter
	Salt and freshly ground pepper to taste
⅓	cup each sieved apricot jam and Dijon mustard mixed together

Make 10 incisions in the loin of pork and stuff each one with an apricot. Let the pork stand for 1 hour. Rub it liberally with butter, salt, and pepper.

Preheat the oven to 325°. Roast the pork, fat side up, for 1½ to 2 hours. About 20 minutes before the roast is finished, coat it generously with the mixture of apricot jam and mustard. When the roast is done, let it rest, lightly covered with foil, in a warm place for 15 minutes before carving. Serve with creamy mashed potatoes.

ROAST PORK WITH LENTILS

⤬

A fine winter meal.

6–8 SERVINGS

1   *4-pound loin of pork*
    Coarse salt
    Dried marjoram or sage
    Lentils Provençale (see page 272)

Preheat the oven to 325°.

Remove excess fat from the loin of pork and rub the meat with salt and marjoram or sage. Roast it on a rack set in a roasting pan for 2½ hours. While the pork is cooking, prepare the lentils provençale.

When the pork is ready, let it rest for 15 minutes, then slice it into serving portions. Season with salt and pepper. Put alternate layers of pork and lentils in a large casserole. Bake, covered, for 30 minutes.

CHOPPED MEAT

Some compliments go straight to the heart. Unforgettable was the poet Marianne Moore's "These meatballs are celestial, my dears," when she came to dinner one evening. "Meatballs for a poet?" you ask. We can only say that at our meatball dinner there was a prolonged discussion with Miss Moore and another of our favorite poets, Elizabeth Bishop, on the merits of meatballs versus steak. All agreed that chopped meat won hands down. "Steak is so *lurid*," said Elizabeth with a shudder. At the poets' urging, we have been serving meatballs to "company" ever since.

Here are some recipes for meatballs (as well as other chopped-meat dishes) that we hope you too may find "celestial."

GALA MEAT LOAF

༽

The addition of *duxelles* elevates the homely meat loaf to company
stature. You will need an 8- by 12-inch baking pan.

10–14 SERVINGS

DUXELLES

2   tablespoons cèpes or other dried mushrooms
1¼ pounds fresh mushrooms
1   stick (¼ pound) butter
    Salt and pepper to taste

3   pounds ground chuck
3–4 chorizos (Spanish sausages) or Italian sausages with
        fennel
1½–2 cups chopped onions
1   tablespoon each butter and oil (or more if needed)
1   clove garlic, minced or passed through a garlic press
    Salt and pepper to taste
3   eggs
1   cup bread crumbs
1   cup coarsely chopped Italian-style tomatoes (drain and
        reserve the juice)
2   tablespoons Dijon mustard
1   tablespoon Worcestershire sauce
2–3 dashes of Tabasco sauce
1   teaspoon curry powder
1   teaspoon dried thyme (or 1 tablespoon fresh, finely
        chopped)
    Salt and pepper to taste

Make the *duxelles*. Soak the dried mushrooms in warm water to cover
for 30 minutes. Drain and pat dry. Chop the fresh and dried mushrooms rather fine and fry them in a heavy pan in the butter over medium heat. Cook for about 30 minutes, or until they are very dark
brown and all their liquid has evaporated. Season with salt and pepper and set aside.

Remove the chopped beef from the refrigerator and bring it to room temperature. Cook the sausages in ½ inch of water for 30 minutes, turning them once. Drain, discard the skins and chop the sausages coarsely. Set aside.

Preheat the oven to 350°.

Fry the onions in the butter and oil over medium heat, stirring often, until golden brown. Stir in the garlic. Add more fat, if needed. Season with salt and pepper. Set aside.

Put the chopped beef and sausage in a large bowl with all the remaining ingredients except the reserved tomato juice. Mix until well combined. Place in a baking dish, and shape into a loaf with a 1-inch space around it. Bake for about 1½ hours, basting frequently with the tomato juice and pan juices. Serve with Carrots in Marmalade (see page 265) and Corn Pancakes (see page 267), increasing the amounts by half, if you like.

CURRIED MEATBALLS
(Boulettes au Cari)

෬෴

4–6 SERVINGS

½ pound veal fillet
½ pound lean pork
1 stick (8 tablespoons) butter
½ cup chopped tart apple
½ cup chopped onion
1 tablespoon curry powder
Salt and freshly ground pepper to taste
1 cup Chicken Broth (see page 48)
1 egg
½ cup heavy cream
½ cup flour
¼ cup minced chives

Grind the veal and pork. Combine the two and mix them well.

Heat 2 tablespoons of the butter in a heavy pan. Add the chopped apple and onion. Cook over low heat, stirring often, till the onions are translucent but not browned. Sprinkle with the curry and add salt and pepper. Heat the chicken broth and add it. Cook, uncovered, stirring occasionally, for 10 minutes, or until the broth has evaporated. Remove from the heat.

Mix together the ground meat, the egg, 2 tablespoons of the cream, 1 tablespoon of flour, and salt and pepper. Add the onion-apple mixture and mix well. Divide this mixture into twelve equal parts. With moistened hands, roll them into balls, then roll them in flour to coat them lightly.

Refrigerate for 30 minutes. Heat a generous amount of butter (about 4 tablespoons) in a heavy frying pan. Sauté the meatballs over medium heat for 15 to 20 minutes, turning them once or twice so that they are well browned. Remove them with a slotted spoon to a warm platter. Add the remaining cream to the pan. Cook over high heat for 2 or 3 minutes, stirring and scraping the brown bits into the cream. Add a pinch or two of curry powder. Taste and correct the seasoning, adding more curry, salt, or pepper if needed. Pour this sauce over the meatballs, sprinkle them with chopped chives, and serve with buttered noodles.

A SUGGESTED MENU

(see Index for recipes)

ASPARAGUS WITH SABAYON SAUCE

CURRIED MEATBALLS

BIBB LETTUCE, VINAIGRETTE

CRUSTLESS TARTE TATIN

wine: CALON-SÉGUR

MOROCCAN MEATBALLS

4 SERVINGS

1   *cup coarsely chopped onions*
2   *cups Beef Broth (see page 47)*
1   *cup finely chopped onions*
1   *pound ground chuck or round steak*
1   *tablespoon uncooked rice, pulverized in a food*
    processor
4   *teaspoons cumin or more to taste*
2   *teaspoons dried coriander or more to taste*

1   cup finely chopped parsley
1   teaspoon salt
½   teaspoon freshly ground pepper
1   egg, beaten
    Bread crumbs
2–3 tablespoons vegetable oil
2   tablespoons tomato paste
1   cup cooked peas
1   cup chopped fresh coriander or parsley

Put ½ inch of water in a large heavy frying pan, stir in the coarsely chopped onions, and bring to a simmer. Cover and cook until tender, adding beef broth as needed to maintain the ½-inch level. Mix together the finely chopped onions, the meat, rice, cumin, coriander, parsley, salt, and pepper. Shape into 1½-inch balls. Roll them in the beaten egg, then in the bread crumbs. Sauté them in oil over medium heat for 10 minutes. Transfer the meatballs to the pan with the onions and water, and simmer gently for 25 minutes, turning them occasionally. Stir the tomato paste, the peas, and an additional bit of cumin into the liquid in the pan and cook just long enough to heat thoroughly. Taste and correct the seasoning. Sprinkle with half the coriander and serve with buttery rice mixed with the remaining chopped fresh coriander.

PERSIAN MEATBALLS IN SWEET AND SOUR WALNUT SAUCE

⌒◡⌒

8–10 SERVINGS

1¼ pounds ground chuck
    Salt and freshly ground pepper to taste

SAUCE

2   cups walnuts, chopped (easily done in a blender)
2   tablespoons pomegranate syrup (available in Middle
        Eastern specialty shops) or 2 tablespoons lemon
        juice, or 1 tablespoon each lemon juice and tomato
        sauce
3   tablespoons sugar

½ *cup chopped onions*
2 *tablespoons butter (or more if needed)*

Season the ground chuck with salt and pepper and roll into small meatballs, no larger than ¾ inch in diameter (you should have about 60). Refrigerate them while you prepare the sauce.

In a large heavy pot, heat the walnuts (without any fat) over low heat for 3 to 5 minutes, stirring often. Do not let them burn. Add water to cover, the pomegranate syrup, and the sugar. Bring to a boil. Reduce the heat and simmer, covered, for 25 to 30 minutes.

While the sauce is simmering, sauté the onions in the butter in a large heavy frying pan until browned. Add some of the meatballs (do not crowd the pan) and sauté them till they are browned on all sides. Remove the onions and meatballs. Add a little more butter if needed and cook the rest of the meatballs.

Add the meatballs and onions to the walnut sauce. Cook over low heat for 10 to 15 minutes, adding a little water if needed. The sauce should be quite thick. Serve with steamed rice.

VARIATIONS: Substitute in place of the meatballs ¾-inch cubes of roasted duck, chicken, pheasant, or quail. An exotic use for leftover roast fowl.

SWEDISH MEATBALLS À LA LINDSTROM

4–6 SERVINGS

1 *pound chuck or sirloin, finely ground three times with*
     the fine blade of a meat grinder
5 *egg yolks*
⅓ *cup heavy cream*
2 *cooked beets, 2 cooked potatoes, 1 onion—all small*
     to medium in size and finely chopped (there
     should be about 1½ cups altogether)
1 *tablespoon capers*
     Salt and freshly ground pepper to taste (about ½
     tablespoon each)
     Butter for frying

Mix the meat, the egg yolks, and the cream, then add all the other ingredients except the butter. Roll into balls no larger than an inch across. Fry them very quickly in a hot skillet with plenty of butter. The outside should be nicely browned, the inside rare and moist. Delicious served hot or cold with Ron Lehrman's Cucumber Salad (see page 305) and imported Swedish lingonberries.

STUFFED APPLES,
OMAR KHAYYAM

၆‿၅

4 SERVINGS

4   *large tart green baking apples*
4   *tablespoons butter*
½   *pound ground chuck*
    Seasonings: ½ teaspoon each salt and freshly ground
        pepper, 1 teaspoon cinnamon or more to taste
1   *medium-size onion, finely chopped*
4   *tablespoons canned chick-peas, drained and mashed*
2   *tablespoons raisins*
    Sauce: 1 tablespoon butter, ¼ cup vinegar, 2 tablespoons
        sugar

Preheat the oven to 350°.

Cut thin slices from the stem ends of the apples and save them to use as lids. With an apple corer, remove and discard the cores and seeds—do not cut through the bottoms of the apples. Use a melon-ball cutter to remove most of the pulp, leaving a shell approximately ½ inch thick. Chop the pulp and reserve.

Heat 1 tablespoon of the butter in a frying pan. Cook the ground chuck, breaking it up with a fork, for about 3 minutes, or until it loses its color. Remove it to a mixing bowl. Add the apple pulp and the seasonings.

Cook the onion in 2 tablespoons of the butter over low heat until translucent. Add to the meat mixture along with the chick-peas and raisins. Stuff each apple with a quarter of this mixture and cover it with its apple-slice lid. Butter a baking dish with the remaining butter and set the apples in it. Bake for 15 minutes. Bring the sauce ingredients to a boil with ¼ cup of water. Remove the apples from the oven, take off the lids, and fill each apple with the sauce. Bake the apples for another 15 minutes, pouring any remaining sauce over them. Baste them once or twice. Before serving, pour the sauce in the baking dish over the apples and replace the lids.

VARIATIONS: The same procedure can be used to stuff green peppers or onions that have been partially cooked and then hollowed out.

LADY PENROSE'S NO-DOUGH PIZZA

You will need a 9-inch pie plate.

6 SERVINGS

CRUST

1 tablespoon olive oil
1 pound ground beef (top round)
2 teaspoons minced onion
½ teaspoon each salt and freshly ground pepper

FILLING

2 cups tomatoes, peeled, seeded, squeezed dry, and
      chopped coarsely, or 2 cups canned Italian-style
      tomatoes, carefully drained and chopped
1 tablespoon capers, drained
10 olives, black and green, pitted and halved
1 can flat anchovy fillets
1 teaspoon basil or oregano
   Mozzarella, thinly sliced, enough to cover the "pizza"

Preheat the oven to 400°.

Spread the oil in a 9-inch pie plate. Mix the beef with the onion, salt, and pepper and spread it evenly in the pie plate, building up the sides to form a "crust." Cover the beef with the tomatoes, then arrange the capers, olives, and anchovies in a decorative pattern. Sprinkle with the herbs. Bake for 25 minutes. Remove from the oven and cover the surface with mozzarella. Bake for 5 minutes, or until the mozzarella melts. If liquid has collected, remove it with a bulb baster and discard it. Serve the "pizza" hot in pie-shaped wedges.

BEEF

BOLLITO MISTO
(Mixed Broiled Meats)

᠔

Italy's glorious version of the French pot-au-feu. A special treat as served at the Ristorante al Cambio, the most beautiful restaurant in Turin. Ideal when prepared and eaten on blustery winter days.

If we give a good deal of space to *bollito misto* and to boiled fillet of beef, it is because these noble dishes, carefully prepared, are as satisfying as domestic happiness itself. In her cookbook Pampille—the daughter-in-law of the writer Alphonse Daudet—assures us that boiled beef is a remedy for fatigue and discouragement. And we believe her.

8–10 SERVINGS

2 *pounds lean short ribs of beef*
1 *veal knuckle*
½ *pound lean salt pork, parboiled*
1 *onion, stuck with 6 cloves*
1 *clove garlic*
2 *carrots, sliced*
2 *small stalks celery, sliced*
2 *tomatoes, peeled, seeded, and coarsely chopped*
   Bouquet garni (2 sprigs each parsley and thyme and
      1 bay leaf tied together with string)
1 *tablespoon salt*
10 *whole peppercorns*

1   1-pound cotechino (Italian sausage)
1   5-pound capon
      Salt and pepper

STUFFING FOR THE CAPON

1   onion, finely chopped
1   clove garlic, passed through a garlic press
2   tablespoons prosciutto or ham, finely chopped
      Liver, heart, and gizzard of the capon, sautéed 5
          minutes in 2 tablespoons butter, then finely
          chopped
3   cups fresh Italian bread cubes, soaked in milk, then
          squeezed dry
2   tablespoons chopped parsley
2   eggs, lightly beaten
      Salt and pepper to taste

      Vegetable garnish: 1 pound each of 5 or 6 vegetables
          in season, such as peas, carrots, green beans,
          zucchini, cabbage, small potatoes, pearl onions
2   quarts Beef Broth (see page 47) or half beef and
          half Chicken Broth (see page 48)
      Optional: a can of frutta in mostarda (fruit in mustard
          syrup, available in Italian specialty shops)

Place the beef, veal knuckle, and salt pork in an 8- to 10-quart soup
pot. Cover with water. Over low heat, slowly bring to a boil and skim.
Add the onion, garlic, carrots, celery, tomatoes, and bouquet garni.
Season lightly with salt and add the peppercorns. Simmer, covered,
for 3 to 4 hours.

Prick the *cotechino* sausage all over with a fork so that it does not
burst when cooking. Soak it in cold water in a separate pot.

Clean the capon. Salt and pepper it inside and out. Mix the stuffing
ingredients together and fill the cavity of the capon. Truss the bird
with metal skewers, laced with string. Tie the wings and legs close
to the bird.

When the beef has simmered for 1 hour, remove the veal knuckle
and salt pork, and add the stuffed capon. After another hour, bring
the *cotechino* to a boil in its pot, reduce the heat immediately to a
simmer, and cook over low heat for about 1 hour, or until tender.
Turn off the heat, leaving the *cotechino* in the hot water. When the
capon is tender and the leg joint can be moved easily, remove it to

a platter or a large bowl, cover it with some of the broth, and keep it warm.

About 40 minutes before the beef is tender, add the garnish vegetables to the pot, timing them so they will be ready when the beef is cooked. (For example, add carrots and potatoes first, zucchini last.)

Remove the strings from the capon. Spoon out the stuffing. Carve the capon and the meats and slice the *cotechino*. Arrange them on a warm large platter around the stuffing and surround them with the boiled vegetables. Serve each guest a portion of everything, the red, white, and green sauces (see below and pages 218, 219)—the colors of the Italian flag—and *frutta in mostarda*.

NOTE: Needless to say, the liquid the meat and capon were cooked in makes a most delicious broth if skimmed of fat and strained. This is done after it has cooled so that the fat is easily removed. Leftover meat, vegetables, and chicken are good cold with the same sauces, although Italians pride themselves on serving freshly made *bollito*.

A SUGGESTED MENU

(see Index for recipes)

BOLLITO MISTO WITH RED SAUCE,

WHITE SAUCE, AND GREEN SAUCE

SALAD OF ARUGULA AND FENNEL

FIG ICE CREAM

wine: BARBARESCO

RED SAUCE
(Bagnet Ross)

You will need a flame tamer.

3–4 CUPS

7 very ripe medium-size tomatoes, unpeeled
2 medium-size onions, peeled
1 carrot, scraped and trimmed
2–3 cloves garlic, peeled
    A pinch of minced hot red pepper (or cayenne pepper,
       pepper flakes, or a dash of Tabasco sauce)

　1　 *teaspoon salt*
1–3　 *teaspoons sugar*
　1　 *teaspoon red wine vinegar*
½–¾　 *cup olive oil*

Mince the tomatoes, onions, carrot, and garlic. Put them all in an earthenware or enamel pot. Add the hot red pepper, salt, sugar, vinegar, and about ¼ cup of oil. Cook, covered, over the lowest heat for 3 to 4 hours, stirring often. A flame tamer under the pot is essential. Stir occasionally and add a little oil as needed to prevent sticking. Start the cooking with the pot covered. Toward the end, remove the cover to thicken the sauce if necessary, stirring constantly.

Pass the sauce through a food mill or a strainer, pressing through as much of it as possible. Discard the tomato skins and seeds. Stir in a little more oil. The sauce should be thick but not dry. Correct the seasoning, adding more salt, sugar, or vinegar as desired. Serve with *bollito misto* or with hamburgers, chops, or steaks.

WHITE SAUCE
(Salsa al Rafano)

❧

ABOUT 1 CUP

1　 *½-inch slice Italian bread, trimmed of crust*
¼　 *cup milk*
4　 *tablespoons freshly grated horseradish (or bottled)*
½　 *teaspoon salt*
½　 *teaspoon superfine sugar*
½　 *cup whipped cream or sour cream, or a combination*
　　 of both
1　 *teaspoon vinegar*

Break up the bread, soak it in the milk, then squeeze it dry. Place it in a bowl with the horseradish. (If you are using bottled horseradish, strain it through a fine strainer to get rid of the liquid.) Stir in the salt, sugar, and cream. Store in the refrigerator. When ready to use, stir in the vinegar. Correct the seasoning, adding more salt or sugar if needed. Serve with *bollito misto* or with cold steamed or poached fish.

GREEN SAUCE
(Salsa Verde)

⟋⟍⟍⟍

ABOUT 2 CUPS

4 *tablespoons finely chopped fresh parsley*
1 *small clove garlic, finely chopped*
2 *anchovies, finely chopped*
1 *small dinner roll or half a peeled boiled potato*
2 *tablespoons vinegar*
2–3 *pickled mushrooms (available in Italian delicatessens*
     and specialty shops), finely diced
     Salt and freshly ground pepper to taste
2 *teaspoons capers*
1 *small sour pickle or cornichon, finely chopped*
1 *tablespoon finely diced green pepper*
½ *teaspoon finely diced hot red pepper, or 2–3 dashes*
     Tabasco sauce
1 *teaspoon finely diced scallion or onion*
1 *hard-boiled egg yolk, mashed*
8–12 *tablespoons Italian olive oil*

In a wooden bowl or large mortar, mash the parsley, garlic, and anchovies together. Discard the crust and break up the roll, then soak
the pieces in vinegar. Squeeze them dry and add them to the bowl.
Mash them with a wooden spoon or pestle. (If using a boiled potato,
cut it up and add it to the bowl with 1 teaspoon of vinegar.)

Add the remaining ingredients except the oil and mash them together into a coarse paste. Add the olive oil gradually, using enough
to make a thick but fairly liquid paste. Store, covered, in a cool place
but not in the refrigerator. Float a bit of olive oil on top to prevent
discoloration.

When ready to use, if most of the oil has become absorbed, gradually stir in a bit more. Correct the seasoning. Serve with *bollito misto*
or with boiled beef or boiled chicken.

TIP: Do as they do in Piedmont and fill scooped-out halves of ripe red
tomatoes with this piquant green sauce, mixed with a bit of mayonnaise. Excellent over hard-boiled eggs or cold poached fish as well.

BOILED FILLET OF BEEF
WITH STRINGS ATTACHED
(Boeuf à la Ficelle, Paul Bocuse)

၆✎

If you do not have the time to make a *bollito misto*, try our adaptation of this luxurious version of boiled beef, a specialty of the great Paul Bocuse. It can be made in about an hour.

8–10 SERVINGS

1   *4-pound fillet of beef*
1   *pound carrots, peeled and cut into ¼-inch julienne strips*
1   *pound turnips, peeled and cut into ¼-inch julienne strips*
6   *small onions, each peeled and stuck with 1 clove*
6   *leeks, white part only, washed thoroughly*
2   *celery hearts (or 2 fennel bulbs), cut into quarters*
3   *tomatoes, peeled, cut in half crosswise, and gently
        squeezed to remove the seeds and juice*
1   *sprig each parsley, tarragon, and chervil (or 3 sprigs
        parsley)*
12 *peppercorns*
    *About 1 tablespoon coarse salt or 2 teaspoons table salt
        or to taste*

CROUTONS

12 *slices French bread, cut ½ inch thick*
3   *tablespoons butter*
6   *tablespoons grated imported Swiss cheese*

1   *tablespoon butter*

Have the butcher tie the beef fillet with strings to hold its shape. Ask him to tie an additional long loop of string to one end. (This will make it easy to remove the fillet from the pot.) Leave the meat out of the refrigerator for 3 to 4 hours before cooking.

Bring 3 quarts of water to a boil in a large copper, earthenware, or enamel-lined pot. Add the meat, looping the string over the pot handle so that later you can pull it out easily. Boil for 5 minutes. Add all the other ingredients except the crouton ingredients and butter. Simmer for about 40 minutes, skimming the bouillon frequently. The beef should be rosy inside. Do not overcook.

While the meat is cooking, prepare the croutons. Toast the bread slices under the broiler on one side. Turn them over, spread them with the butter and sprinkle them generously with grated cheese. Toast until the cheese is golden brown.

Transfer the meat to a platter. Remove the vegetables with a slotted spoon and arrange them around the meat. Spoon a little bouillon over all and keep the meat and vegetables warm in a low oven. Pour the remaining bouillon through a cheesecloth-lined sieve into a heated tureen. Correct the seasoning and swirl in 1 tablespoon of butter. Serve the delicate, light bouillon as a first course, putting a crouton in the bottom of each soup plate and pouring the hot bouillon over it.

For the second course, slice the meat and arrange it on the platter with the vegetables around it. With it, serve bowls of coarse salt, Dijon mustard, gherkins (*cornichons*), and cocktail onions in vinegar.

MIROTON
(Baked Leftover-Beef and Potatoes)

⌒～⌒

One of the finest leftover meat dishes imaginable.

6 SERVINGS

1½–2   *pounds leftover boiled beef*
6   *medium-size onions, peeled and chopped fine*
2   *tablespoons butter*
1   *tablespoon oil*
1   *heaping tablespoon flour*
2   *tablespoons red wine vinegar*
2   *cups Beef Broth (see page 47)*
3   *medium-size ripe tomatoes, peeled, seeded, and*
      coarsely chopped

1   teaspoon tomato paste
2   cloves garlic, peeled and bruised
    Sugar, salt, and freshly ground pepper to taste
4   boiled potatoes, sliced
1–3 tablespoons chopped fresh parsley
1–3 tablespoons bread crumbs
2   tablespoons melted butter
6   sour gherkins (cornichons), finely sliced or chopped

The leftover boiled beef should be at room temperature before preparing the *miroton*.

Boil the onions for 5 minutes. Drain and pat them dry on paper towels. In a heavy pot, cook the onions in the butter and the oil over low heat, stirring often with a wooden spoon for 10 to 15 minutes, or until translucent but not browned. Sprinkle the flour over the onions and cook, stirring, for 4 to 5 minutes, pressing out any lumps. Stir in the vinegar, cook for a few seconds and remove from the heat.

Bring the beef broth to a boil in another pot and gradually add it to the onion mixture. Cook over low heat, stirring constantly to prevent lumps from forming. Add the tomatoes, tomato paste, garlic, a pinch of sugar, a bit of salt, and a generous twist of freshly ground pepper. Bring to a boil, reduce the heat, and simmer for 20 minutes. (The recipe can be prepared ahead of time to this point.)

About 20 minutes before serving time, preheat the oven to 350°. Spread a third of the onion-tomato sauce on the bottom of a buttered baking dish. Cut the beef into ½-inch slices and arrange them over the onions in a single overlapping layer. Spread a third of the onion-tomato sauce over the beef. Arrange the boiled potatoes in a row of overlapping slices on top of the beef. Season them lightly with salt and pepper and cover them with the remaining sauce. Sprinkle with the chopped parsley, bread crumbs, and melted butter. Bake for 15 minutes and serve. Sprinkle the chopped gherkins over all just before serving.

NOTE: If you want to increase the number of servings, the *miroton* can be stretched by arranging slices of boiled sausage (such as French cervelat) under the potato slices.

BEEF SALAD, PARMENTIER
(Salade de Boeuf Parmentier)

❧

A simple way to use leftover boiled beef and delicious, too.

Mix equal amounts of leftover boiled beef (at room temperature), cut into ¾-inch cubes, and boiled potatoes, cut into ¼-inch slices while they are hot. Season them immediately with salt and freshly ground pepper. Add oil and one-third as much red wine vinegar. Add finely chopped scallions (including a bit of the green) and chopped fresh herbs, such as parsley, tarragon, and chervil. Serve at room temperature.

BELGIAN BEEF STEW
(Carbonnades de Boeuf)

❧

4–5 SERVINGS

4	tablespoons peanut oil
2½	pounds stewing beef, cut into 1- to 1½-inch cubes
2	large onions, sliced
2	tablespoons vinegar
1	tablespoon brown sugar
2–3	cloves garlic (or more to taste), passed through a garlic press
2	bay leaves
1	sprig thyme
2	cups malt beer
1	cup beef broth
1	thick slice French bread, crust removed
1–2	tablespoons Dijon mustard
¼	cup chopped parsley

Heat the oil in a large casserole until very hot. Add the beef, several pieces at a time. Sear them over high heat until well browned on all sides. Transfer the beef to a warm platter. Cook the onions in the same oil over low heat until translucent but not browned.

Return the beef to the casserole, raise the heat to medium, add the vinegar, sugar, garlic, bay leaves, and thyme. Add only enough beer and beef broth to cover. Spread the French bread with mustard. Bury the bread in the center of the casserole. Bring to a boil, then reduce the heat, cover and simmer for 2 hours, or until tender, skimming the top several times.

Remove the beef to a platter and keep it warm. Discard the bay leaves. Reduce the liquid over high heat to about 1 to 1½ cups. Replace the beef and heat it thoroughly. Sprinkle with chopped parsley and serve with buttered noodles or boiled potatoes rolled in chopped chives.

GENOESE BRAISED BEEF

6 SERVINGS

½   cup olive oil
3   tablespoons rendered bacon fat
1   4½-pound bottom round or rump of beef
2   cups good red wine (Barolo is ideal)
2   cloves garlic, peeled and finely chopped
1   large onion, chopped
1½ cups chopped carrots
1   cup chopped celery
2   ripe tomatoes, peeled, seeded, and coarsely chopped
        (reserve the juice) or 7 ounces of drained canned
        Italian tomatoes
    Salt and pepper to taste
3   sprigs parsley
2   cloves
10 basil leaves or 2 teaspoons dried basil
2   cups Beef Broth (see page 47)
2   ounces dried mushrooms
    Garnish: ½ cup chopped parsley

In a large, heavy casserole, heat the oil and bacon fat until hot but not smoking. Brown the meat well on all sides. Add the wine and cook till it is reduced by one-third. Add the garlic, onion, carrots, celery, and tomatoes (without their juice). Season with salt and pepper and add a bouquet garni of parsley, cloves, and fresh basil wrapped in a cheesecloth bag. (If you are using dried basil, add it separately.)

Simmer over medium heat with the casserole tightly covered for 4 hours, adding some of the juice from the tomatoes after 1 hour. Moisten the meat from time to time with some of the beef stock.

Soak the mushrooms in 1½ cups of hot water for 30 minutes. Drain and chop them. Set aside.

Half an hour before the meat is ready, add the mushrooms, and more salt and pepper if needed.

Remove the meat to a platter and keep it warm. Rub the sauce through a food mill fitted with the medium sieve. Return the sauce to the casserole and heat it thoroughly. Slice the meat into medium-thick slices. Arrange them on a serving platter. Pour the sauce over the meat. Serve with *orzo*, the Italian pasta that looks like rice.

MANOUCHER YEKTAI'S
PERSIAN BEEF STEW WITH
VEGETABLE SAUCE

⌒⌣⌒

The distinguished Iranian painter Manoucher Yektai, who lives in New York, entertains his friends with Persian banquets. Most of our Persian recipes were inspired by his remarkable cooking.

4–6 SERVINGS

½   cup chopped onions
3   tablespoons butter
3   tablespoons oil (preferably peanut oil)
1¼ pounds stewing beef, cut into ¾-inch cubes
     Seasonings: Salt and freshly ground pepper to taste,
       ¼ teaspoon turmeric (or a pinch or two of saffron)

2   bunches scallions (both white and green parts),
       chopped
3   large bunches fresh parsley, stems removed and
       chopped
3   teaspoons limoo amani (dried limes, available at Middle
       Eastern grocers) or the juice of 1 lemon
½   cup kidney beans, boiled and drained (or canned
       kidney beans)

Brown the onions in a deep heavy pot in 1 tablespoon each of the
butter and oil over medium heat for 10 minutes, stirring often. Remove the onions with a slotted spoon and reserve. Raise the heat to
high and add the cubes of meat. Cook for 10 minutes, turning the
meat so that it browns well on all sides. Return the onions to the pot.
Add the seasonings (larger amounts can be used according to taste)
and just enough water to cover. Bring to a boil, then lower the heat
and simmer for 20 minutes.

Meanwhile, sauté the scallions for 10 to 12 minutes in a large
heavy frying pan in 1 tablespoon each of the butter and oil. Push
them to one side, add the remaining butter and oil to the empty side,
then add the parsley and sauté for 5 minutes without mixing it with
the scallions (a Persian refinement). Then stir the scallions and
parsley together and cook for 2 to 3 minutes.

Add the parsley-scallion mixture and the dried limes or lemon
juice to the meat. Cook over low heat for 30 minutes. No harm will
be done if you cook the stew for 30 to 60 minutes more over very
low heat, adding a small amount of water from time to time as
needed. For the last 10 minutes of cooking, add the kidney beans.

MANOUCHER YEKTAI'S TIPS: This dish can be prepared in advance
and reheated before serving, adding small amounts of water as
needed.

Cubes of lamb or veal can be used in place of the beef.

In the south of Iran, cubes of fish are substituted for the meat.
Bass, swordfish, eel, etc., can be used or, better still, a combination
of several kinds of fish. The recipe is followed exactly, except that
saffron would be used in preference to turmeric and lemon juice
would be substituted for part of the water.

T-BONE STEAK WITH MARROW SAUCE

᧬

2 SERVINGS

5   *1-inch slices of marrowbone*
1   *heaping tablespoon finely chopped shallots*
1   *tablespoon butter*
    Salt and pepper to taste
¼ *cup white wine*
¼ *cup sour cream or crème fraîche*
1   *1½-pound T-bone steak*
    Coarse salt and freshly ground pepper to taste
    Oil for frying
2   *tablespoons finely chopped parsley or chervil*

Put the slices of marrowbone in a pot and cover them with cold water. Simmer for 5 minutes, then remove them. Scoop the marrow out of the bones. Sauté the shallots in butter and season them with salt and pepper. When the shallots are soft but not browned, add the wine, raise the heat, and cook till the wine is reduced by half. Then add the marrow and sour cream. Cook over low heat, stirring often.

Season the steak with coarse salt and freshly ground pepper and fry it in very hot oil to the desired degree of doneness. Sprinkle the sauce with parsley or chervil and pour it over the steak before serving.

STEAK IN A COCOTTE WITH GREEN PEPPERCORNS, LÉON DE LYON

᧬

2 SERVINGS

1   *1½-inch-thick boneless shell steak, trimmed of all excess*
    fat
4   *teaspoons whole green peppercorns (available in*
    specialty food shops)

3   *tablespoons butter*
¼   *cup cognac or brandy*
¾   *cup dry white wine*
¾   *cup Beef Broth (see page 47)*
     Coarse salt to taste
¼   *cup French peanut oil*

Preheat the oven to 450°.

The steak must be at room temperature. Leave it out of the re-frigerator for 3 to 4 hours before cooking.

Reserve 1 teaspoon of the peppercorns. Put the remaining pepper-corns on a wooden board and crush them with the bottom of a heavy cast-iron pan. Put the crushed pepper into a 3- to 4-cup saucepan with 2 tablespoons of the butter. Cook over medium heat for a minute or two. Add the cognac, raise the heat, and light it with a match. When the flame dies down, add ½ cup of the wine and the broth. Cook over high heat, stirring occasionally, till reduced to half its volume. Then add the salt.

Meanwhile, pour the oil into a flameproof oval baking dish, with a cover, which should not be much larger than the steak. Place over high heat. When the oil is sizzling hot, brown the steak for a minute or two on each side. Place the steak, uncovered, in the oven. Bake it for 8 to 10 minutes for rare, 12 to 15 minutes for medium rare. Remove the baking dish from the oven, and now act quickly.

Place the steak on a heated dish and keep it warm. Pour the oil out of the baking dish. Put the remaining wine in the baking dish, and deglaze quickly by scraping the brown bits into the wine. Return the steak to the baking dish. Add the reserved whole peppercorns and the remaining butter. Pour in the reduced sauce and place over high heat till the sauce bubbles up. Cover the baking dish and bring it to the table.

At the table, let your privileged guest inhale the aroma, slice the steak, and serve half the sauce over each portion.

Excellent accompaniments would be Gratin of Potatoes and Tur-nips (see page 284) and Old-Fashioned Country String Beans (see page 264).

VEAL

RACK OF VEAL WITH
ROSEMARY, PARIOLI ROMANISSIMO

೧∾౨

A recipe given to us by Signor Rubrio Rossi, the genial host of Parioli Romanissimo, one of New York's greatest Italian restaurants.

6 SERVINGS

1   *rack of veal (6–7 chops)*
    Salt and freshly ground pepper to taste
6   *sprigs fresh rosemary or 1 tablespoon dried*
½   *cup olive oil*
6   *bacon strips, blanched 1 minute in boiling water, then
    drained and dried on paper towels*
2   *cups dry white wine*
1   *tablespoon glace de viande (concentrated meat glaze)*
1   *cup Chicken Broth (see page 48)*
2   *tablespoons butter*

Preheat the oven to 450°.

Wipe the veal with a damp cloth. Place it, bone side up, on a rack in a roasting pan. Season it with salt, pepper, and rosemary. Brush it with the olive oil and roast it in the oven for 15 minutes.

Turn the roast, meat side up and cover it with the bacon strips. Roast for another 15 minutes.

Reduce the heat to 350°. Add the wine to the pan, and roast for 30 minutes, or until the meat thermometer reads 160°–165°. Heat the meat glaze and chicken broth together in a small saucepan, until the meat glaze has dissolved. Pour this liquid into the roasting pan and roast the veal for 45 minutes more. Remove the veal to a hot serving platter and cover it lightly with foil. Transfer the liquid from the roasting pan to a saucepan and boil it for about 5 minutes, or until it becomes fairly thick. Swirl in the butter, taste and correct the seasoning. Carve the rack into separate chops, and pour the sauce over them before serving.

Serve with Green Peas Roman Style (see page 277) and Devilish Potatoes (see page 283), specialties of Parioli Romanissimo.

VEAL SCALLOPS IN LEMON SAUCE
(Piccata di Vitello)

4 SERVINGS

1   pound veal scallops, pounded as thin as possible, then
    cut into 3- by 4-inch pieces
¼   cup flour
    Salt and freshly ground pepper to taste
4   tablespoons butter
2   tablespoons olive oil
2   tablespoons lemon juice
2   tablespoons finely chopped parsley
10 lemon slices

Lightly dredge the veal scallops in the flour. Season them with salt
and pepper. Heat 2 tablespoons of the butter with the oil in a large
frying pan until it bubbles. Brown the scallops on each side for a
minute or two. Do not cook more scallops at a time than can be
placed in a single layer. Remove them to a warm serving platter.
Pour off all the fat in the pan and add the remaining butter, the
lemon juice, and the parsley. Put the scallops back in the pan and
cook for 2 to 3 minutes, spooning the pan juices over them. Arrange
the lemon slices between the pieces of veal and serve. A purée of
potatoes and leeks makes a satisfying accompaniment.

SAUTÉED VEAL SCALLOPS
(Sauté de Veau, Henriette)

4 SERVINGS

4   veal scallops
    Salt and freshly ground pepper to taste
1   egg, lightly beaten
    Bread crumbs

¼ cup freshly grated imported Parmesan cheese
3 tablespoons butter
1 tablespoon oil
½ pound mushrooms, thinly sliced
¼ cup beef broth (or 2 tablespoons each broth and wine)

Preheat the oven to 375°.

Have the butcher pound the veal scallops as thin as possible; then ask him to pound a bit more! Cut them into 2- by 4-inch rectangles. Season them with salt and pepper. Dip each piece in beaten egg until lightly coated on both sides, letting any excess egg run off. Coat them lightly on both sides with the bread crumbs and grated cheese.

Heat the butter and oil in a large heavy pan and fry the scallops over medium heat until browned on both sides (about 2 minutes on each side). As each piece is browned, place it in an ovenproof casserole with a lid. When all the veal is in the casserole, fry the mushrooms for 1 to 2 minutes in the same pan in which you fried the veal. Add more butter if necessary. Season them and add them to the casserole. Pour in the broth. Bake, covered, for 10 minutes. Serve with buttered spinach.

STUFFED VEAL SCALLOPS
(Involtini di Mozzarella)

❧

4 SERVINGS

8 veal scallops
4 slices mozzarella cheese (about ⅛ inch thick), diced
8 fresh basil leaves, chopped (or 1 teaspoon dried)
1 small Italian sausage, skinned, diced, and fried for 10 minutes
¼ cup freshly grated imported Parmesan cheese
Salt and freshly ground pepper to taste
¼ cup flour
2 tablespoons olive oil
¼ pound (8 tablespoons) butter
1 cup vermouth
Lemon wedges

Ask your butcher to prepare veal scallops so that they are as thin and flat as possible and then trim them into 6- by 3-inch pieces.

Mix the mozzarella, basil, sausage, and grated cheese. Season lightly with salt and pepper. Roll the mixture with your hands into balls small enough to be wrapped in the veal scallops. (The mozzarella will soften and hold the other ingredients together.) Place a ball of this filling on each scallop. Make packages by folding two opposite corners of the veal over to meet and doing the same with the other two corners. Fasten them securely with toothpicks. Season the stuffed scallops with salt and pepper and dip them in flour to coat them lightly on all sides.

Put the oil and 6 tablespoons of the butter in a heavy frying pan large enough to hold the scallops in a single layer without crowding. Heat the fat to sizzling. Sauté the scallops on both sides for about 10 minutes, or until well browned, turning them carefully with a spatula so that the filling does not come out.

Remove them to a warmed platter and discard the toothpicks. Add the vermouth to the pan, scraping up all the brown bits. Cook, stirring, till the liquid is reduced to a syrupy sauce. Swirl in the remaining butter. Correct the seasoning and serve, garnished with lemon wedges.

VEAL CHOPS IN FOIL
(Côtelettes de Veau en Papillotes)

❧

4 SERVINGS

4   *veal chops (the whitest, youngest veal you can find)*
4   *tablespoons butter*
2   *tablespoons oil*
    Salt and freshly ground pepper to taste
4   *shallots, finely chopped*
4   *strips bacon*
8   *tablespoons mixed fresh herbs (tarragon, chives,*
      parsley, chervil), finely chopped

Wipe the chops with a damp cloth. In a large heavy frying pan, sauté them in the butter and oil for about 10 minutes, or until they are golden brown on both sides. Remove them to a platter and season them with salt and pepper. Add the shallots to the pan and cook, stirring often, for 1 to 2 minutes. Set aside.

Put the bacon in a pot with 1 quart of cold water. Bring to a boil and simmer for 10 minutes. Drain the bacon, rinse it in cold water, dry it on paper towels, and cut each strip in half. Cut four pieces of aluminum foil, each large enough to wrap one chop easily. Put a half-strip of bacon in the center of each piece of foil, then a chop, sprinkled on both sides with 2 tablespoons of the herbs. Pour some of the shallot-butter-oil mixture on each chop, cover with another half-strip of bacon, and fold the foil so that each chop is tightly sealed.

Put the foil-wrapped chops over an outdoor grill or in a preheated 400° oven for 15 minutes. Serve in the foil. As each guest unseals his chop he will be greeted by an aroma heady and appetizing.

VEAL CHOPS IN SORREL SAUCE, À LA LYONNAISE

୧୦

4 SERVINGS

½ *pound fresh sorrel (or 1 13-ounce jar of imported Belgian sorrel, available in specialty shops)*
4 *veal chops, cut 1 inch thick and trimmed of fat*
   Salt and freshly ground pepper to taste
   About ¼ cup flour plus 3 tablespoons flour
1 *stick (¼ pound) butter, at room temperature*
2 *tablespoons peanut oil*
⅓ *cup dry white wine*
1 *cup Crème Fraîche (see page 151), sour cream, or heavy cream*

Wash the sorrel. Pull off and discard the coarse large stems and any wilted leaves. Pat dry and shred coarsely. Set aside.

Season the chops with salt and pepper, and coat them lightly with flour on both sides. In a heavy frying pan large enough to hold the chops in a single layer, heat 3 tablespoons of the butter with the oil.

Brown the chops for about 4 minutes on each side. Cover the pan and cook over moderate heat for 15 to 20 minutes, or until the chops are tender, turning them once after 10 minutes. Transfer the chops to a warm platter, cover them loosely with foil and keep them in a low oven while you prepare the sauce. Do not wash the pan.

Prepare a *beurre manié* by working together with your fingers 3 tablespoons of the butter and 3 tablespoons of flour until well mixed. Set aside in the refrigerator.

Place the pan in which you cooked the chops over low heat, add the wine, and, with a wooden spoon, scrape all the brown bits on the sides and bottom of the pan into the wine. Add the sorrel and cook it, stirring, over medium heat for 4 to 5 minutes, or until it is wilted. (If you use the bottled sorrel, 1 to 2 minutes would be enough.) Stir in the *crème fraîche* or cream and mix well. Add the *beurre manié*, bit by bit, and cook, stirring, until the sauce is fairly thick. Taste and correct the seasoning. Swirl the remaining butter into the sauce. Pour the sauce over the chops and serve immediately.

VEAL STEW WITH SAUSAGES AND CHESTNUTS

◦◡◦

One of our favorite dishes for large dinner parties.

12–14 SERVINGS

1 *5-pound neck of veal, cut into 2-inch cubes*
2 *cups vegetable oil or French peanut oil*
1 *cup chopped onion*
2 *pounds ripe tomatoes, peeled, seeded, and coarsely
    chopped, or 1 can (1 pound 3 ounces) Italian
    tomatoes, drained and coarsely chopped*
½ *cup dry white wine*
1 *teaspoon sugar
   Salt and freshly ground pepper to taste*
3 *tablespoons coarsely chopped fresh basil or 1
    tablespoon dried*
½ *pound dried chestnuts (available in specialty shops)
   About 1 quart Chicken Broth (see page 48)*

30   pearl onions, as uniform in size as possible
8   tablespoons butter
1   tablespoon sugar
½   cup dried mushrooms
2   pounds fresh mushrooms
12   chorizo sausages (or good Italian sausages, 6 hot and
        6 sweet)
1   cup chopped fresh parsley

Preheat the oven to 350°.

Wipe the veal with a damp cloth. Heat the oil in one or two large heavy pans until smoking hot. Sear the veal without crowding the pieces until very well browned on all sides. As each piece is finished, transfer it to a large casserole. Discard most of the oil, leaving enough in one of the pans to sauté the chopped onions. Cook them, stirring, until browned. Transfer them with a slotted spoon to the casserole. Add the tomatoes, wine, sugar, salt, pepper, and basil to the casserole. Bring to a boil. Cover the casserole and bake in the oven for 1½ hours.

Meanwhile, in a small saucepan, simmer the dried chestnuts, in enough broth to cover them, just until they are tender. Add more broth to cover as it cooks away. Remove and let the chestnuts cool in the broth. Drain. When cool enough to handle, pick out and discard the dark hard membrane with the point of a sharp knife. Leave the chestnuts as nearly whole as possible.

To peel the pearl onions, put them in boiling water for 2 minutes, then drain them in a sieve under cold running water. Trim the stem ends. The onions will slip out of their skins easily. Put the peeled onions in a pan. Add enough broth to cover them. Boil, uncovered, until they are almost tender. Add a little more broth from time to time if needed. When the onions are almost done, let the broth boil down, add 2 tablespoons of the butter, the sugar, salt, and pepper to taste and cook over low heat, stirring often, until the onions are browned and glazed. Remove them from the heat and reserve.

Soak the dried mushrooms in warm water to cover for 30 minutes. Drain the liquid through a cheesecloth and reserve. Rinse the mushrooms and pat them dry.

Break off the stems of the fresh mushrooms and chop them. If the mushroom caps are large, halve or quarter them; if small, leave them whole. Sauté the fresh and dried mushrooms in 4 tablespoons of the butter just till tender. Season to taste.

Cut each sausage in four pieces. Sauté them in 2 tablespoons of the butter over low heat until well cooked. Drain them on paper towels. Reserve.

When the veal is tender, add the reserved mushroom liquor and all the other ingredients except the parsley. Mix well and return to the oven for 15 minutes.

Transfer the stew to a hot platter, putting most of the sausage and chestnuts on top so that each person can be served some of everything. Sprinkle with parsley and serve with buttery boiled rice.

VARIATION: Substitute three 2½- to 3-pound chickens for the veal.

A SUGGESTED MENU

(see Index for recipes)

ROASTED ANCHOVIES AND PEPPERS

VEAL STEW WITH SAUSAGES AND CHESTNUTS

ENDIVE AND GRAPE SALAD

SLICED ORANGES WITH LEMON SQUARES

wine: RED RIOJA OR GRIGNOLINO

VEAL STEW WITH TOMATOES

ᕲᕰ

4 SERVINGS

2   *pounds stewing veal, cut into 1½-inch cubes*
2   *tablespoons sweet butter*
4   *tablespoons olive oil*
⅓   *cup vermouth*
1   *clove garlic, passed through a garlic press*
1½ *pounds ripe tomatoes, peeled, seeded, and coarsely*
      chopped
1   *bay leaf*
4–5 *sprigs each parsley and fresh thyme, tied together*
      Salt and freshly ground pepper to taste
¼   *cup chopped chives*

Wipe the veal cubes with a damp cloth. Dry them well with paper towels. Heat the butter and oil in a heavy pot until very hot. Brown the veal, a few pieces at a time, on all sides, then remove them to a warm platter. Do not crowd the meat or it will not brown properly; it must be well seared on all sides. Return the veal to the pot, add the vermouth, and cook until it has almost evaporated.

Add all the remaining ingredients except the chives, bring the stew to a boil, then lower the heat and simmer, covered, for about 1½ hours, or until the meat is tender. Remove the herbs and bay leaf. Taste and correct the seasoning. Transfer the stew to a warmed platter. Sprinkle it with the chopped chives. Serve with buttered noodles.

VEAL KIDNEYS BORDELAISE
(Rognons de Veau, Bordelaise)

4 SERVINGS

2   *veal kidneys*
1   *beef marrowbone, cut into 2-inch pieces*
1   *cup Beef Broth (see page 47)*
1   *tablespoon cornstarch*
6   *tablespoons butter*
4   *tablespoons finely chopped shallots (or scallions)*
½   *cup red Bordeaux (the better the wine, the better the*
    sauce)
1   *large pinch each thyme and powdered bay leaf*
    Salt and freshly ground pepper to taste
2   *tablespoons bread crumbs*
3   *tablespoons finely chopped fresh parsley*

Preheat the oven to 450°.

Ask the butcher to trim the fat from the veal kidneys and give it to you. Trim off any fat that may have escaped his notice. Wash the kidneys, slice them in half horizontally, and pat them dry on paper towels. Put all the kidney fat in a baking dish. Place the kidneys, cut side up, on the layer of fat. The kidneys will be more tender if they do not touch the bottom of the baking dish.

Dig the marrow out of the pieces of bone. (A grapefruit knife makes a good tool.) Bring the beef broth to a boil in a small saucepan. Drop the marrow into it, then remove the pot from the heat immediately. After 3 or 4 minutes, remove the marrow with a slotted spoon and reserve. Cool the broth, add the cornstarch, and stir until it has dissolved.

Melt 4 tablespoons of the butter in a saucepan over medium heat. Add 2 tablespoons of the chopped shallots. Cook, stirring, for 2 minutes. Add the wine, raise the heat, and boil until reduced to half its volume. Lower the heat, add the broth and the marrow, and cook over lowest heat for 2 to 3 minutes. Season with thyme, bay leaf, salt, and pepper. Keep warm on a flame tamer.

Place the kidneys in the oven. Test them after 10 to 12 minutes by piercing them with a kitchen fork with metal tines. Leave the fork in for a minute or two. If the tines are hot, the kidneys are done; if not, return them to the oven and test them again after about a minute.

Over medium heat, sauté the remaining shallots in the remaining butter for 1 to 2 minutes. Stir in the bread crumbs and cook for 1 minute. Remove from the heat and set aside.

Serve the kidneys on very hot dishes. Sprinkle them with the mixture of shallot and bread crumbs and the chopped parsley. Pass the sauce separately. Garnish this dish with fresh garden vegetables: broccoli, carrots, spinach, and new potatoes, boiled separately, then heated in butter and seasoned with salt and pepper.

A SUGGESTED MENU

(see Index for recipes)

TOMATOES À LA CRÈME

VEAL KIDNEYS BORDELAISE

GREEN SALAD

APPLE CRANBERRY TART

wine: LYNCH-BAGES OR BEYCHEVELLE

CALF'S LIVER WITH RAISINS

૦✑

2 SERVINGS

¼ *cup wine vinegar mixed with 1 tablespoon water*
2 *tablespoons sugar*
2 *tablespoons raisins*
4 *fresh sage leaves or 1 teaspoon dried sage*
   Salt and freshly ground pepper to taste
2 *tablespoons butter*
4 *very thin slices calf's liver*
2 *tablespoons chopped parsley*

In a saucepan, heat the vinegar, sugar, raisins, sage, salt, and pepper
to the boiling point and cook for exactly 1 minute. Meanwhile, heat
the butter in a heavy frying pan and sauté the liver for about a
minute on each side. (It should be brown on the outside, pink inside.) Remove it to a hot platter.

Bring the vinegar-raisin sauce to the boil once more. Pour it into
the pan in which you cooked the liver. Stir, scraping the brown bits
clinging to the pan into the sauce, and pour it over the liver. Sprinkle
with parsley and serve. Delicious with mashed potatoes.

A SUGGESTED MENU

(see Index for recipes)

DOUBLE SALMON MOUSSE

CALF'S LIVER WITH RAISINS

SALAD OF GREENS WITH ARUGULA

ANKA BEGLEY'S QUICK AND EASY CHOCOLATE CAKE

wine: CHABLIS, FOLLOWED BY GLORIA

LAMB

ARMENIAN MOUSSAKA
(Eggplant–Lamb Casserole)

❧

A marvelous way to use leftover roast lamb. You will need a 14- by
10- by 2-inch baking dish.

8–10 SERVINGS

 2 *large eggplants*
   Salt
 1 *large onion, finely chopped*
 6 *tablespoons butter*
   About 1 cup vegetable oil or more if needed
   Freshly ground pepper
 ½ *teaspoon sugar*
 1 *clove garlic, minced*
 1 *pound mushrooms*
 1½ *pounds leftover roast lamb (or ground raw lamb)*
 ½ *teaspoon cinnamon*
 1 *teaspoon cumin*
 1 *teaspoon allspice*
   Hot red pepper flakes to taste
 1 *cup chopped parsley (or coriander)*
 2 *cups Tomato Sauce (see page 36) or Italian-style*
   canned tomatoes, drained and coarsely chopped

Wash the eggplants but do not peel them. Trim the ends. Slice them
into rounds ⅜ inch thick. Put the slices on a platter, salting each layer
as you go. Cover with another platter and a heavy weight. This will
release the eggplants' bitter juices. Set aside for 1 hour.

 Sauté the onion in 2 tablespoons of butter and 1 tablespoon of oil,
stirring often, until lightly browned. Season with salt and pepper to
taste. Add a pinch or two of sugar. Stir in the minced garlic and
sauté, stirring, for about a minute. Set aside.

Wipe the mushrooms clean with a damp cloth and trim the stem ends. Chop the mushrooms fine. Sauté them in 2 tablespoons of butter until their liquid has evaporated and they are dark in color. Season with salt and pepper to taste. Set aside.

Grind the meat coarsely or chop it by hand. Sauté it in 2 table-spoons of butter until it is warm. (If using uncooked lamb, sauté it until it is browned.) Season it with salt and pepper to taste, cinnamon, cumin, allspice, and hot pepper flakes. Add the parsley, onions, and tomato sauce. Cook, stirring, for 2 minutes. Taste and correct the seasoning, adding a little sugar if you like.

Wipe the salt off the eggplant slices. Press down on them to drain off the liquid. Pat them dry with paper towels. Heat 2 tablespoons of oil in a large heavy pan and sauté the eggplant slices in a single layer until lightly browned on both sides, adding more oil as needed. Repeat until all the eggplant is sautéed. Season with pepper but do not add salt.

Preheat the oven to 375°. Line the bottom of the baking dish with slightly overlapping eggplant slices. Spread the meat mixture over the eggplant. Spread the mushrooms over the meat. Cover with the remaining eggplant. Bake for about 40 minutes and serve hot. Serve with rice, wheat pilaf, or Roesti (see page 281).

VARIATIONS: Make beef moussaka by substituting ground chuck for the ground lamb.

ARMENIAN KEBABS

৵

4–6 SERVINGS

2 *pounds lean lamb, trimmed of fat and cut into 1-inch cubes*

MARINADE

2 *cups yogurt*
1 *teaspoon salt*
1 *cup chopped onion*
3 *bay leaves, crumbled*

1   teaspoon powdered thyme
3   shakes cayenne pepper
½   cup chopped fresh dill or 3 tablespoons dried
3   tablespoons chopped fresh mint or 1 tablespoon dried
    Juice of 1 lemon

VEGETABLES
18 pearl onions, boiled just until tender but still firm
4   green peppers, seeds and membranes removed, and
        cut into 1-inch squares
1   quart cherry tomatoes, stemmed

Put the lamb cubes in a large bowl. Combine the marinade ingredients, pour over the lamb, and mix well. Cover and marinate in the refrigerator for a day or two, turning occasionally. Remove the lamb cubes, wipe off the marinade clinging to them, and dry them thoroughly on paper towels.

Preheat the broiler for 30 minutes. Alternate the cubes of meat and the vegetables on skewers. Broil 3 inches from the heat for 3 to 5 minutes on each side, or until the meat is tender and browned. Superb broiled over charcoal.

DOROTHY LICHTENSTEIN'S BUTTERFLY LAMB, BROILED OR BARBECUED

ᗆᔈ

8–10 SERVINGS

1   7-pound leg of lamb (have your butcher butterfly it)

MARINADE
3   cloves garlic, crushed or passed through a garlic press
4   tablespoons mixed dried herbs
1   teaspoon finely ground pepper
1   tablespoon dried thyme
1½ cups tamari soy sauce (the sugarless organic sauce
        available in health food stores)

Salt and freshly ground pepper to taste

Wipe the lamb with a damp cloth and dry it with paper towels. Combine all the marinade ingredients except the soy sauce and rub them into the lamb on both sides. Place in a deep dish and pour the soy sauce around it. Marinate in the refrigerator for 24 hours or more, turning occasionally.

Remove the lamb from the refrigerator 3 to 4 hours before cooking and let it come to room temperature in the marinade. Turn once during this time. Drain the lamb well, pat it dry with a paper towel, and season it with salt.

If you are not barbecuing the lamb on an outdoor grill, preheat the oven broiler, closed, to its highest point for 1 *hour* before broiling.

Broil the lamb for 5 minutes, the fat side up. Turn it and broil it 10 minutes longer for rare lamb.

Let the lamb rest in a warm place for 15 minutes before carving it. Serve with wheat pilaf or rice.

DOROTHY'S TIP: Leave the door of the broiler partially open while broiling. The circulation of air gives a drier heat, which is more like that of an open fire.

MICA ERTEGUN'S
TURKISH LAMB CHOPS

つ

Mica Ertegun, one of the world's most accomplished interior decorators, gave us this superb recipe. Ideal for charcoal broiling.

2–4 SERVINGS

8   rib lamb chops, cut very thin (not more than ½ inch
       thick)
1   medium-size onion
1   teaspoon salt
     Freshly ground pepper to taste
2   tablespoons olive oil
¼   cup finely chopped fresh herbs (thyme or oregano)

Ask your butcher to trim the chine bone and flatten the chops as much as possible.

Grate the onion in a food processor or by hand and save the juice. Stir the salt and pepper into the onion juice. Add olive oil and mix until well combined. Rub this marinade into both sides of the chops. Sprinkle the chops on both sides with the herbs. Lay them in a single layer on a sheet of waxed paper and cover them with another sheet of waxed paper. Let them marinate for 2 hours in a cool place. Broil them close to the heat for 1 or 2 minutes on each side.

LAMB CHOPS, PROVENÇALE
(Côtelettes d'Agneau Provençale)

6∿⁀

4 SERVINGS

8 *loin lamb chops*
2 *tablespoons peanut oil*
4 *tablespoons butter*
 Salt and freshly ground pepper to taste
3 *onions, minced*
¼ *cup beef broth*
 Beurre manié (made by rubbing together with your
  fingers 2 tablespoons each of cold butter and flour)
½ *cup milk*
2 *egg yolks*
2 *cloves garlic, minced*
2 *tablespoons fresh rosemary, finely chopped, or 2*
  teaspoons dried
2 *whole eggs*
 Bread crumbs

Preheat the broiler.

Brown the chops quickly on both sides in the peanut oil and 2 tablespoons of the butter. Transfer them to a warm platter. Salt and pepper them. Set aside.

Sauté the onions in 2 tablespoons of butter until they are translucent but not browned. Add the broth and cook, covered, for about 5 minutes.

Add the *beurre manié*, a bit at a time, till the sauce begins to thicken and brown. Bring the milk to a boil and pour it in. Cook for 3 to 4 minutes. Remove the pan from the heat for a minute or two. Whisk in the two egg yolks, one at a time, till well blended, then stir in the garlic and rosemary.

Beat the whole eggs with a whisk and dip one side of each chop in them. Then dip the same side in bread crumbs. Broil the chops, breaded side up, for 4 minutes. Remove them. Turn them over and spread the unbreaded sides with the onion mixture. Brush with the remaining beaten egg and top with bread crumbs. Broil for 5 minutes and serve at once. Pour any juice from the broiler pan over the chops. Serve with puréed spinach or sautéed mushrooms.

LAMB STEW
WITH LEMONS AND PARSLEY

6–8 SERVINGS

 5 tablespoons olive oil
 3 pounds boned lamb for stew, cut into 2-inch squares
 1 tablespoon butter
12 scallions, chopped (including some of the green part)
 2 cloves garlic, peeled
 2 tablespoons flour
    Seasonings: ½ teaspoon sugar; 1 teaspoon each salt,
       pepper, paprika; 1 bay leaf
 1 tablespoon tomato sauce
    About 2 cups Beef Broth (see page 47)
1½ cups chopped parsley
10 lemon slices
 3 egg yolks
 ½ cup sour cream

In a large heavy pan, heat 4 tablespoons of the oil until it bubbles. Sear the lamb well on all sides, a few pieces at a time. Do not crowd the pan. As soon as they are browned, remove them to a warm platter.

Meanwhile, in a heavy casserole, melt the butter with the remaining tablespoon of oil, add the scallions and garlic, and cook over low heat till the scallions are wilted. Discard the garlic. Add the browned pieces of lamb to the casserole, sprinkling each layer with a little flour. Stir till the flour browns. Add the seasonings, the tomato sauce, and just enough of the broth to cover the meat. Cover and simmer for 30 minutes.

Add the parsley and the lemon slices and simmer, covered, for another 20 to 30 minutes, or until the lamb is tender. Let the stew cool to tepid. Lightly beat together the egg yolks and sour cream. Stir them into the stew and reheat slowly. Do not boil, or the egg mixture will curdle. Serve with pilaf or boiled potatoes.

PORK

PORK CHOPS, NORMANDY STYLE
(Côtes de Porc, Vallée d'Auge)

ᧁﾉ

4 SERVINGS

12	pearl onions
1½	pounds mushrooms
4	pork chops
2–3	tablespoons vegetable oil
	Salt and freshly ground pepper to taste
2–3	tablespoons butter
½	cup Crème Fraîche (see page 151) or sour cream
2	tablespoons Calvados

Peel the onions and boil them for 5 to 8 minutes, or until they are barely tender. Drain and set aside. Wipe the mushroom caps with a damp cloth. Slice them and set aside. (Reserve the stems for soup.)

Wipe the pork chops with a damp cloth and pat them dry with paper towels. Heat the oil until it is almost smoking in a frying pan large enough to hold the chops in a single layer. Sear the chops for 3 to 4 minutes on each side. Transfer them to a warm platter. Discard the hot oil. Season the chops with salt and pepper. Heat the butter in the pan. Put the chops back in the pan and cook them, covered, for 10 minutes, turning them once or twice. Add the onions and mushrooms and cook for about 25 minutes, or until the chops are tender. Remove them to a hot serving platter. Arrange the vegetables on and around them. Keep the platter warm while you prepare the sauce.

Add the *crème fraîche* to the pan, stirring and scraping the brown bits from the bottom and sides of the pan into the cream. Taste and correct the seasoning. Add the Calvados and bring it just to a boil, always stirring. Pour the sauce over all and serve.

PORK CHOPS, VINEYARD STYLE
(Côtes de Porc, Vigneronnes)

4 SERVINGS

4 large pork chops, ¾ inch thick, trimmed of excess fat

MARINADE
Salt
Freshly ground pepper
1 clove garlic, peeled and crushed
2–3 sprigs thyme or 1–2 teaspoons dried thyme
4 tablespoons olive oil or French peanut oil
Juice of 2 lemons
1 bay leaf

TOMATO SAUCE (about 1½ cups)
2 tablespoons butter
¾ cup chopped onion
1 large clove garlic, peeled and crushed
1½ cups ripe tomatoes, peeled, seeded, and chopped, or
1½ cups drained Italian-style canned tomatoes, coarsely chopped
1 teaspoon tomato paste
Salt and freshly ground pepper to taste

2   tablespoons olive oil or French peanut oil
½   cup dry white wine
1   tablespoon Dijon mustard
1   tablespoon butter
2   tablespoons chopped chives

Marinate the pork chops in the combined marinade ingredients for about 2 hours, turning them occasionally.

Meanwhile, prepare the tomato sauce. In a heavy saucepan, heat the butter, add the chopped onion and cook, stirring often, over medium heat until the onions are limp but not browned. Add the garlic clove, the tomatoes, the tomato paste, and the salt and pepper. Stir until the tomato paste has dissolved. Cook until quite thick, stirring more often as it thickens, to prevent sticking. Set aside.

Remove the chops from the marinade. Drain and dry them well with paper towels. Heat the oil in a frying pan large enough to hold the chops in a single layer. Sauté the chops for 5 to 6 minutes on each side. Remove them to a warm platter.

Pour off and discard all but 2 tablespoons of the fat. Deglaze the pan with the wine, scraping in all the brown bits. Return the chops to the pan and pour the tomato sauce over them. Cover and cook over low heat for 25 to 30 minutes, or until tender. Remove the chops and keep them warm. Reduce the sauce by half.

Stir in the mustard and butter until well blended. Pour the sauce over the chops, sprinkle with chives and serve.

PORK SCALLOPS

༄

4 SERVINGS

2   tablespoons butter
1   small onion, thinly sliced
1   large green apple, peeled, cored, and sliced
¼   cup dry white wine
¼   cup tarragon vinegar
1   teaspoon sugar

1½   pounds pork scallops, pounded very thin
      Dijon mustard to coat the scallops
      Flour for dredging
      About ½ cup olive oil
      Salt and freshly ground pepper to taste
½   cup chopped parsley

Melt the butter in a large pan over low heat. Add the onion slices and
cook, stirring, until they are limp. Add the apple slices and cook for
10 minutes, or until they are soft. Add the wine, vinegar, and sugar.
Cover and cook for 20 minutes. Remove from the heat and cool.
Purée the mixture through the medium blade of a food mill. Set
aside.

Spread the pork scallops on both sides with a little mustard, and
dredge them lightly with flour. Heat half the oil in a large frying
pan until it is hot but not smoking. Add the scallops, a few at a time.
Brown them for 2 minutes on each side. Transfer them to a platter
and keep them warm. Repeat the process with the remaining scallops,
adding more oil as needed. Combine the purée and scallops in the
same pan. Simmer, covered, for 10 minutes. Season with salt and a
generous amount of pepper. Garnish with chopped parsley and serve
with buttered wide noodles.

SAUSAGES WITH FLAGEOLET BEANS
(Saucisses aux Flageolets)

೧∾

6–8 SERVINGS

1   1-pound box (about 2¼ cups) imported flageolet beans
      (available at specialty shops and in some
      supermarkets)
2   cups chopped onions
3   tablespoons oil
2–3 tablespoons butter
1   14-ounce can Italian-style tomatoes
3   sage leaves or 1 teaspoon dried sage

   1   *bay leaf*
   1   *teaspoon dried thyme or a few sprigs of fresh thyme*
½–1 *cup chicken broth*
     Salt and freshly ground pepper to taste
12–16 *French or Italian sausage links*
     About 4 tablespoons lard

Follow the directions on the package for soaking the beans. (They
may have to be soaked the night before.) Drain the beans. Then cook
them in water to cover by an inch for 2 hours, or until they are almost
soft. As the water cooks away, add more to keep the beans covered.
Sauté the onions in the oil and butter in a casserole, stirring often
until they are wilted. Drain the beans and add them to the onions
along with all the other ingredients except the sausage and lard.
Season to taste with salt and pepper. Cook for 15 minutes. Separate
the sausage links. Prick the sausages with the point of a sharp knife
in several places so they will not burst when cooking. Cook in one
layer in a little lard until well browned on both sides. Add them to
the beans (with or without the fat in the pan, as you prefer). Simmer
for 10 to 15 minutes and serve. Hearty and delicious.

SAUSAGES WITH MUSHROOMS
(Saucisses aux Champignons)

❧

6 SERVINGS

  12 *Italian sausage links made with fennel if possible*
       (available at Italian delicatessens and butchers)
3–4 *tablespoons lard*
1½ *cups chopped onion*
1½ *tablespoons flour*
  2 *cups Chicken Broth (see page 48)*
 ¼ *cup tomato sauce*
  1 *large clove garlic, put through a garlic press*
  1 *bay leaf*
     Salt and freshly ground pepper to taste
1½ *pounds mushrooms, wiped clean and sliced*

3–4 *tablespoons butter*
Beurre manié (made by working together with your
fingers 2 tablespoons each flour and butter)
¼ *cup chopped fresh parsley*

Separate the sausage links. Prick them with the point of a sharp knife in several places so that they do not burst when cooking. Sauté them in one layer in the lard over medium heat until they are well browned on both sides. Remove them to a warm platter. Put the chopped onion in the same pan and sauté, stirring, till they are lightly browned. Add the flour. Cook, stirring, to coat the onions with the flour. Return the sausages to the pan and add the chicken broth, the tomato sauce, the garlic, and the bay leaf. Season to taste with salt and pepper. Simmer, covered, for 20 to 30 minutes, or until the sausages are well cooked. Meanwhile, sauté the mushrooms separately in the butter for 5 to 6 minutes. Add them to the sausages and cook over low heat for 10 minutes. Add bits of the *beurre manié* as needed, and cook, uncovered, until you have a fairly thick sauce. Correct the seasoning and serve piping hot. Garnish with parsley.

VARIATION: Omit the mushrooms. Reduce the quantity of butter to 1 to 2 tablespoons. Gently warm ¼ cup of drained capers in it and pour over the sausages. Serve with mashed potatoes.

COTECHINO AND ZAMPONE

Two of the finest Italian sausages are *cotechino* and *zampone*. If you have never tasted them and have an Italian butcher, or *salumeria*, within reach, you are in for a great treat. The Italians traditionally serve *cotechino* and lentils on New Year's Eve—the *cotechino* because it is delicious, the lentils because they will make you rich. *Zampone* sliced thin and eaten with lentils or white beans is equally good. To cook the *cotechino*, simply prick the skin in several places with the sharp end of a knife and simmer it in water for a couple of hours.

The *zampone*, which is larger (about 4 pounds), should be wrapped in cheesecloth and simmered for 3 or 4 hours. An onion and some celery added to the water can do no harm.

Serve with Green Sauce (see page 219), Dijon mustard, and pickles, or the traditional specialty from Cremona, *frutta in mostarda* (fruits preserved in a mustard syrup), available at Italian specialty shops.

SMITHFIELD HAM
WITH APRICOT NECTAR GLAZE

Hams from Virginia, particularly from Smithfield, Virginia, were exported to England from earliest Colonial times. In fact, the name Smithfield is as jealously protected by law as Champagne and Cognac are in France. Only hams cut from "peanut-fed hogs, raised in the peanut belt of the State of Virginia or the State of North Carolina, and which are cured, treated, smoked, and processed in the town of Smithfield, in the State of Virginia" are legally allowed to be called Smithfield hams. They appeared on Thomas Jefferson's table at breakfast, dinner, or supper.

To cook *any* aged country ham, soak it overnight in cold water to cover. When ready to cook, drain it, cover it with cold water again, and simmer it for 2 hours. Cool it in the liquid. Cut the rind off the ham, score the fat in a diamond pattern, stud it with cloves, and glaze it. Bake it for 30 minutes at 400°. Slice it thin and serve it hot or cold.

A very simple glaze can be made by pouring 1 can of apricot nectar over the ham before baking it. Baste it frequently. As the apricot juice thickens, it forms a delicious glaze.

HAM WITH JUNIPER BERRIES

4 SERVINGS

4   *quarter-inch-thick slices baked him (if using Virginia
      ham, soak in milk to cover for 30 minutes, then
      drain and dry)*
2   *tablespoons lard, peanut oil, or rendered ham fat*
1   *tablespoon butter*

2 tablespoons flour
1 cup dry white wine
¾ cup beef broth
1 teaspoon crushed juniper berries
1 tablespoon chopped fresh tarragon or 1 teaspoon dried
¼ cup tarragon vinegar
10 crushed peppercorns
3 tablespoons Crème Fraîche (see page 151) or sour cream

In a frying pan, sauté the ham slices in the hot fat until they are brown on both sides. Remove them to a warm platter. Pour off the fat. Add the butter and flour to the same pan. Cook over low heat, stirring, until the mixture thickens. Stir in ¾ cup of the wine and the beef broth. Mix well, pressing out any lumps of flour with the back of a spoon. Stir in the juniper berries and tarragon. Return the ham to the pan and simmer for 15 minutes.

In a small saucepan, combine the remaining ¼ cup of wine with the vinegar and the crushed peppercorns. Cook until the liquid is reduced by half.

Remove the ham. Add the wine-vinegar mixture to the pan and mix well. Return the ham to the pan and cook for another 15 minutes.

Remove the ham to a warm platter. Strain the sauce. Add the cream, stirring until it is well mixed. Pour the sauce over the ham. Serve with new potatoes boiled in their jackets and cabbage simmered in butter until tender.

CANADIAN BACON AND CABBAGE

⌒〰⌒

4 SERVINGS

1 medium-large cabbage, cored and coarsely shredded
   Salt and freshly ground pepper to taste
1½ cups heavy cream
4 tablespoons butter
16 slices Canadian bacon
½ cup dry white wine
4 sage leaves or 1 tablespoon dried sage
¼ cup freshly grated Parmesan cheese

Boil the cabbage in a pot of salted water until it is almost tender. Drain it well and return it to the pot. Season it with salt and pepper. Add the cream and cook over medium heat until the cabbage is tender and the cream has reduced and thickened somewhat.

Melt 3 tablespoons of the butter in a pan. Add the bacon and sauté it for a minute or two on each side. Add the wine and the sage. Cook until the liquid reduces to a syrupy glaze.

Butter a baking dish with the remaining tablespoon of butter. Spread the cabbage in the baking dish. Lay the bacon on the cabbage in overlapping slices. Pour the sauce from the pan over all. Sprinkle with the Parmesan cheese and put under the broiler for 2 to 3 minutes, or until the cheese is lightly browned.

VARIATION: Substitute slices of smoked pork butt for the bacon.

A SUGGESTED MENU

(see Index for recipes)

TOMATO-SORREL SOUP

CANADIAN BACON AND CABBAGE

GREEN SALAD

HILDE'S PLUM TART

wine: CABERNET

CASSOULET

∽

Cassoulet takes a long time to make. But was *War and Peace* written in a day? This dish is a perfect way to welcome the autumn season. Drink a Julienas or a robust Médoc throughout the meal. Or, if you are feeling extravagant, Champagne is even better. Follow the cassoulet with sliced oranges or other fresh fruit.

10–12 SERVINGS

2 *pounds pea beans or navy beans*
   Salt and freshly ground pepper to taste
1 *leek, sliced*

1   onion, sliced

1   carrot, sliced

2   tomatoes, peeled, seeded, and chopped

1   tablespoon tomato paste

4   cloves garlic, put through a garlic press
       Bouquet garni, made by enclosing in a cheesecloth
           bag 2 cloves, 1 bay leaf, 3 sprigs parsley, and
           3 sprigs fresh thyme (if unavailable, 1 teaspoon dried
           thyme can be added directly to the pot)

¾   pound pork rind

1   pound lean, unsliced bacon

5   cups Chicken Broth (see page 48)

1   pound garlic sausage, skinned and sliced

2   cups dry white wine

1   2- to 3-pound pork shoulder or pork butt

2   cans imported French confit d'oie (preserved goose,
       available in specialty shops) or, if not available,
       3–4 pieces roast duck and ½ cup goose fat

2   cups fresh white bread crumbs mixed with ½ cup
       chopped parsley

Soak the beans overnight. Drain and rinse them in cold water. Put them in a large pot. Season them lightly with salt and generously with pepper. Add the leek, onion, carrot, tomatoes, tomato paste, garlic, and bouquet garni. Blanch and dice the pork rind and the bacon. Add them to the pot along with 1 quart water and the chicken broth.

Bring slowly to a boil, then simmer for about 1 hour, or until the beans are partially cooked but not soft. (*Caution:* Be sure the beans are still firm. Keep the beans covered with liquid throughout their cooking.) Add boiling water as needed. Add the sausage and the wine, and cook over low heat for 30 minutes. Set the beans aside in their cooking liquid.

Meanwhile, roast the pork for 1½ to 2 hours. Cut it into 1½-inch serving pieces, deglaze the fat in the roasting pan, scraping in the brown bits, and set aside.

In a large earthenware or enamel-lined casserole, assemble the cassoulet. Drain the beans, discarding the bouquet garni. Reserve the liquid. Fill the casserole with alternating layers of beans, the roast pork, and the *confit d'oie* with its fat (or roast duck with a little goose fat). The bottom and top layers should be beans. Add enough of the reserved cooking liquid to bring it just to the top layer of beans. Sprinkle the bread crumbs over the top. Put some of the fat from both the roast pork and the *confit d'oie* on top of the bread crumbs.

Preheat the oven to 375°.

Put the casserole, uncovered, in the top third of the oven for 1 hour. As soon as the bread crumbs form a golden crust, break the crust into the beans with the back of a spoon and baste with the liquid in the casserole. Repeat this process two or three times as the crust re-forms. But leave a crust at the end of the baking. When serving, be sure to include some of everything in each portion.

VEGETABLES

ealth-conscious Americans, who jog where angels
fear to tread, dote on vegetables. To eat vegetables, once
a sober duty, is now considered a sybaritic pleasure. Yester-
day's child, threatened with no dessert unless he finished
his spinach, is delighted to skip dessert if he is promised
his *risotto verde con spinaci*. We no longer think of vegetables as supporting actors but as stars that glow in spotlit
splendor. Some cookbook writers have a tendency to fanta-
size about tripping out to a mythical vegetable patch to
pick their corn and tomatoes at the perfect moment of
ripeness. And a fine thing that can be if you have a garden.
Otherwise, our advice is to find the freshest available
vegetables and treat them with loving care. Of course, if
you do have a vegetable garden, there is perhaps no
better way of cooking vegetables than steaming or boiling
them (they don't *always* have to be crunchy) and adding

a good pat of butter, salt, pepper, and your favorite herb. We ourselves have made sumptuously successful molded vegetable pâtés
with vegetables bought at a supermarket and wonderful corn pancakes with frozen corn kernels. And as we all know, imported Italian
canned tomatoes are far tastier than those pallid fresh tomatoes
available in winter. Unfortunately, our vegetable section is not long
enough to include the endless possibilities. But here are a few suggestions.

Rub a piece of hot red pepper on buttered cooked corn on the cob.
The pungent heat of the pepper makes a fiery contrast to the bland
corn.

Crumble feta cheese over leeks vinaigrette. Serve a perfectly roasted
chicken with three purées: a thick applesauce heightened with a dash
of Calvados or a spoonful of horseradish, mashed potatoes flecked
with lemon rind, a purée of celery root mixed with cream and Dijon
mustard. These tips and the following recipes, we hope, will make
you feel as the poet Andrew Marvell felt when he said, "My vegetable
love should grow vaster than empires and more slow."

MOLDED VEGETABLE PÂTÉS,
DANIEL BOUCHÉ
(Gourmandises de Légumes)

〜

A superb first course for a serious dinner.

This dish was served us at Daniel Bouché's Le Petit Montmorency,
one of our favorite Paris restaurants. It takes time to prepare, but
when unmolded, its layered look and its subtle contrasts of taste and
color will be ample reward for your labors.

6 SERVINGS

1 *pound mushrooms, finely chopped*
4 *scallions, finely chopped*
1 *stick (¼ pound) butter*
1 *pound spinach, trimmed, carefully washed, and*
      coarsely chopped
8 *carrots, sliced*

1   *cauliflower, medium to large (or 2 small ones), broken*
into florets

4   *egg yolks*
Salt and freshly ground pepper to taste

1   *teaspoon sugar*

Sauce

1   *leek (or 4 scallions), white part only*
1   *carrot*
3   *dried mushrooms (or 3–4 mushroom caps)*
1   *stalk celery*
2   *tablespoons butter*
Salt and pepper to taste
⅓   *cup Crème Fraîche (see page 151) or sour cream*

Sauté the mushrooms with the scallions in 2 tablespoons of the butter for about 5 minutes. Set aside. Boil the spinach in salted water for 2 to 3 minutes. Drain, pressing out as much liquid as possible. Boil the carrots and cauliflower in separate pots until tender. Purée each of the vegetables separately in a blender, food processor, or food mill until very smooth. Return to the pot in which each was cooked, after first drying the pot carefully. Wash the blender or processor between operations, since you do not want to mix the colors of the vegetables. Add 1 tablespoon of butter, 1 lightly beaten egg yolk, salt and pepper to each purée. Add the sugar to the carrot purée. Put each purée in its pot over low heat, stirring constantly, until the mixture is thick.

Generously butter 6 ¾-cup-size custard cups or metal timbale molds. Make equal layers in each mold of the four purées in this order: cauliflower, spinach, carrot, and mushroom. Set the molds in a deep ovenproof dish. Put them in the oven. Carefully add boiling water until it comes halfway up the sides of the molds. Bake at 375° for 30 minutes, or until a knife inserted into the purées comes out clean.

Prepare the sauce. Cut the leek, carrot, dried mushrooms, and celery into 1-inch lengths, then into the thinnest possible matchstick strips. Put them in a heavy pan with a tight-fitting cover, add the butter and cook, covered, over medium heat for 10 minutes, stirring often. Season with salt and pepper and remove from the heat.

When the purées are ready, remove them from the oven and wipe the molds dry. Run a knife around the inside edges of the molds and invert them onto individual dishes.

Add the *crème fraîche* to the vegetable strips, return to low heat, and stir until the cream is hot. Do not let it boil. Correct the seasoning, spoon some of the sauce over each unmolded purée, and serve.

TIP: Any vegetable can be puréed and unmolded following the same procedure, as long as it has 1 egg beaten into it for each cup of purée.

A SUGGESTED MENU

(see Index for recipes)

MOLDED VEGETABLE PÂTÉS

ROAST TURKEY, NORMANDY STYLE

GREEN SALAD

CHOCOLATE MOUSSE CAKE, MICHEL GUÉRARD

wine: CABERNET SAUVIGNON

RATATOUILLE

The secret of this recipe is that the vegetables are cooked separately, then combined. The result is fragrant, crisp, robust, and not too oily.

Whenever we make this recipe we think of our French friend Angelo Torricini. And he, in turn, thinks of his mother, who taught him the dish. First, he gathers the eggplants, the red-ripe tomatoes, the purple onions, the fresh garden herbs—all the good things that go into a *ratatouille*. He arranges them in a wooden bowl. The enthusiasm when he invites you to admire his vegetable still life! A kitchen painting, he calls it. Then, when the garlic and onions begin to simmer in olive oil, he breathes a sigh of satisfaction and mutters to himself, *"Quel parfum délicieux!"* He cubes and slices, chops and minces, shakes the pan, smells and tastes so ardently that you know the dish will be superb.

12–14 SERVINGS

2   *large eggplants, unpeeled, cut into 1½ inch cubes*
2   *tablespoons salt*
    About 2 cups olive oil

4 green peppers (or even better, a combination of green,
    yellow, and red peppers), each cut into 8 pieces,
    and stems, white membrane, and seeds discarded
3 fairly large unpeeled zucchini, scrubbed and cut into
    1½-inch slices
2 large Spanish onions, peeled and cut into 1½-inch slices
3 (about 2 pounds) large, ripe tomatoes, peeled and
    seeded
4 cloves garlic, coarsely chopped
2 bunches parsley, stems removed and finely chopped
3 sprigs thyme or 1 teaspoon dried
1 bay leaf
2 slices lemon
    Salt and freshly ground black pepper to taste

Sprinkle the eggplant cubes with 2 tablespoons of salt. Let them
stand in a colander for 1 hour with a heavy weight to rid them of
their bitter juice. Squeeze out as much of their juice as you can.
Drain them well on paper towels.

Line four large platters with a double thickness of paper towels,
which you will use to drain the vegetables separately as they are
cooked.

Heat ½ cup of the olive oil in a large heavy frying pan until it
bubbles. Fry the peppers over high heat for 6 to 8 minutes, stirring
frequently, until they are slightly charred. Remove them with a
slotted spoon and drain on one of the paper-lined platters. Fry the
zucchini in the same pan, adding a little oil only if needed. Cook,
stirring often, for 2 to 3 minutes. Remove them with a slotted spoon.
Drain them well. Fry the onions in the same pan over high heat,
stirring constantly until golden, adding more oil as needed. Remove
them with a slotted spoon, and drain them well.

Dry the eggplant carefully. Add 6 tablespoons of the oil to the
pan and fry a single layer of eggplant, turning until browned on all
sides. Remove them and drain. Repeat the process with the rest of
the eggplant, adding oil as needed.

Coarsely chop the tomatoes and put them in a bowl. Add the
garlic to the tomatoes along with the parsley, thyme, bay leaf, and
lemon slices. Mix well.

Cover the bottom of a casserole large enough to hold all the ingredients with a thin layer of oil. Add a third of the tomato mixture,
then half of each vegetable to the casserole, seasoning them lightly

with salt and generously with pepper as you go. Cover with a third of the tomato mixture. Repeat the process. Then top with the remaining third of the tomato mixture.

Cover the casserole and simmer over low heat for 10 minutes. Stir occasionally and use a bulb baster to baste the vegetables with the liquid at the bottom. Raise the heat and cook, uncovered, for another 10 to 15 minutes, just until the vegetables are cooked and the liquid is reduced to 2 or 3 tablespoons.

Wonderful served hot with steak, hamburgers, or roasts; tepid or cold, as a first course in itself. We always make the full recipe even if we are not planning to serve it all, as it is a versatile leftover. Reheat it slowly and use it to fill omelets, or as a sauce for spaghetti or grilled swordfish. Serve it cold with cold roast chicken or as a sauce over cold poached fish. Or mix it with flaked tunafish, olives, capers, and some diced celery for added crispness, and serve as an appetizer.

A SUGGESTED LUNCH MENU

(see Index for recipes)

RATATOUILLE

OMELET WITH CROUTONS AND WALNUTS

INSTANT BANANA BLITZ

ANKA BEGLEY'S QUICK AND EASY CHOCOLATE CAKE

wine: CAHORS

ASPARAGUS WITH SABAYON SAUCE

Sabayon is the French word for that mixture of egg yolks, sugar, and Marsala wine the Italians call *zabaglione*. Substitute white wine for the Marsala, omit the sugar and you have a perfect sauce for asparagus—or fillet of sole, for that matter.

6 SERVINGS

2 *pounds asparagus*
1 *teaspoon salt*

SAUCE

3   egg yolks
½   cup dry white wine (such as Chablis)
½   teaspoon salt
    Several turns of freshly ground white pepper
1   teaspoon lemon juice
    A pinch of sugar

To prepare the asparagus: With a vegetable scraper, peel the stems of the asparagus. Break off the tough bottom ends so that all the stalks are of the same length. Tie the asparagus stalks into bundles. Fill an asparagus steamer half full of water and add the salt. Or use a tall pot with a cover. The stems must boil; the tips must steam. Bring to a fast boil, then stand the bundles upright in the steamer or pot. Cook, covered, for 10 minutes, or until tender but still crisp. Test the stems with the point of a sharp knife. If the knife goes in easily, they are done. Do not overcook. Remove the asparagus and drain them.

Lay the asparagus in a lightly buttered shallow ovenproof dish.

Prepare the sauce. Put all the ingredients in the top of a double boiler over just simmering water. With a wire whisk or rotary egg beater, beat constantly for about 5 minutes, or until the sauce foams up and doubles in volume.

Pour the sauce over the asparagus *at once.* Place under the broiler, 4 inches from the heat, until lightly browned.

VARIATION: Sprinkle 2 tablespoons of grated Gruyère or Parmesan cheese over the sauce before putting it under the broiler.

TIP: If you have a baby-bottle warmer, use it to steam asparagus. Just stand a bunch of asparagus in each metal circle where you would normally put a bottle.

ASPARAGUS WITH MUSTARD SAUCE

6 SERVINGS

2   pounds asparagus
4   egg yolks
8–10 tablespoons crème fraîche or heavy cream
1   teaspoon Dijon mustard or more to taste

Steam the asparagus following the procedure for Asparagus with
Sabayon Sauce (see page 262).

Meanwhile, prepare the sauce. In a heavy-bottomed saucepan, beat
the egg yolks with a wire whisk for a minute or two. Whisk in the
cream and place the saucepan over medium heat. Cook, whisking
constantly, for about 6 to 8 minutes, or until the mixture thickens.
Do not let the sauce come to a boil, or it may curdle. Stir in the
mustard, adding a little more if you like, until well combined. Remove from the heat immediately. Whisk for a minute, then spoon
the sauce over the asparagus and serve.

The sauce is equally good over other steamed vegetables, such as
broccoli or cauliflower, or with poached fish.

OLD-FASHIONED
COUNTRY STRING BEANS

6–8 SERVINGS

2–2½   pounds young string beans
       Salt and freshly ground pepper to taste
  1   stick (¼ pound) butter
  1   small onion, very finely chopped (or 4 tablespoons
          finely chopped shallots)
       Juice of 1 lemon
  ⅓   cup finely chopped parsley
  1   lemon, cut into 6 wedges

String the beans. Put 6 quarts of water and 3 tablespoons of salt into
an 8-quart pot and bring it to a rolling boil. Drop the beans, a handful
at a time, into the water. Bring the water back to a boil. Reduce the
heat somewhat and boil the beans slowly for about 8 minutes, or
until they are tender but still bright green. As soon as the beans are
done, drain them in a colander, pouring cold water over them to
stop the cooking. Dry on paper towels.

In a large frying pan, toss the beans over medium heat to remove
excess moisture. Season with salt and pepper. Add half the butter and
the onions. Cook, stirring, for 2 to 3 minutes. With a slotted spoon,

remove the beans and onions to a warm serving platter. Pour the lemon juice into the hot pan, stir it, then immediately pour it over the beans. Cut the remaining butter into bits. Add to the beans along with the chopped parsley. Toss, correct the seasoning, and serve with lemon wedges. Splendid with lamb chops or roast chicken.

CARROTS IN MARMALADE

6–10 SERVINGS

3 *cups thinly sliced carrots*
3 *tablespoons butter*
½ *cup chicken broth*
½ *teaspoon each salt and freshly ground pepper*
½ *cup ginger marmalade or a combination of orange and*
   ginger marmalade
   Optional: a dash of Grand Marnier

Put the carrots, butter, and broth in a heavy pot. Cook, covered, for 10 minutes. Add the remaining ingredients. Cook, uncovered, until the carrots are tender and the sauce has become a thick glaze. Stir often as the sauce thickens.

Serve with Gala Meat Loaf (see page 208), grilled ham slices, or roast turkey.

BAKED CAULIFLOWER, ITALIAN STYLE

4–6 SERVINGS

1 *2-pound head cauliflower with its leaves*
4 *tablespoons butter*
2 *tablespoons oil*
1 *medium-size onion, finely chopped*

1   *clove garlic, minced or put through a garlic press*
1   *cup Tomato Sauce (see page 36)*
    Salt and pepper to taste
    A few fresh basil leaves or 1 teaspoon dried basil
    A pinch of sugar
4–6   *tablespoons freshly grated Parmesan cheese*
½   *cup cubed mozzarella*

Preheat the oven to 350°.

Bring a large pot of salted water to a boil. Trim the head of cauli-flower, discarding the hard core and any damaged outer leaves. Boil the remaining leaves for 10 minutes. Add the cauliflower and cook for about 20 minutes, or just until tender. Remove it with a slotted spoon. It should be *al dente*, but the leaves must be wilted enough to be pliable. Break the cauliflower into florets and drain them well. Dry the leaves on paper towels. Butter a baking dish just large enough to hold the florets in a single layer. Wrap each in a leaf and set the florets in the baking dish, close together, stem side down.

Heat the oil and 2 tablespoons of the butter in a small saucepan. Add the onion and cook, stirring, over low heat for 2 to 3 minutes. Do not let them brown. Add the garlic and cook for 1 minute. Add the tomato sauce. Season with salt, pepper, basil, and sugar. Cook over low heat for 10 to 15 minutes.

Sprinkle the cauliflower with the grated cheese and the mozzarella. Dot with the remaining butter and pour tomato sauce over all. Cover with foil and bake for 20 minutes. Remove the foil for the last 5 to 10 minutes of cooking. Serve hot.

SAUTÉED CELERY ROOT

6~

4–6 SERVINGS

1   *large celery root, peeled and cut into ¾-inch cubes*
3   *tablespoons oil*
    Juice of 1 lemon
    Salt, freshly ground pepper, and cumin to taste
¼   *cup chopped fresh coriander or parsley*

Sauté the cubes of celery root in the oil for 5 minutes over medium heat. Add the lemon juice and enough water to cover. Season with salt, pepper, and cumin. Simmer, uncovered, turning occasionally, for about 10 minutes, or until the celery root is tender. Over high heat, reduce the liquid to 2 or 3 tablespoons. Garnish with chopped coriander and serve hot. Excellent with baked or sautéed fish or served cold as a salad.

CORN PANCAKES

∽

A delicacy when fresh corn is in season.

6–8 SERVINGS

2   cups fresh corn kernels, scraped off the cob
2   eggs
¼   cup plus 1 tablespoon flour
½   teaspoon baking powder
½   teaspoon salt
¼   teaspoon pepper
1   stick (¼ pound) butter, for frying, or more if needed

Place the corn kernels in a food processor along with all the other ingredients except the butter. Using the steel knife, process for a few seconds until the mixture is well combined but the corn is still in fairly coarse pieces. Transfer to a bowl and refrigerate for 1 hour.

Heat about 2 tablespoons of the butter in a large frying pan. When it is sizzling, drop in the batter by level tablespoonfuls, widely spaced, and reduce the heat to medium. When bubbles appear in the pancakes, turn them carefully with a spatula and brown the other side. Add more butter as needed. Keep the pancakes warm in a low oven while you repeat the process. Very fine with Gala Meat Loaf (see page 208) or fried chicken. Or try them for breakfast with maple syrup.

FRIED CUCUMBERS

❧

4–6 SERVINGS

2   medium-size cucumbers
2   scallions, trimmed and thinly sliced (including some
       of the green)
2   tablespoons butter
     Salt and freshly ground pepper to taste
4   tablespoons sour cream
2   tablespoons chopped fresh dill or chives

Peel and cut the cucumbers into thin slices. Sauté the scallions gently
in half the butter for 1 minute. Add the remaining butter and cucumber slices and sauté, shaking the pan occasionally. When the
cucumber slices begin to wilt, season them generously, stir in the
sour cream, and sprinkle with dill. Cook until the sour cream is warm.
Serve with grilled salmon steaks.

CHINESE STEAMED EGGPLANT

❧

4 SERVINGS

1   medium-size (about 1 pound) eggplant

DRESSING

1   tablespoon sesame oil (Chinese or Japanese)
2   teaspoons rice vinegar or white wine vinegar
1   tablespoon light soy sauce
1   teaspoon sugar
⅛   teaspoon cayenne pepper
1   clove garlic, passed through a garlic press

Wash the eggplant and trim the ends, but do not peel it. Cut into quarters lengthwise. Cook, covered, in a vegetable steamer over boiling water for 20 minutes, or until tender. Turn off the heat, but let the eggplant stand, covered, in the steamer for 10 minutes longer. Drain on paper towels. Use a fork to separate the eggplant into long strips. Discard the seeds and the tough pith. Place in a serving bowl.

Mix all the dressing ingredients well and pour over the eggplant. Toss and chill for 1 hour before serving.

EGGPLANT IN CREAM
(Aubergines à la Crème)

6 SERVINGS

2   *medium-size eggplants*
    Salt
6   *tablespoons butter and 2 tablespoons peanut oil (or*
      more if needed)
2   *tablespoons Crème Fraîche (see page 151)*
    Freshly ground pepper
1   *tablespoon chopped fresh parsley or chives*

Peel the eggplants and cut them into ¼-inch slices. Sprinkle them generously with salt and let them sit for 30 minutes. Press out the bitter juices, drain, and pat them dry. Cook them, covered, in 4 tablespoons of the butter and the oil in a heavy frying pan over low heat. Turn them so that they are golden brown on both sides. Add the remaining butter as needed. Season with pepper only. Add the cream and cook over medium heat until the cream has reduced by half. Correct the seasoning. Remove the eggplant from the heat, and add the chopped herbs. Excellent with broiled chops or fish.

BRAISED ENDIVES
(Endives Braisées)

෴

6 SERVINGS

12   *medium-size endives*
 1   *stick (¼ pound) butter*
     Salt and freshly ground pepper to taste
     Juice of half a lemon
 ¼   *cup chicken broth or water*

Preheat the oven to 350°.

Trim off the root ends with a small sharp knife, and discard any wilted outer leaves. Never let endive sit in water, as that will exaggerate the bitterness. If they are fairly clean to start with, just wipe them with a damp cloth.

Generously butter the bottom of a 3-quart flameproof enameled casserole and arrange the endives close together in two layers. Season each layer with salt, pepper, and lemon juice. Dot with the remaining butter. Add the broth or water. Simmer, covered, for 10 minutes; then boil, uncovered, for another 10 minutes, or until the liquid has reduced to a few tablespoons. Cut a round of paper to fit the top of the casserole and butter it well. Lay the paper, buttered side down, on the endives, cover the casserole and bake for about 1 hour.

OPTIONAL: When cooked, arrange the braised endives in a shallow baking dish, dot with more butter, and brown under the broiler for a minute or two.

BRAISED ENDIVES WITH HAM
(Endives Braisées au Jambon)

෬～

This enrichment of the basic recipe for braised endives makes a marvelous first course or luncheon dish.

6 SERVINGS

Braised Endives (see preceding page)
12 thin slices boiled ham
4 tablespoons butter
3 tablespoons flour
1½ cups milk, heated just to the boiling point
Salt and freshly ground pepper (white pepper if possible) to taste
½ cup heavy cream or Crème Fraîche (see page 151)
¼ cup grated Gruyère cheese

Make the basic braised endives. Remove them from the casserole and wrap each one in a slice of ham, then place it in a generously buttered shallow baking dish.

Melt 2 tablespoons of the butter in a heavy saucepan over low heat. Blend in the flour with a wire whisk and cook, stirring, for 2 to 3 minutes. Remove from the heat. Add the milk and start beating with the whisk immediately, scraping the edges of the pan to blend the flour and milk together. Return the saucepan to medium heat and whisk until the sauce comes to a boil. Boil, whisking constantly, for 1 minute.

Heat the cream in a small saucepan and gradually whisk it into the sauce. Season with salt and pepper. Pour the sauce over the ham-wrapped endives, sprinkle with the grated cheese, and dot with the remaining 2 tablespoons of butter. Place under a medium-hot broiler until the cheese is golden brown. Serve at once.

VARIATION: Give this dish an Italian accent by substituting slices of prosciutto for the ham and using freshly grated imported Parmesan cheese instead of Gruyère.

LENTILS PROVENÇALE

❧

8 SERVINGS

2 cups dried lentils
2 onions, coarsely chopped
3 tablespoons olive oil
1 cup dry white wine
1½ teaspoons salt
½ teaspoon sugar
2 bay leaves
1 cup Tomato Sauce (see page 36), puréed in a blender,
      or canned Italian tomato purée
   Freshly ground pepper
   Chopped parsley for garnish

Pick over the lentils, discarding any stones. Sauté the onions in the oil in a large heavy casserole with a tight-fittng cover until translucent but not browned. Add the wine and cook, uncovered, until it has evaporated. Add the lentils, salt, sugar, bay leaves, tomato sauce or purée, and enough boiling water to cover. Bring to a boil, cover tightly, simmer for 1 hour, or until the lentils are soft. Add more boiling water if necessary to keep the lentils covered while they are cooking. When cooked, discard the bay leaves. Correct the seasoning, garnish with the parsley, and serve.

RAGOUT OF MUSHROOMS

❧

If you like mushrooms, you will become addicted to this dish.

6 SERVINGS

1 1-ounce package dried French chanterelle mushrooms
      (available in specialty shops)
1½ pounds fresh mushrooms

1   *4-ounce can imported German Steinpilze mushrooms*
      (available in specialty shops)
1   *stick (¼ pound) butter*
1   *clove garlic, peeled and crushed*
2   *tablespoons brandy*
1   *cup Crème Fraîche (see page 151), sour cream, or heavy*
      cream
      Salt, pepper, and cayenne pepper to taste
¼   *cup chopped parsley*

Soak the chanterelles in warm water to cover for ½ hour. Drain and rinse them two or three times. Dry them carefully on paper towels.

Wipe the fresh mushrooms clean. Trim the stems. Cut the mushrooms into thin slices.

Drain the canned mushrooms and cut the larger ones into two or three small pieces.

Heat the butter in a large heavy frying pan. Add the garlic and chanterelles and sauté over medium heat for 3 to 4 minutes, stirring often. As soon as the garlic begins to turn color, discard it. Add the fresh mushrooms and cook, stirring, for 4 to 5 minutes. Stir in the canned mushrooms and the brandy. When the brandy is hot, ignite it and let it burn, shaking the skillet till the flames die down.

Add the cream, salt, pepper, and cayenne. Cook over high heat, stirring constantly, until the cream thickens. Sprinkle with parsley and serve as a glorious solo, accompanied by triangles of white bread fried in butter, or as a most luxurious sauce over a sautéed veal chop. Sybaritic!

A SUGGESTED MENU

(see Index for recipes)

RAGOUT OF MUSHROOMS

RISOTTO WITH CHICKEN LIVERS

QUINCE CRISP

wine: CHALOSSE

STUFFED MUSHROOMS

໓∾

4 SERVINGS

8 *large mushrooms*
2 *shallots, finely chopped*
½ *stick (4 tablespoons) butter*
  Salt and freshly ground pepper to taste
1 *cup cooked peas (or canned tiny peas), drained*
½ *teaspoon curry powder*
1 *teaspoon brandy, kümmel, or vermouth*
1 *teaspoon sugar*
2 *tablespoons freshly grated imported Gruyère or*
  Parmesan cheese

Break off the mushroom stems and chop them fine. Wipe the mushroom caps clean. Sauté the shallots in 1 or 2 tablespoons of the butter over medium heat, stirring, for a minute or two. Do not let them brown. Add the chopped mushroom stems. Season with salt and pepper. Sauté for 3 to 5 minutes. Set aside.

Preheat the oven to 325°.

Purée the peas in a food processor. Add them to the shallot-mushroom mixture along with the curry powder, brandy, and sugar. Add salt and pepper and heat the mixture through, stirring to mix well. Remove from the heat and fill the mushroom caps with this mixture. Sprinkle with grated cheese and dot with butter. Bake in a buttered baking dish for about 20 minutes. Serve as a first course or with Coulibiaca (see page 133).

VARIATION: Sauté ½ cup of finely shredded sorrel along with the shallots.

BAKED ONIONS

᠗

6 SERVINGS

6 medium-size Spanish onions, left unpeeled
1 stick (¼ pound) butter
  Salt and freshly ground pepper to taste
1 hard-boiled egg, finely chopped
2 tablespoons finely chopped parsley

Bake the unpeeled onions at 350° in a greased baking dish for 45 minutes, or until tender when pierced with a knife. Peel them. Slice each onion in half horizontally. Butter them lavishly and sprinkle them with salt, pepper, chopped egg, and parsley. Serve hot or at room temperature.

PARSNIP–TURNIP PURÉE

᠗

6 SERVINGS

1   cup sliced parsnips
2   cups sliced small white turnips
2   tablespoons butter
2   tablespoons sour cream or Crème Fraîche (see page 151)
1–2 egg yolks
2–4 tablespoons freshly grated Parmesan cheese
    Salt and freshly ground pepper to taste
    Optional: 2 tablespoons chopped chives or parsley

Boil the parsnips and turnips together in salted water until tender. Drain them well and dry them on paper towels. Place the vegetables in a food processor, using the knife blade. Add all the remaining ingredients and purée until smooth. (If you are using a food mill, put the boiled, drained, and dried parsnips and turnips through the mill using the fine disk. Stir in all the remaining ingredients, reheat and serve.)

The purée can be kept warm in the top of a double boiler over simmering water. Dot the purée with bits of butter to prevent a crust from forming. Stir well just before serving. Garnish with chopped chives or parsley. Serve hot with roast duck or pork.

COLD DILLED PEAS

A Russian accompaniment to cold roast meat or chicken, or to chicken salad.

6 SERVINGS

2   *cups shelled garden-fresh peas, boiled, or canned tiny*
       peas
1   *cup sour cream*
¾   *cup chopped fresh dill, chives, or a combination*
       of both
       combination of both
    Salt and freshly ground pepper to taste
    Optional: ½–1 teaspoon curry powder

Drain the peas thoroughly. Cool to room temperature. Mix the other ingredients together and, using two forks in order not to crush them, combine with the peas. Transfer to a glass serving bowl. Chill in the refrigerator for 1 hour and serve.

PEAS WITH MINT

6–8 SERVINGS

3 pounds fresh peas
4 tablespoons butter
Salt and freshly ground pepper to taste
Chopped fresh mint to taste

Bring a large pot of salted water to a boil while you shell the peas. Cook the peas just until they are tender. Drain, dot generously with butter, and season to taste. Stir in the chopped mint and serve.

GREEN PEAS, ROMAN STYLE
(Piselli alla Romana)

6 SERVINGS

3 pounds (about 3 cups) fresh green peas
4 tablespoons butter
3 tablespoons light oil (such as French peanut oil)
½ cup finely chopped onions
⅛ pound prosciutto, thinly sliced, then cut into julienne
     strips
1 teaspoon dried sage, rubbed in your hands till
     powdery, or 3 fresh leaves, minced
1 cup Chicken Broth (see page 48)
2 large romaine lettuce leaves, cut into julienne strips
   Salt and freshly ground pepper to taste

Shell the peas just before cooking them. Boil them in lightly salted water for 3 minutes, or until tender. Drain. Heat the butter and oil in a pan. Add the onions, prosciutto, and sage. Sauté, stirring occasionally, until the onions are translucent. Add the peas, and sauté for 5 minutes. Add the chicken broth, lettuce, salt, and pepper. Simmer over low heat until tender. Drain and serve with Rack of Veal with Rosemary (see page 229) and Devilish Potatoes (see page 283).

PURÉE OF SPLIT PEAS

༄

6–8 SERVINGS

1 pound dried split peas
¼ cup salt pork or a thick slice of bacon, diced
3 tablespoons butter
1 medium-size onion, chopped
1 carrot, chopped
1 parsnip, chopped
4 lettuce leaves, shredded
1 teaspoon sugar
1 tablespoon brandy, kümmel, or whiskey
   Salt and freshly ground pepper to taste

Put the peas in a pot with enough water to cover. Bring to a boil,
then lower the heat and simmer, covered, adding boiling water if
needed to keep the peas covered.

Parboil the salt pork for 5 minutes. Drain. Sauté it in 1 tablespoon
of the butter for 5 minutes. Discard the pork. Add the chopped onion,
carrot, and parsnip to the fat and cook until lightly browned. Add
the lettuce and cook 3 to 4 minutes. Add this mixture to the split peas
and stir well. If necessary, add a little more boiling water to keep
the vegetables covered. Cook, covered, over low heat for 1 to 1½ hours,
or until the mixture is thick. Stir occasionally to prevent sticking.

Purée the mixture through a food mill. Return to the pot over low
heat. Stir in the remaining 2 tablespoons of butter, the sugar, brandy,
salt, and a generous amount of pepper. Serve piping hot with roast
pork or baked ham.

VARIATION: A hearty, delicious split-pea soup can easily be made by
adding good chicken or beef broth to the pea purée in the proportion
of 1 cup of broth to 2 cups of purée, and mixing it well over medium
heat. Use a little less broth if you like a very thick soup, a little more
if you prefer a thinner soup. In any case, taste and correct the
seasoning and serve hot with croutons.

ROASTED PEPPERS

∽

12 SERVINGS

10   *red, green, or yellow sweet peppers*
½   *cup olive oil*
     Salt and freshly ground pepper to taste

To char and skin the peppers: Spear the peppers, one at a time, with a long-handled fork and hold them over a gas flame, turning them constantly until they are charred and blistered all over. Or place the peppers on a foil-lined baking sheet 2 to 3 inches from the broiler. Broil, turning them often, until they are charred on all sides. Put them in a plastic or brown paper bag and fold the bag to seal it tightly. When the peppers are cool enough to handle, peel the skins with a small knife. *Do not* wash them, as they will become soggy.

Dry the peppers and cut them in half. Remove and discard the stems, seeds, and white membranes. Put the pepper halves in a baking dish with the oil. Season them with salt and pepper. Bake at 350° for about 20 minutes. Delicious hot or cold, alone or with hamburgers or barbecued chicken.

PURÉE OF SWEET PEPPERS

∽

4 SERVINGS

4   *large or 6 medium-size green peppers*
2–4   *tablespoons butter*
½   *cup rice*
1–1½   *cups Chicken Broth (see page 48), at room temperature*
     Salt and freshly ground pepper to taste
     A dash of cayenne pepper
2   *tablespoons Crème Fraîche (see page 151) or sour cream*

Char and skin the peppers according to the directions given for Roasted Peppers (see preceding page). Remove and discard the white membranes, stems, and seeds. In a heavy saucepan over low heat, cook the peppers, covered, in 2 to 3 tablespoons of butter until tender.

Meanwhile, put the rice and the broth in a pot and boil for about 20 minutes, or until the rice is very soft. Drain the rice and purée it, along with the peppers, in a blender or food processor (using a little of the broth if necessary) until it is smooth. Put the mixture in the saucepan and cook it over the lowest heat, stirring constantly until it is fairly thick. Season with salt, pepper, and cayenne. Stir in the *crème fraîche* and mix well over the heat. Correct the seasoning, swirl in 1 tablespoon of butter, and serve.

PEPPERS AND TOMATOES, ITALIAN STYLE
(Peperonata)

4 SERVINGS

¼   *cup olive oil*
1   *medium-size onion, thinly sliced*
4   *green peppers*
    Salt, sugar, and freshly ground pepper to taste
3   *tablespoons vinegar*
6   *ripe tomatoes, peeled and seeded*
2   *tablespoons chopped fresh basil*

Heat the oil in a heavy pot with a cover. Sauté the onion slices over medium heat till translucent but not browned.

Discard the stems, seeds, and white membranes and cut the peppers into slices. Add them to the onions, season with salt, sugar, and pepper. Add the vinegar. Stir, cover and cook until the peppers are tender.

Chop the tomatoes coarsely, add them to the mixture and cook, uncovered, for 6 to 7 minutes. Sprinkle with the basil. Serve hot or at room temperature. Wonderful with steaks or chops, or as a first course.

VARIATION I: Lightly butter individual ramekins or soufflé dishes. Fill two-thirds full with the *peperonata.* With the back of a spoon, press a hollow in the middle of the *peperonata.* Break an egg into each hollow and sprinkle it with salt, pepper, and 1 teaspoon of grated Parmesan cheese. Bake in a preheated 375° oven until the white of the egg is set. A satisfying light lunch.

VARIATION II: Use *peperonata* as a sauce for spaghetti by cooking it down, uncovered, to a thick pulp for 20 to 25 minutes after the tomatoes have been added. Pass grated Parmesan cheese separately.

ROESTI
(Swiss Potato Pancake)

෧෴

One good reason to go to Switzerland is to enjoy the crusty golden potato pancake called *roesti.* When we first visited Fredy Girardet's world-renowned restaurant near Lausanne, it had a workingmen's café adjoining it. The same chefs cooked for both. We found Girardet's inspired inventions as great as food can be, yet nothing gave us more pleasure than the simple *roesti* served in the rustic room across the hall. Here is our recipe for this traditional Swiss specialty.

You will need a 10-inch nonstick frying pan with sloping sides, a 9-inch dinner plate, and a flexible spatula.

4–6 SERVINGS

3   *large baking potatoes (preferably Idaho)*
½   *cup minced shallots (or onions)*
1   *stick (¼ pound) butter*
    Salt and freshly ground pepper to taste
    Optional: 2 slices bacon, crisply fried

Wash the potatoes and boil them in their skins until barely tender. Peel them and dry them a little in a pot over low heat for a minute or two. Set them aside to cool.

Sauté the shallots in 2 tablespoons of butter until they are wilted but not browned. Transfer the shallots with the butter to a large bowl. Grate the potatoes coarsely with a grater or in a food processor with the grating disk. Add them to the shallots. Melt 2 tablespoons of butter and pour it over the potatoes. Mix the potatoes and shallots lightly and season them with salt and pepper.

Heat the remaining butter in a nonstick frying pan. Spread the potato-shallot mixture in the pan in a thin even layer, pressing it down with the back of a spoon. Sprinkle with 1 tablespoon of cold water. Cover with an inverted plate that fits inside the rim of the pan and rests on the potatoes. Cook over medium heat, shaking the pan from time to time. After fifteen minutes, gently raise an edge of the pancake to see if it is browning properly. When the bottom is golden brown, carefully loosen it all around. Remove the pan from the heat. Cover it with a warmed plate and invert the *roesti* onto the plate. Slide it back into the pan and brown the other side. Serve at once.

If you like, scatter hot, crumbled bacon over the *roesti* before serving it, as they do in some parts of Switzerland.

POTATO AND CELERY MOLDS

You will need six ¾-cup molds: timbales or custard cups.

6 SERVINGS

1   cup minced hearts of celery
5   tablespoons butter
¼   cup minced shallots
    Salt and freshly ground pepper to taste
1½ pounds potatoes, peeled and quartered
½   cup light cream or half-and-half
5   egg yolks
½   cup grated Parmesan cheese

Preheat the oven to 450°.

Sauté the celery in 2 tablespoons of the butter until tender. Stir in the shallots and sauté for 2 minutes. Season with salt and pepper. Set aside in the pan.

Boil the potatoes until tender. Drain them thoroughly. Heat the cream but do not let it boil. Mash the potatoes with 1 tablespoon of butter, then gradually stir in the hot cream. When it is absorbed, beat in the egg yolks, one at a time. Stir in the celery and shallots with the butter in the pan. Stir in the cheese.

Grease the molds generously with the remaining butter. Fill them to within ¼ inch of the top. Place them in a fairly deep baking pan and add enough hot water to come halfway up the sides of the molds. Bake for 30 to 40 minutes, or until a knife inserted in the molds comes out clean. Run a knife around the edges of the molds and unmold onto a serving platter. Serve with roast meat or baked fish.

VARIATION: Bake in a generously buttered pie dish and serve it from the dish. A much simpler procedure.

DEVILISH POTATOES, PARIOLI ROMANISSIMO
(Patate al Diavolicchio)

6 SERVINGS

6   *medium-size baking potatoes, peeled and thinly sliced*
¼   *cup olive oil or more if needed*
2   *tablespoons butter or more if needed*
1   *teaspoon finely chopped garlic*
2   *hot peppers, very thinly sliced, or 1–2 teaspoons hot red pepper flakes*
½   *teaspoon rosemary*
    Salt and freshly ground pepper to taste

Keep the potato slices in a bowl of cold water until ready to use, then drain and dry them carefully. Heat the oil and butter together in a large pan over medium heat. Sauté the garlic for 1 to 2 minutes, or until golden brown. Add the potatoes, hot peppers, and rosemary. Season with salt and pepper. Sauté for 5 minutes, stirring often. Add a bit more oil and butter if needed. Cover and cook for 5 minutes. Remove the cover and cook for about 15 minutes, turning the potatoes often until they are tender and evenly browned. Serve with Rack of Veal with Rosemary (see page 229) and Green Peas, Roman Style (see page 277).

LEMON POTATOES SAINT-TROPEZ

6 SERVINGS

2   cups onions, thinly sliced
2   tablespoons olive oil
1   teaspoon each salt and freshly ground pepper
1   stick (¼ pound) butter
2   pounds potatoes, peeled and cut into thin uniform
      slices
8   anchovies, chopped
4   tablespoons chopped parsley
    Rind of 1 lemon, grated
    Juice of 1 lemon
1   cup milk

Preheat the oven to 400°.
Sauté the onions in the oil until translucent but not browned.
Season with salt and pepper. Grease a baking dish generously with
butter. Add a layer of potatoes, a layer of onions, and a layer of
anchovies, parsley, and lemon rind mixed together, dotting each layer
with butter. Repeat the process, ending with a layer of potatoes. Pour
the lemon juice and milk over all. Cover with foil, and bake for 1½
hours, or until the potatoes are tender. Remove the foil for the last
15 minutes to brown the potatoes. Serve with poached salmon.

GRATIN OF POTATOES AND TURNIPS
(Gratin de Pommes de Terre et Navets)

6 SERVINGS

1   pound boiling potatoes, peeled
1   pound small white turnips, peeled
1   stick (¼ pound) butter
    Salt and freshly ground pepper to taste
1   cup grated imported Gruyère or Parmesan cheese
⅔   cup beef broth

½   cup Crème Fraîche (see page 151) or ¼ cup each heavy
cream and sour cream whipped together
1   large or 2 small egg yolks

Preheat the oven to 425°.

Cut the potatoes and turnips into slices ⅛ inch thick. Boil them
separately for 5 minutes, drain, and dry them carefully on paper
towels. Use 1 tablespoon of the butter to grease a baking dish 2
inches deep and 10 inches in diameter. Arrange alternating layers of
potatoes and turnips, dotting each layer with butter, seasoning them
with salt and pepper, and sprinkling them with cheese. Reserve
about 2 tablespoons of the cheese.

Bring the broth to a boil and pour it carefully over the potatoes
and turnips. Bake for 1 to 1½ hours, or until the potatoes are tender.
(If the top begins to brown too much, cover it loosely with a sheet
of foil.)

Beat the cream and egg yolks together until well combined. Spoon
them over the top of the potatoes and turnips. Season with a little
salt and pepper and sprinkle with the remaining cheese and butter.
Return the dish to the oven until the top is well browned, or place
it under the broiler, watching carefully so that it does not burn.

Delicious served with Pork Chops, Vineyard Style (see page 247).

SORREL MOLDS

༄

You will need six ¾-cup molds: timbales or custard cups.

6 SERVINGS

2   pounds fresh sorrel or spinach, or 1 pound of each
1   stick (¼ pound) butter
Salt and freshly ground pepper to taste
3   tablespoons finely chopped shallots
1¼   cups freshly made bread crumbs (easily done
in a blender or processor)
6   eggs
2   cups light cream or half-and-half
½   cup freshly grated Parmesan or Gruyère cheese

Preheat the oven to 350°.

Wash and trim the sorrel carefully, discarding the coarse stems. Drain, chop and set it aside. Use 1 tablespoon of the butter to grease the molds. Heat 3 tablespoons of butter in a large pan, add the chopped sorrel and cook, stirring, for a few minutes, just until the sorrel wilts. Season with salt and pepper. Transfer to a large bowl.

Heat the remaining butter in the pan and sauté the shallots for 2 to 3 minutes. Add the bread crumbs and cook, stirring, for another 2 to 3 minutes. Season lightly with salt and pepper. Add to the sorrel and mix well.

Whisk the eggs lightly in a large bowl. Heat the cream for 1 to 2 minutes. Do not let it boil. Whisking constantly, add it to the eggs, then stir in the cheese. Add the sorrel mixture and stir it in well. Fill the molds to within ⅛ inch from the top. Place them in a baking pan and add enough hot water to come halfway up the sides of the molds. Bake for 30 to 35 minutes, or until the custards are set. Run a knife around the edges of the molds and unmold the custards onto a platter. Very fine with roast chicken.

SPINACH, GENOA STYLE
(Spinaci alla Genovese)

ᴄ◡ᴐ

4–5 SERVINGS

2	*pounds fresh spinach*
3–4	*tablespoons olive oil*
1	*clove garlic, peeled*
3	*anchovies, coarsely chopped*
4	*tablespoons chopped fresh parsley*
¼	*cup pine nuts (pignoli)*
¼	*cup raisins, soaked in warm water for a few minutes,* *then drained*
	Salt, pepper, and nutmeg to taste

Trim the spinach, discarding the larger stems. Wash it thoroughly in several changes of water. In a large enamel pot, cook it, covered, over low heat, with only the water clinging to the leaves. Cook until wilted, for 5 to 7 minutes. Drain again. When cool enough to handle, squeeze out as much water as possible, a handful at a time. Set the spinach aside.

Put the oil, garlic, anchovies, and parsley in a large heavy frying pan. Cook over low heat for 2 to 3 minutes. Discard the garlic. Add the spinach, pine nuts, and raisins. Season with salt, pepper, and nutmeg. Mix well. Cook over low heat, stirring often, for 5 to 7 minutes. Serve hot.

VARIATION I: Add 2 to 3 hard-boiled eggs, sliced while warm, and a can of rolled anchovies, drained. Arrange the spinach in a flat layer on a serving platter. Place the slices of egg on top, with an anchovy on each egg slice.

VARIATION II: Add 4 eggs and ¼ cup of grated Parmesan cheese. Spread the spinach in a lightly oiled baking dish. Make four hollows in it with the back of a large spoon. Break an egg into each hollow. Sprinkle with cheese. Bake in a preheated 350° oven till the eggs are set. Serve at once. An excellent dish for lunch.

PURÉE OF SPINACH AND SORREL

4–6 SERVINGS

2 *pounds fresh spinach*
1 *pound fresh sorrel*
4 *tablespoons butter*
3 *tablespoons chopped onions*
   Salt, freshly ground pepper, and nutmeg to taste

Trim the spinach, snapping off the stem ends of the small leaves and removing the stems from the large leaves. Wash carefully in several changes of cold water. Trim the sorrel in the same way, but keep it separate.

Cook the spinach, with just the water clinging to its leaves, in a glass or enamel pot with a cover for about 6 minutes, or until tender but still bright green. Drain immediately. When it is cool enough to handle, squeeze the spinach with your hands to remove as much water as possible.

Cook the sorrel in an enamel or glass pot in 2 tablespoons of the butter, stirring often, for 2 or 3 minutes, or until it has wilted.

Sauté the onions in the remaining butter over low heat for 6 to 7 minutes, stirring often. Do not let them brown.

Purée all the ingredients together in a blender or food processor (using the knife blade) until smooth. Season with salt and pepper and add a generous sprinkling of nutmeg.

Serve hot with grilled salmon slices, swordfish steaks, or roast chicken.

BAKED TOMATOES, ITALIAN STYLE

4 SERVINGS

4   medium-size ripe but firm tomatoes
    Salt and freshly ground pepper to taste
2   tablespoons butter
¼   cup chopped fresh basil leaves
¼   cup freshly grated Parmesan cheese
3   tablespoons olive oil

Preheat the oven to 400°.

Scoop out some of the pulp from each tomato, leaving a thick shell. Chop the pulp coarsely. Sprinkle the inside of the tomato shells with salt and invert them to drain.

Mash together the pepper, butter, basil, tomato pulp, and cheese. Fill the shells with the mixture. Dribble a little oil on each and set them in a lightly oiled baking dish. Bake in the upper third of the oven for 10 minutes, or until the tomatoes are tender but still hold their shape. Serve with an omelet or a chop—or as a separate vegetable course.

VARIATION: For baked tomatoes provençale, fill the shells with the tomato pulp, ¼ cup of bread crumbs, 4 teaspoons of chopped scallions or shallots, and 4 teaspoons of chopped fresh parsley.

TOMATOES À LA CRÈME

⟋⟍

One of the finest and most quickly prepared tomato recipes we know.

2 SERVINGS

2   ripe tomatoes
1   tablespoon butter
1   clove garlic, bruised
2   tablespoons heavy cream
1   tablespoon finely chopped fresh basil or tarragon
    Salt and freshly ground pepper to taste

Cut the tomatoes in half horizontally. Prick the skins in several places with the point of a sharp knife.

Heat the butter and the garlic in a heavy frying pan over medium heat. Sauté the tomato halves, cut side down, for 2 to 3 minutes, pressing them lightly with the back of a spoon to release some of the juice. When the tomatoes are tender but still firm, remove them to a warm serving dish. Discard the garlic. Add the cream and basil to the pan and season with salt and pepper. Cook, stirring constantly, until slightly thickened. Pour the cream over the tomatoes. Serve with broiled steak or veal chops.

TOMATOES AU GRATIN

⟋⟍

4 SERVINGS

4   large ripe tomatoes, thickly sliced
1   clove garlic, put through a garlic press or minced
2   tablespoons finely chopped Italian parsley
¼   cup freshly grated imported Gruyère cheese
    Salt and pepper to taste
    ¼ cup bread crumbs
2   tablespoons butter

Lightly grease a baking dish. Arrange the tomato slices in layers, sprinkling each layer with minced garlic, parsley, grated cheese, salt, and pepper. Sprinkle the top with bread crumbs and dot with the butter. Bake the tomatoes for 15 to 20 minutes in a medium oven until their tops are lightly browned. Or pass them under the broiler for a few seconds. Serve warm.

PURÉED TURNIPS WITH ORANGES

4 SERVINGS

1   *pound small white turnips, peeled and quartered*
2   *shallots, finely chopped*
3–4   *tablespoons butter*
⅓   *unpeeled orange, seeded and coarsely chopped*
1   *teaspoon sugar*
½   *cup milk*
  Salt and freshly ground pepper to taste

Boil the turnips for 8 to 10 minutes, or until tender. While they are cooking, sauté the shallots in 1 tablespoon of the butter, stirring, for 1 minute. Add the chopped orange, sugar, and another tablespoon of butter if needed. Sauté, stirring, for another minute or two.

When the turnips are cooked, drain and return them to the pot. Bring the milk to a boil and add it to the turnips with the remaining butter. Add salt and pepper and mash the turnips until they are creamy. Stir in the shallot-orange mixture. Serve hot with duck or chicken.

VARIATION I: Spread the turnip mixture in a buttered shallow baking dish and bake for 10 to 15 minutes in a preheated 350° oven. Place under the broiler for a minute or two to brown before serving.

VARIATION II: Substitute potatoes for half the turnips.

SHREDDED ZUCCHINI

2 SERVINGS

2   *medium-size zucchini, carefully washed but not peeled*
2   *scallions, white part only*
    Salt and freshly ground pepper to taste
2   *tablespoons butter*

Cut the zucchini to fit the feeder tube of a food processor. Using the pusher, press the zucchini through the shredding disk along with the scallions. (Or grate the zucchini and chop the scallions by hand.) Season with salt and pepper. Sauté in butter over fairly high heat for 3 to 5 minutes. Serve with grilled fish.

SALADS

*It takes four men to dress a salad: a wise man for
the salt, a madman for the pepper, a miser for the
vinegar and a spendthrift for the oil.*

ANON.

*M*aking salads is the most permissive form of cooking.
While it takes strict discipline and classical procedure to
prepare a mousse, a soufflé, or even a good apple pie, when
you invent a salad you can throw restraint—well, almost—
to the winds. "Salad" comes from the old Provençal word
salada, a salted dish. In French slang it means a mixture of
things haphazardly tossed together—in a word, a mess. A
very Parisian example: At a cocktail party in Paris we met
a couple who were old friends of ours. Drowning their
embarrassment in various corners of the room were the
husband's former wife with her new husband, his former
mistress, and two of his present mistresses, one of whom
muttered, *"Quelle salade!"*

Contrary to the human comedy, it would be difficult to
go so far wrong when combining salad ingredients. Even
our preference for 4 tablespoons of oil to 1 tablespoon of

vinegar can be altered if you prefer a sharper taste. The Hungarians, after all, make a delicious cucumber salad with no oil—just vinegar, water, and a little sugar. In Italy, on the other hand, your waiter is apt to pause after pouring the olive oil and ask if you would like *"un po' di aceto,"* as though a little vinegar required a certain daring. Ask for mustard mixed into your vinaigrette and your daring becomes total depravity.

Here are a few shorthand recipes to add to your collection.

For cooked zucchini salad: Cook tomato juice down by half, let it cool and add it to an ordinary vinaigrette.

For any cooked vegetable salad: Cook 2 tablespoons of chopped onion in oil. Add curry powder to taste. Then make an ordinary vinaigrette with the addition of a little diced garlic.

For cauliflower salad: Cook the smallest cauliflower you can find until tender. Leave it whole but separate the florets a little. Add a minced anchovy to a simple vinaigrette and decorate with black and green pitted olives.

For a sauerkraut salad: Rinse the sauerkraut thoroughly. Press out all the water. Add some raisins, broken-up walnuts, quartered hard-boiled eggs, and slices of beets. Moisten with a mustardy vinaigrette.

For a Scandinavian salad: Chop a cup of matjes or Bismarck herring. Add ½ cup of diced cold potatoes that have been boiled in consommé, 2 to 3 cups of diced boiled beets, ½ cup of chopped apple, as much chopped onion as you like, ½ cup of chopped dill pickle, and 6 table-spoons of chopped fresh dill. Dress with a mustardy vinaigrette mixed with a little cream.

For shrimp salad: Add to a mustard mayonnaise some finely chopped, blanched sorrel leaves. Mix the shrimp with this dressing an hour or more before serving.

VINAIGRETTE DRESSING

Like perfumes, salad dressings are chameleon and should be chosen to enhance the particular green they cloak.

Simple Vinaigrette: A delicate Bibb lettuce, meticulously washed and just as meticulously dried will respond to the simplest mixture of 4 tablespoons of olive oil, 1 tablespoon vinegar or lemon juice, salt and freshly ground pepper to taste. Cream can be substituted for the oil in a dressing for cucumber or raw mushroom salads. An interesting version of simple vinaigrette is made by adding a chopped hard-boiled egg and 3 teaspoons of chopped tarragon.

Mustard Vinaigrette: A stronger salad like escarole, chicory, or endive wants a headier dressing: 1 tablespoon Dijon mustard, salt, pepper, 8 tablespoons oil, and 2 tablespoons vinegar. Put the mustard in a small bowl. Add 1 tablespoon of oil and, whisking vigorously, as you would for a mayonnaise, add the rest of the oil in a thin trickle. Stir in the vinegar (shallot vinegar is particularly good).

MAYONNAISE

1½–2 CUPS

3 egg yolks, at room temperature
1 tablespoon vinegar
½ teaspoon salt
½ teaspoon pepper
1 teaspoon dry or prepared mustard
1½ cups olive oil, French peanut oil, or a combination
of both, at room temperature

Rinse a bowl in warm water and dry it. Add the yolks, vinegar, salt, pepper, and mustard and beat until frothy and well blended. Add the oil, drop by drop, beating constantly, until the mixture thickens.

(Stop adding oil every 10 seconds, but continue to whisk vigorously.) Now add the oil in a thin trickle, always whisking. The sauce should now have the consistency of thick cream. Beat in the remaining oil in a slow, steady stream. Add lemon juice, vinegar, or cream if you want a thinner mayonnaise. To prevent curdling, beat 2 tablespoons of boiling water into the mayonnaise. Store the mayonnaise covered tightly with foil.

GREEN MAYONNAISE: Add spinach, watercress, basil, parsley, and tarragon. Blanch all the greens, blend them in a processor and add to the mayonnaise.

SAUCE RÉMOULADE: Add 1 tablespoon Dijon mustard, 1 teaspoon of anchovy paste, chopped *cornichons* (small French pickles), capers, parsley, and tarragon or basil to the mayonnaise when it is finished.

GAZPACHO MAYONNAISE: Combine equal amounts of chopped cucumbers, tomatoes, scallions, and green peppers with enough mayonnaise to bind the chopped vegetables together.

LIGHT MAYONNAISE SAUCE: Miraculously, a light mayonnaise sauce can be made by reversing the usual procedure and adding the egg at the end. Simply make the Mustard Vinaigrette (see preceding page) and then whisk in an egg yolk. Stir vigorously, and those of you who suffer from mayonnaise failure will be rewarded with a fine light version of mayonnaise. Refrigerated, this mayonnaise sauce will thicken somewhat.

ALGERIAN CAULIFLOWER
AND OLIVE SALAD

A pungent aromatic salad.

6 SERVINGS

- 1   *head cauliflower*
- 1   *lemon*
- 1   *cup black olives (Calamata olives are particularly good)*

3–4   tablespoons olive oil
1   teaspoon paprika
1   teaspoon sugar
1   teaspoon cumin powder
   A dash of cayenne pepper
   Salt and pepper to taste

Cook the cauliflower in boiling salted water for about 20 minutes, or until tender but still crisp. Drain, cool, and break it into florets. Cut the lemon in half and, with a grapefruit knife, scoop out all the sections of pulp. Cut the olives in half. Put all the ingredients in a salad bowl. Add the oil and the seasonings. Toss thoroughly and serve as a salad or first course.

ARUGULA AND BEET SALAD

4–6 SERVINGS

1   large bunch arugula
1   bunch beets, trimmed but not peeled, and baked for
   1–1½ hours, or until tender
6   tablespoons olive oil
2   tablespoons wine vinegar
2   tablespoons chopped fresh chives or parsley
   Salt and freshly ground pepper to taste
1   hard-boiled egg, finely chopped

Wash the arugula, dry it thoroughly, and remove the coarse stems. Slice the baked beets and marinate them for 30 minutes in a dressing made by combining the oil, vinegar, chives, salt, and pepper. Add the arugula and the chopped egg. Toss and serve.

French *mâche*, upland cress, or field salad are equally good with beets.

ASPARAGUS CHICKEN SALAD

6 SERVINGS

3 whole chicken breasts, skinned, boned, and trimmed
of tendons and fat

MARINADE

7 tablespoons oil (a mixture of French peanut oil and
olive oil)
4 tablespoons lemon juice
1 medium-size onion, sliced
2 tablespoons mixed fresh or dried herbs, such as thyme,
tarragon, rosemary, chervil, basil, and parsley
1 bay leaf
Salt and freshly ground pepper to taste

24 asparagus tips, about 3 inches long (reserve the stems
for asparagus soup)
1–1½ cups Vinaigrette Dressing (see page 295)

Cut the chicken into rather large cubes and place them in a bowl.
Combine the marinade ingredients. Add them to the chicken, and
mix well. Marinate for 4 hours, or overnight, turning the chicken
from time to time.

Drain the cubes of chicken, discarding the marinade, and cook them
in a steamer over boiling water. Test for doneness after 3 or 4 minutes.
Do not overcook.

Boil or steam the asparagus tips for about 5 minutes, or until they
are tender but still firm and bright green. Drain them thoroughly.

Toss the chicken with half of the vinaigrette dressing and mound
it in the center of a serving platter. Arrange the asparagus around it,
spooning the remaining dressing over it. Serve at room temperature.

AVOCADO–PAPAYA–SHRIMP SALAD

᠀

2 SERVINGS

½ *pound shrimp*
¾ *cup French dressing made with 3 tablespoons wine*
    vinegar, 9 tablespoons olive oil, Dijon mustard,
    salt, and freshly ground black pepper to taste
1 *ripe papaya*
    Juice of 1 lemon
1 *large ripe avocado*
2 *tablespoons chopped fresh chives*

Boil the shrimp for 2 or 3 minutes. Shell them as soon as they are cool enough to handle. Beat the dressing with a whisk until all the mustard is dissolved. Pour ½ cup of the dressing over the shrimp and let them marinate while you prepare the fruit.

Cut the papaya in half lengthwise without peeling it. Discard the the seeds and strings. With a sharp knife, cut lengthwise slices through to the skin. Use a large spoon to detach the slices from the shell. Sprinkle them with half the lemon juice. Prepare the avocado in the same way. Sprinkle with the remaining lemon juice to prevent discoloration.

Arrange the avocado and papaya slices, alternating them, on individual plates and pour the remaining dressing over them. Arrange the shrimp with their dressing around and over the fruit slices. Sprinkle with chives and serve.

VARIATION: Omit the shrimp, make half the amount of French dressing, and serve a colorful avocado-papaya salad before or after a main dish.

SALAD OF BAKED BEETS
AND ONIONS

〜

4–6 SERVINGS

Wash but do not peel 2 or 3 medium-size beets and 2 or 3 onions of the same size. Wrap them in two separate foil packages and bake at 450° for 1 hour, or until tender. (The beets will have to bake much longer than the onions.) Let them cool, peel them, and cut them into slices. Dress them with salt, freshly ground pepper, and 1 part of wine vinegar to 3 parts of olive oil. Sprinkle with chopped fresh parsley or chervil.

ALTERNATE DRESSING: Season the vegetables with salt and pepper to taste. Mix together lemon juice, *Crème Fraîche* (see page 151) or sour cream, and Dijon mustard in the proportion of 2 tablespoons of cream and 1 teaspoon of mustard to the juice of 1 lemon. Mix the dressing with the beets and onions. Top with a tablespoon of chopped fresh tarragon or dill.

BEET AND YOGURT SALAD

〜

4 SERVINGS

2   *large baked beets, peeled, cut into ½-inch cubes, and*
        cooled
1½   *cups yogurt*
½   *teaspoon salt*
½   *cup chopped fresh mint*

Combine all the ingredients in a serving bowl, reserving a third of the mint to decorate the top. Serve cold or at room temperature. Can be eaten as a salad or a relish.

CAIRO CHEESE AND CUCUMBER SALAD

෧෮

3–4 SERVINGS

¾ *pound feta cheese*
   Juice of 1½ lemons
4 *tablespoons olive oil*
2 *tablespoons finely chopped Spanish onion or 4*
      scallions with some of the green, finely chopped
1 *cucumber, peeled and diced*
2 *tablespoons minced green pepper*
1 *tablespoon finely chopped fresh parsley, dill, or basil*
   Freshly ground pepper to taste

With a fork, mash the cheese together with the lemon juice and olive oil. Stir in the onion, cucumber, and green pepper. Sprinkle with the chopped herbs and freshly ground pepper. Chill and serve.

CHINESE CHICKEN SALAD

෧෮

Even if you do not fancy yourself a Chinese cook, we urge you to include this recipe in your repertory.

6 SERVINGS

2 *whole chicken breasts, skin, bones, and tendons*
      removed
2 *chicken bouillon cubes*

SAUCE
2 *tablespoons ground sesame-seed paste (such as Sahedi*
      or Krinos brand)
½ *teaspoon salt*
2 *tablespoons sugar*

½ teaspoon crushed Szechuan hot red peppers (or
 bottled hot red pepper flakes)
2–4 tablespoons chili oil (such as Kame brand)
2 tablespoons light Oriental soy sauce
1 tablespoon rice-wine vinegar or white wine vinegar
1 tablespoon sesame oil (use only the Oriental kind,
 such as Kame brand)

1 head Chinese cabbage or iceberg lettuce
2 cloves garlic, finely chopped
2 tablespoons scallions, finely sliced
1 large bunch fresh coriander (cilantro), available at
 Oriental and Latin greengrocers (reserve a few
 sprigs for garnish and chop the rest)

Place the chicken breasts in a pot just large enough to hold them. Add just enough water to cover. Remove the chicken and add the bouillon cubes. Bring to a boil and mash the cubes with a fork. As soon as the water boils, return the chicken to the pot. Bring back to a boil, then lower the heat to a simmer. (Add some boiling water if needed). Cover and simmer 8 minutes, remove from heat and let the chicken cool in the bouillon for at least 2 or 3 hours before making the salad.

Prepare the sauce. If the oil in the sesame paste has separated and floated to the top, stir with a spoon to mix it in well. Put 2 tablespoons of the paste in a mixing bowl and add 2 tablespoons of warm water. Stir with a wooden spoon until well blended. Add the salt, sugar, crushed peppers, chili oil, soy sauce, vinegar, and sesame oil.

About 30 minutes before serving, remove the chicken breasts from the bouillon. Shred them into strips ½ inch wide. Then shred the cabbage coarsely and spread it on a serving platter. Cover the cabbage with the shredded chicken. Stir the garlic, scallions, and chopped coriander into the sauce and pour over all. Garnish with the coriander sprigs and serve. Really superb!

A SUGGESTED MENU

(see Index for recipes)

CHINESE STEAMED EGGPLANT

CHINESE CHICKEN SALAD

WATERMELON

wine: VERDICCHIO OR CHINESE BEER

CHINESE STRING BEAN SALAD

∾

3–4 SERVINGS

1   *pound fresh young string beans*
½   *teaspoon baking soda*
1   *tablespoon fresh ginger root, peeled and finely*
      shredded, or put through a garlic press
⅓   *cup slivered almonds*

DRESSING

2   *teaspoons mustard powder (Chinese, if available)*
      mixed with ½ tablespoon cold water to make a
      smooth paste
1   *teaspoon sugar*
1   *teaspoon salt*
1   *tablespoon Oriental sesame oil, available in Oriental*
      groceries and in many supermarkets
1½ *tablespoons white vinegar*
1   *tablespoon light soy sauce*

Trim the beans and break them into pieces about 2 inches long. Bring 1 quart of water to a boil, stir in the soda and cook the beans until tender but still very crisp. Drain and rinse them with cold water to stop the cooking. Dry them carefully on paper towels and put them in a serving bowl. Add the ginger root and almonds.

Combine all the ingredients for the dressing and mix thoroughly. Pour over the string beans and toss well. Let the salad rest in a cool place until ready to serve.

FRENCH STRING BEAN SALAD
(Salade de Haricots Verts)

6 SERVINGS

1½ pounds of the freshest, thinnest young string beans
     you can find
Vinaigrette dressing: 1 part wine vinegar to 4 parts
     olive and walnut oil combined
Salt and freshly ground pepper to taste
Garnish: 1 hard-boiled egg and 1 shallot, minced and
     mixed together

String the beans. Boil or steam them for 5 minutes, or until tender but still crisp. Dress them with the vinaigrette and, just before serving, sprinkle the garnish over all.

VARIATION: Cook shelled fresh young lima beans until tender but still crisp. Mound them in the center of a platter and surround them with the darker green string beans. Pour vinaigrette dressing over all. A refreshing combination of color and taste. Superb with cold poached salmon.

A SUGGESTED VEGETARIAN MENU

(see Index for recipes)

RISOTTO WITH WHITE TRUFFLES OR
RISOTTO WITH FENNEL
FRENCH STRING BEAN SALAD
MANGO ICE CREAM
NUT THINS
wine: ORVIETO

COLE SLAW WITH CHERRIES

Marinate finely shredded cabbage and pitted ripe cherries in French dressing for 1 hour, tossing from time to time. Add mayonnaise, salt, and pepper to taste.

RON LEHRMAN'S CUCUMBER SALAD

Peel cucumbers and cut them in half lengthwise. Remove the seeds, then cut the cucumbers into ⅛-inch slices. Salt them and set them aside for 30 minutes. Squeeze them to remove any excess moisture and drain them on paper towels. Marinate them in French dressing for 1 hour, then drain.

Add a little Dijon mustard to mayonnaise. Before serving, dress the cucumbers, using just enough of the mustard-mayonnaise to coat them. Sprinkle them with chopped parsley and serve.

Ron, a great oenophile, is disturbed by the fact that, in France, wine is rarely served with salad because the vinegar in the salad destroys the taste of the wine. His genial solution is to whisk French dressing into an egg yolk, which makes it compatible with wine.

HENRIETTE DE VITRY'S CHICKEN SALAD

6–8 SERVINGS

1   roasted or boiled chicken, boned and cut into large
      dice
3   avocados, peeled and sliced
3   bulbs fennel or 6 stalks celery, diced
3   endives, leaves separated
1   cup coarsely broken walnut meats
12 black olives, pitted and halved
2   tablespoons chopped fresh tarragon (or half parsley,
      half chives)
1   cup Vinaigrette Dressing (see page 295)
    Salt and pepper to taste
1   cup Mayonnaise (see page 295)

Combine all the ingredients except the mayonnaise in a large salad bowl. Set aside for 1 hour, tossing occasionally. Mix the mayonnaise into the salad, correct the seasoning, and serve.

VARIATION: For a low-calorie chicken salad (4–6 servings), use only the chicken, fennel, endives, chopped scallions, and herbs. Season them lightly with salt and pepper and toss them with a dressing made by mixing together a cup of yogurt, the juice of half a lemon, 1 teaspoon of Dijon mustard, and 2 tablespoons of drained capers. Garnish with two quartered tomatoes.

CURRIED RICE SALAD

6–8 SERVINGS AS PART OF AN ASSORTED ANTIPASTO

2   *cups boiled rice (cooked al dente)*
¼   *cup coarsely diced fennel or celery*
1   *roasted green pepper (see page 279), diced*
½   *cup cooked shrimp or drained canned tuna, cut into*
      pieces
6   *pitted black olives, halved*
4   *mushroom caps, thickly sliced*
1   *tablespoon dried currants*
2   *tablespoons each finely chopped parsley and chives*
2   *teaspoons curry powder*
½   *teaspoon cinnamon*
1   *teaspoon Pernod*

VINAIGRETTE SAUCE

6   *tablespoons oil*
2   *tablespoons lemon juice or vinegar*
      A 2-inch ribbon of anchovy paste
      Freshly ground pepper to taste

Put the salad ingredients in a serving bowl. Combine the ingredients for the vinaigrette sauce and beat vigorously. Pour it over the salad and toss lightly but thoroughly.

VARIATION: Cut slices off the tops of 8 ripe tomatoes and save them to use as lids. Remove and discard the pulp. Fill the tomatoes with the curried rice salad. Cover with the lids, and serve at room temperature.

DOUBLE TOMATO TREAT

∽

A salad that can be turned into a soup.

I. TOMATO SALAD

8 SERVINGS

8   *fairly large ripe tomatoes, peeled, seeded, and cut into small wedges*
4   *cups yogurt*
2   *cloves garlic, passed through a garlic press*
    Salt and freshly ground pepper to taste
¼   *cup chopped fresh mint, or more to taste*
¼   *cup chopped fresh dill*
2–4 *tablespoons coarsely chopped walnuts*

Put the tomatoes in a salad bowl. Mix all the remaining ingredients together and pour them over the tomatoes. Toss gently but thoroughly. Chill and serve.

II. TOMATO SOUP

Purée all the ingredients in a food processor. Serve in soup bowls with one or two ice cubes in each bowl. The soup is very low in calories and as refreshing as a cold shower.

NOTE: To take full advantage of this double treat, serve half as a salad with dinner, then process the remainder for lunch the next day.

ENDIVE SALAD WITH ALMONDS

∽

2–4 SERVINGS

¼   *cup blanched whole almonds*
2   *tablespoons slivered almonds*
1   *tablespoon vegetable oil*
½   *teaspoon powdered sugar*

2   *large or 4 small endives*
2   *hard-boiled eggs, sliced*
4   *radishes, thinly sliced*
2   *tablespoons chopped fresh parsley*

DRESSING

6   *tablespoons French peanut oil (or 3 tablespoons each*
        peanut and walnut oil)
2   *tablespoons wine vinegar*
2   *teaspoons Dijon mustard*
    Salt and freshly ground pepper to taste

Put the whole almonds and the slivered almonds in separate pie tins brushed with vegetable oil and toast them in a low oven until golden brown. (Remove the slivered almonds first.) Drain them on paper towels. When cool, grind the whole almonds in a blender or food processor. Stir in the powdered sugar.

Trim the endives and slice them into thin rounds. Put all the salad ingredients in a bowl. Mix the dressing well and pour it over the salad. Toss and serve.

ENDIVE SALAD
WITH WALNUTS AND GRAPES

If you can find the tiny champagne grapes, they are ideal for this salad. The slight bitterness of the endives with the sweetness of the grapes make this the freshest salad imaginable.

4 SERVINGS

2–3 *fairly large endives*
1   *cup ripe seedless grapes, stems removed*
¼   *cup coarsely broken walnut meats*

DRESSING

4   *tablespoons French peanut oil*
2   *tablespoons imported French walnut oil*
2   *tablespoons wine vinegar*
    Salt and freshly ground pepper to taste

Trim the endives and cut them into rounds. Place them in a salad bowl with the grapes and walnuts. Just before serving, mix the dressing well and pour it over the salad. Toss thoroughly.

Excellent with cold roast duck or lamb.

FLEMISH SALAD

In Belgium and Holland, fresh herring is greeted with the same enthusiasm as new Beaujolais in France. If you like herring and potatoes—one of the great European peasant dishes—you will enjoy this salad.

8–10 SERVINGS

1 *large onion, unpeeled*
4 *medium-size potatoes, unpeeled*
Salt and freshly ground pepper to taste
9 *tablespoons olive oil*
3 *tablespoons wine vinegar*
4 *endives*
1 *head chicory*
2–3 *tablespoons chopped fresh chives*
2–3 *tablespoons chopped fresh chervil or dill*
1 *6-ounce jar matjes herring*
3 *radishes, thinly sliced*

Wrap the onion tightly in foil and bake it in a 400° oven for 1 hour, or until tender but still quite firm. Drain, peel, and slice them. Place coarsely.

While the onion is baking, boil the potatoes for about 20 minutes, or until cooked but still quite firm. Drain, peel, and slice them. Place them in a bowl with the chopped onions while they are still warm. Add a pinch of salt, pepper to taste, oil, and vinegar. Toss well and let them sit at room temperature for 1 hour, turning them frequently.

Trim the endives and cut them into rounds. Wash the chicory and dry it well. Save some nice green outer leaves to line the serving platter. Tear the white center leaves into coarse pieces. Add them

along with the endives to the potatoes and onions. Add the chopped
chives and chervil. Mix well. Taste and add more oil, vinegar, salt and
pepper, if needed.

Arrange the green chicory leaves at the bottom of a serving platter.
Mound the salad on them in a dome shape. Drain the herring and
cut it into uniform pieces. Arrange the herring and the sliced radishes
on top of the potato-endive salad.

GREEN SALAD WITH
CHICKEN LIVER DRESSING
(Salade Bourguignonne)

6 SERVINGS

2   *chicken livers, trimmed*
1   *teaspoon Dijon mustard (or a little more to taste)*
1   *tablespoon vinegar*
1   *egg yolk, lightly beaten*
1   *shallot, finely chopped*
    Salt and pepper to taste
3   *tablespoons olive oil*
1   *large or 2 small heads Boston lettuce*

Boil the chicken livers in lightly salted water for 4 to 5 minutes. Drain,
cool, and chop them fine. Put them in a wooden bowl and mash them
to a paste. Dissolve the mustard in the vinegar and add it to the
livers. Add the egg yolk, shallot, salt and pepper. Mix well with a
fork. Continue to mix while you add the oil gradually. Pour over
lettuce or mixed salad greens and toss well. Very appropriate after
a roast chicken.

LEMON-CREAM MUSHROOM SALAD

4–6 SERVINGS

18 *large raw mushroom caps, sliced*
4   *teaspoons lemon juice*

½ teaspoon Dijon mustard
4 tablespoons heavy cream
   Salt and pepper to taste
3 hard-boiled eggs, cut into wedges
1 tablespoon chopped chives

Put the mushrooms in a serving bowl. In another bowl, combine the lemon juice, mustard, cream, salt and pepper. Mix well. Pour this dressing over the mushrooms. Garnish with the eggs and sprinkle with chives.

LENTIL SALAD

6–8 SERVINGS

1 cup dried lentils
1 bay leaf
2 tablespoons finely chopped fresh coriander or tarragon
½ Spanish onion, cut into paper-thin slices, then
       separated into rings (or 4 scallions, finely
       chopped)
   About ½ cup Vinaigrette Dressing (see page 295)

Pick over the lentils, discarding any stones. Put the lentils and the bay leaf in a pot with 3 cups of cold water. Bring to a boil, reduce the heat, and simmer for 30 to 40 minutes, or until the lentils are cooked but still firm. Drain them immediately and put them in a bowl. Add the remaining ingredients while the lentils are still hot. Combine all the ingredients by lifting the lentils from below with two forks in order not to mash them. Serve the lentils cool or at room temperature.

TIP: We often double this recipe, as leftover lentil salad makes one of our favorite soups. Just add 2 cups or more of homemade chicken broth (see page 48) for each cup of leftover salad and purée it all in a blender or food processor. Heat and serve.

LIMA BEAN SALAD

⟡

8 SERVINGS

2½   *pounds fresh lima beans or fava beans, shelled*
2   *teaspoons paprika*
1   *large clove garlic*
1   *bay leaf*
5   *tablespoons oil*
2–3 *tablespoons lemon juice*
       Salt, pepper, and cayenne to taste
3   *tablespoons chopped fresh coriander or parsley*

Put all the ingredients except the coriander in a pot, and add just enough water to cover. Cook over low heat for about 10 minutes until tender. Drain thoroughly. Allow the salad to cool, add the coriander, toss and serve.

MOZZARELLA-TOMATO SALAD

⟡

6–8 SERVINGS AS PART OF AN ASSORTED ANTIPASTO

3   *fairly large ripe tomatoes*
¼   *pound mozzarella cheese*
       Salt and freshly ground pepper to taste
4   *tablespoons olive oil*
1   *tablespoon vinegar*
3   *tablespoons chopped fresh basil or oregano (or 1½*
        tablespoons dried)

Cut the tomatoes and mozzarella into ⅛-inch slices and trim them so that they are the same size. Salt and pepper them. Arrange them on a long narrow dish, alternating and overlapping the tomato and mozzarella slices. Dribble the oil over all and sprinkle with vinegar and basil.

MUSSEL AND CELERY ROOT SALAD

⌒

8–10 SERVINGS

2   *celery roots*
    Juice of 1 lemon
2   *quarts mussels*
4   *tablespoons butter*
4   *shallots, minced*
1   *teaspoon each parsley and thyme*
1   *cup hard cider (available at liquor stores) or ½ cup*
    each apple cider and dry white wine
1   *tablespoon Dijon mustard*
1½ *cups Mayonnaise (see page 295)*
½   *cup mixed herbs, such as parsley, chives, dill, and*
    tarragon
    Salt and pepper to taste

Peel the celery roots and cut them into shoestring strips. Parboil them for 1 minute. Drain and pat them dry. Sprinkle them with the lemon juice.

Scrub the mussels well under cold running water and remove the beards. Place the butter, shallots, parsley, and thyme in a large pot with the cider. Bring to a boil and add the mussels. Cook, covered, over medium heat, shaking the pot occasionally. Remove the mussels as soon as they open. Discard any with broken or unopened shells. Remove the mussels from their shells and let them cool. Carefully avoiding the sediment at the bottom of the pot, spoon out 1 tablespoon of hot mussel liquid into a large bowl, beat in the mustard, then the mayonnaise. Place the celery root and the mussels in a serving bowl, add the mayonnaise and mix well.

Let the salad rest in a cool place until ready to serve. Chop the mixed herbs and stir them into the salad. Taste and correct the seasoning.

A SUGGESTED LUNCH MENU

(see Index for recipes)

MUSSEL AND CELERY ROOT SALAD

WATERCRESS SALAD

STRAWBERRIES AND ORANGES IN MARSALA

GINGER MARMALADE COOKIES

wine: MUSCADET

MUSSEL AND POTATO SALAD
(Salade Françillon)

◦~◦

A great scandal was created by Alexandre Dumas *fils* when a character in one of his plays gave this recipe onstage. Despite the shock to the literary, gourmets in the audience scrambled for their pencils to jot down the recipe. Parisians have been enjoying this extravagant salad ever since.

4–6 SERVINGS

3   *quarts fresh mussels*
1   *pound medium-size potatoes, unpeeled*
¼   *cup champagne or chablis*
     Salt and freshly ground pepper to taste
5   *tablespoons olive oil*
1   *tablespoon white wine vinegar*
1   *cup minced celery*
3   *scallions, white part and a bit of the green, minced*
½–1 *cup Mayonnaise (see page 295)*
1   *black truffle, sliced*
4   *tablespoons chopped fresh chives*

Clean and scrub the mussels well and pull off their beards. Place them in a large pot and add ¼ cup of water. Cook over high heat. Remove the mussels to a platter as soon as they open, and set them aside. Discard any that do not open.

Boil the potatoes for about 30 minutes, or until tender but still firm. Drain them well and spread them out on paper towels. As soon as they are cool enough to handle, peel and slice them into a large bowl. While the potatoes are still warm, add the champagne, salt and pepper, and toss gently so that the potato slices do not break. Add the oil and vinegar and toss gently again.

Remove all but a few mussels from their shells, reserving the unshelled mussels for garnish. Add the mussels, celery, and scallions to the potatoes and toss carefully once again. Keep the salad in a cool place.

When ready to serve, gradually add the mayonnaise, using only enough to bind the ingredients. Add more salt, pepper, or vinegar if desired. Arrange the salad in a serving bowl or platter. Garnish the salad with truffle slices, chopped chives, and a few mussels in their shells.

A SCALLOP SALAD FOR JIM

6⌒⊃

4–6 SERVINGS

1   *pound bay scallops or sea scallops, quartered*
1   *pound asparagus*

DRESSING

1   *shallot*
2   *sun-dried tomatoes (or 1 tablespoon tomato sauce)*
    Juice of 1 lemon
1   *teaspoon Dijon mustard*
    A 1-inch ribbon of anchovy paste
½   *teaspoon hot red pepper flakes*
1   *cup olive oil*
2   *tablespoons walnut oil*

1   *cup white wine*
1   *small green or red pepper, peeled, seeded, and diced*
2–3 *stalks celery, diced*
½   *cup chopped parsley (or dill)*
8   *cherry tomatoes, halved*

Pick over the scallops, discarding any black bits or pieces of shell, but do not wash them. Set them aside.

Steam the asparagus for about 5 minutes, or until they are tender but still firm and bright green. Drain and dry them on paper towels. Cut the tips into 2-inch lengths and the tender part of the stems into 1-inch lengths. Set aside.

Prepare the dressing. Put the shallot, dried tomatoes, lemon juice, mustard, anchovy paste, pepper flakes, and the olive and walnut oils in a food processor with the knife blade. Process until the shallots and tomatoes are finely chopped and the dressing is well combined. (To make by hand, mince the shallot and tomatoes, then whisk in all the remaining dressing ingredients until well combined.)

Bring the wine and 1 cup of water to a boil in a medium-size pot. Add the scallops, lower the heat and simmer, covered, for 2 to 3 minutes. Stir once or twice during the cooking. Drain the scallops well, put them in a bowl, and mix them with the dressing while they are still hot. Add the asparagus, diced pepper, celery, and parsley. Mix carefully but thoroughly. Do not refrigerate. Serve cool or at room temperature garnished with the cherry tomatoes.

TOMATO SALAD
(Salade de Tomates)

᠗

In August and September, when tomatoes are at their sun-ripened best, nothing is better than the classic French *salade de tomates* served as a first course.

8 SERVINGS

4 *large ripe tomatoes (if yellow tomatoes are available,*
  use 2 yellow and 2 red)
1 *small Spanish onion*
6 *tablespoons oil (half olive oil and half French peanut*
  oil)
2 *tablespoons wine vinegar*
  Salt and freshly ground pepper to taste
¼–½ *cup chopped fresh basil, tarragon, or chervil*

Score the bottoms of the tomatoes. Plunge them into a pot of boiling water for 30 seconds. Peel them, trim the stem ends, and cut them into ¼-inch slices with a serrated knife. Arrange the tomatoes in overlapping slices on a large platter.

Peel and slice the onion paper-thin. Separate the onion rings and place them over the tomatoes.

Whisk together the oil, vinegar, salt and pepper. Pour the dressing over the tomatoes 1 hour before serving. Baste the tomatoes with the dressing periodically—three or four times—using a bulb baster. Scatter the chopped herbs over the tomatoes, baste well once again and serve.

For a simple hors d'oeuvre, serve sardines sprinkled with lemon juice and chopped shallots along with the salad.

ZUCCHINI SALAD

8 SERVINGS

2   *pounds zucchini, cut into small cubes*
1   *cup minced onions*
4   *tablespoons French peanut oil*
1   *tablespoon sweet paprika*
1   *large clove garlic, minced*
    Salt and pepper to taste
1   *tablespoon cumin*
2   *tablespoons vinegar*
1   *tablespoon honey*

Put the zucchini and onions in a pot with ¾ cup of water, the oil, paprika, garlic, salt and pepper. Cook over medium heat for 3 to 4 minutes, or just until the zucchini and onions are tender. Remove them with a slotted spoon.

Add the cumin, vinegar, and honey to the water in the pot and reduce by half. Pour this sauce over the vegetables and serve when the salad has cooled.

ZUCCHINI–TOMATO SALAD

~

6–8 SERVINGS AS PART OF AN ASSORTED ANTIPASTO

4   *small zucchini*
    Olive oil
2–3   *ripe plum tomatoes*
    Salt and freshly ground pepper to taste
1   *tablespoon fresh thyme or 1 teaspoon dried*
    A dressing made of 4 parts olive oil to 1 part vinegar,
      with salt and freshly ground pepper to taste

Wash and dry the zucchini carefully. Trim the ends. Cut the zucchini on a slant to make long oval-shaped pieces ¼ inch thick. Fry them in hot oil until nicely browned on both sides. Remove them with a slotted spoon and drain them on paper towels.

Slice the tomatoes. Season the zucchini and tomato slices with salt and pepper and arrange them on a long narrow dish in alternate overlapping slices. Sprinkle them with thyme and pour the dressing over them.

DESSERTS

Do I dare to eat a peach?

T. S. ELIOT,
"The Love Song of J. Alfred Prufrock"

Beulah! Peel me a grape!

MAE WEST,
She Done Him Wrong

The only friends we have who "never touch desserts" are either dedicated dieters or alcoholics. We are neither. In fact, when we look at a cookbook we are apt to turn to the dessert section first. Our interest lies not only in our love of sweets but in the question of how to end a meal. Like the dilemma that confronts the playwright in the third act, it is the problem of the *dénouement*, the right ending, that is difficult to solve. Recently we enjoyed a perfectly prepared and—by nature—heavy cassoulet at a friend's house. A salad followed. But then came the most imperfect of *dénouements*: a chocolate fudge cake sluggishly floating in whipped cream. We, of course, had been wondering if we dared to eat a peach.

The sun has set, or is setting, on rich cakes for dessert. Those sumptuous layered confections have for the most part been relegated to birthday parties, festive holidays,

and trips to Austria. Fruit in all its guises is always a welcome way
to finish a meal. Perfect ripe apricots, peaches, plums, and cherries,
fresh or in a glazed open-faced tart, never disappoint. Nor do sherbets
and ice creams with a cookie or two. We have noticed a sad tendency
to serve three or even four desserts at the same time. It is probably
the influence of that wretched *nouvelle cuisine* invention, the *menu
dégustation*, in which all the dishes the chef makes are trotted out
at once. The palate is hopelessly confused and subtleties of differing
flavors and textures are destroyed. In fact, we have always thought
the *menu dégustation* was appropriate only for the last meal of a
condemned prisoner. Let the rest of us enjoy the desserts that follow,
one at a time.

APPLE CAKE

𝒞𝒱

You will need a 10-inch angel-food-cake pan.

10–12 SERVINGS

2   *eggs*
2   *cups sugar*
1½ *cups vegetable oil*
2   *teaspoons vanilla extract*
1   *tablespoon grated lemon rind*
2   *tablespoons lemon juice*
1   *teaspoon salt*
3   *cups flour*
1¼ *teaspoons baking soda*
1   *teaspoon cinnamon*
3   *cups peeled and freshly grated apples*
2   *cups chopped pecans*
    *Optional garnish: 1 cup heavy cream, whipped until
        stiff with 1 tablespoon Calvados or apple brandy*

Preheat the oven to 325°.
Beat the eggs well in a large mixing bowl. Add the sugar, oil,
vanilla, lemon rind and juice, and salt. Beat until well combined.

Sift the flour before measuring it. Sift it again with the baking soda and cinnamon. Add gradually to the egg mixture, beating thoroughly after each addition until well combined. Stir in the apples and pecans.

Grease the bottom but not the sides of the cake pan with vegetable oil. Flour it lightly and shake out any excess.

Bake for 1½ hours, or until a toothpick inserted in the cake comes out clean.

If you like, pass the Calvados-flavored whipped cream separately or mound it in the center of the cake.

ANKA BEGLEY'S QUICK AND EASY CHOCOLATE CAKE

ᏻᴗᴖ

You will need a 9-inch cake pan with a removable rim and a 2-quart heavy-bottomed saucepan.

8–10 SERVINGS

6 ounces semisweet chocolate morsels or semisweet
   baking chocolate
1 stick (¼ pound) butter, at room temperature
¾ cup sugar
½ teaspoon salt
4 eggs, separated
½ teaspoon baking powder
½ cup flour
   Optional: 1 cup heavy cream, whipped, or 2 cups
      vanilla ice cream

Preheat the oven to 350°.

Butter the bottom and rim of the cake pan. Flour the pan lightly, shaking out any excess. Melt the chocolate in the saucepan over low heat. Stir in the butter and mix until no trace of it is visible. Stir in the sugar and salt, and beat until the mixture is smooth. Remove from the heat and beat in the egg yolks, one at a time. Mix the baking powder and the flour and carefully fold them into the mixture.

Beat the egg whites in a large bowl until stiff. Stir a quarter of the beaten whites into the chocolate mixture until well incorporated. Pour the mixture over the egg whites remaining in the bowl and fold them in lightly and carefully with a spatula.

Pour the batter into the cake pan and bake for 30 minutes. Lower the heat to 250° and bake for 20 to 30 minutes more. Test with a toothpick. (It should come out not quite clean if you like the center of the cake to be rather moist. If you prefer a drier cake, bake until the toothpick comes out clean.)

Cool on a cake rack for 15 minutes. Run a knife around the sides of the cake and remove the rim. With a wide spatula, loosen the bottom of the cake and transfer it to a platter.

If you like, pass whipped cream or softened vanilla ice cream separately.

CHOCOLATE MOUSSE CAKE, MICHEL GUÉRARD
(Marquise Fondante au Chocolat)

෴

The "Marquise" is aptly named. Like a seventeenth-century lady, it is pert, tasty, and—with its surprising coffee sauce—as sophisticated as a Molière heroine. Michel Guérard, who invented *la cuisine minceur*, was kind enough to give us the recipe. Here is our version of this wickedly rich dessert.

You will need a 7-cup loaf pan 9½ by 5½ by 2¾ inches. This dessert must be chilled for 3 hours or more before it is served.

8 SERVINGS

6 *ounces (6 squares) bitter chocolate or semisweet*
8 *medium-size egg yolks*
1¼ *cups sugar*
2 *sticks (½ pound) unsalted butter, softened*
1 *cup unsweetened Dutch cocoa*
2 *cups heavy cream*
¼ *cup (4 tablespoons) confectioners' sugar*

24 double lady fingers (2 packages will usually provide
  as many as you need)
¾ cup boiling water mixed with 5 teaspoons instant
  espresso coffee, then cooled to room temperature

COFFEE CUSTARD SAUCE (SAUCE AUX GRAINS DE CAFÉ)

1¼ cups milk
⅓ cup sugar
1 teaspoon freshly ground coffee beans (medium grind)
3 egg yolks

1 cup heavy cream

Melt the chocolate in a double boiler over simmering water. Remove it from the heat to cool. Whisk the egg yolks and the sugar for a few minutes, or until the mixture lightens in color. When the chocolate is tepid, add the eggs, folding them in until well combined.

In a large bowl, beat the softened butter with a wooden spoon until it is very smooth. Then beat in the cocoa very gradually until no lumps are left. Pour in the chocolate-egg mixture and stir until well combined and uniform in color.

Whip the cream with the confectioners' sugar until stiff. Stir it into the chocolate mixture until no trace of cream is visible.

Separate the lady-finger halves and brush them lightly with the espresso coffee. Line the loaf pan with plastic wrap. Arrange the lady fingers to line first the bottom and then the sides of the pan. (Use scissors to trim the lady fingers if necessary.) Fill the pan with the chocolate-mousse mixture almost to the top, then cover with a layer of lady fingers. Cover with plastic wrap. Place a weight on top of the cake and refrigerate it for 3 hours or overnight.

Meanwhile, prepare the coffee custard sauce. In a heavy-bottomed saucepan, bring the milk and half the sugar to a boil, stirring until the sugar has dissolved. As soon as the milk begins to boil, remove it from heat, add the ground coffee and cover the saucepan. Let the coffee steep in the milk for 15 minutes.

Put the egg yolks and the remaining sugar in a bowl and whisk together for a few minutes, or until the eggs lighten in color. Gradually pour the milk into the eggs, whisking constantly. Pour the mixture back into the saucepan. Cook over low heat, stirring slowly and steadily with a wooden spoon for 6 to 8 minutes, or until the custard coats the spoon. (The French test for custard: Run your finger across the back of the spoon—if your finger's track remains visible, the custard is ready and will thicken properly as it cools.)

Pour the custard into a bowl to cool (without straining it, as the ground coffee gives this sauce its special texture). Stir the sauce from time to time. When it is cool, refrigerate it.

Remove the weight and plastic wrap on top of the cake. Cover the cake with an inverted platter, then holding the platter and the pan firmly together, invert them. Carefully lift off the pan and peel off the plastic wrap. Whip the cream until stiff and, with a pastry bag, pipe rosettes on the top and around the bottom of the cake. Or spread the cake with the whipped cream. Pass the coffee sauce separately.

ELIZABETH TORSTENSON'S ICE CREAM CAKE

⟅∼⟆

Elizabeth Torstenson is the best Swedish cook we know. This confection, one of her finest accomplishments, is a sterling example of her light hand. A delicate three-tiered oatmeal cake, it is filled with layers of coffee ice cream and served with hot chocolate sauce. We like to fill it with our own cappuccino ice cream, a soft ice cream that is easy to make and easy to spread.

When ripe berries are in season, Mrs. Torstenson fills the cake with layers of sweetened raspberries or strawberries mixed into whipped cream and serves it with Raspberry Sauce (see page 383).

8–10 SERVINGS

¾ cup quick-cooking oats
6 tablespoons butter
⅔ cup sugar
1 tablespoon flour
1 teaspoon baking powder
1 egg, lightly beaten
   Cappuccino Ice Cream (see page 380) or 1 quart good
      coffee ice cream
2 tablespoons confectioners' sugar

Hot Chocolate Sauce

1   *cup dark brown sugar*
½   *cup granulated sugar*
    A pinch of salt
2   *squares unsweetened chocolate*
1   *tablespoon unsweetened cocoa*
1   *tablespoon instant espresso coffee*
⅔   *cup milk*
1   *tablespoon butter*
1   *tablespoon corn syrup*
2   *teaspoons brandy or vanilla or 1 teaspoon of each*

Preheat the oven to 400°.

Put the oats in a bowl. Melt the butter and stir it in until well mixed. Add the sugar. Mix the flour and baking powder together and stir them in. Add the egg and mix until well combined.

Line three baking sheets with kitchen parchment paper (which needs no oiling). Use an 8- or 9-inch pie pan to draw circles on each baking sheet. Spread a third of the batter very thinly and evenly to fill in each circle. (Do not be alarmed if there are a few small holes, as the batter will spread during baking.)

Bake the cakes for about 8 minutes, or just until they are lightly browned, and remove them immediately. Carefully slide the parchment paper with the cakes off the baking sheets and onto cake racks to cool. As soon as they are cool and crisp, carefully use a spatula to separate them from the paper and set them back on the racks.

To assemble, put one cake, flat side down, on a round platter. Spoon half a quart of the cappuccino ice cream or softened coffee ice cream over it. With a spatula, gently spread it to make an even layer. Cover it with the second cake and the remaining ice cream. Top with the third cake. Sprinkle generously with confectioners' sugar. Carefully wrap the cake in foil and put it in the freezer immediately.

Prepare the hot chocolate sauce. Put all the ingredients except the brandy and vanilla in a heavy saucepan. Cook, stirring, over low heat until the chocolate melts. Raise the heat and boil, covered, for 2 minutes. Remove the cover and cook until a little of the mixture dropped into cold water forms a soft ball. Remove from heat, add the brandy and vanilla, and beat vigorously for 1 to 2 minutes.

About 15 minutes before you are ready to serve, place the sauce over simmering water in a double boiler to reheat, and remove the cake from the freezer. At the table, pass the hot chocolate sauce separately.

MERINGUE SHELL
WITH LEMON FILLING

❦

A most festive dessert for gala occasions. You will need 2 large baking sheets, kitchen parchment paper to line them, and a pastry bag fitted with a no. 5 star tube.

ABOUT 16 SERVINGS

Lemon Curd (see next page)
6   egg whites, 4 in one bowl, 2 in another
½   teaspoon cream of tartar
1½ cups sugar divided into 2 bowls, a cup of sugar in one,
        half a cup in the other
1½ cups heavy cream

Prepare the lemon curd and refrigerate it until you are ready to use it.

Preheat the oven to 225°. Cut two pieces of parchment paper to fit your baking sheets exactly. Draw two 9-inch circles on one sheet and one on the other.

Beat 4 egg whites with half the cream of tartar in an electric mixer until soft peaks form when the beaters are lifted. Continue to beat while you gradually add 1 cup of sugar. Beat until stiff peaks form.

Put a dab of the meringue mixture near the four corners of each baking sheet. Place the sheets of parchment paper on the baking sheets, pressing down on the bits of meringue to glue the paper into place.

Fill the pastry bag with the meringue and pipe a 9-inch ring just inside one of the circles. Fill in the ring with a continuing spiral of meringue. (This will serve as the base of the meringue shell.) Inside the other two circles pipe 9-inch rings about ¾ inch wide. Use the remaining meringue to pipe rosettes for decoration. Bake for about 45 minutes. Turn off the heat, but leave the meringues to dry in the oven with the door closed for another 45 minutes. Set the meringues on racks to cool for a few minutes. Carefully peel the paper off.

Preheat the oven to 225° again. Following the same procedure, make a second batch of meringue with the remaining 2 egg whites, cream of tartar, and sugar. Line one of the baking sheets with fresh parchment paper. Set the base (the baked circle of meringue) on the paper. Fill the pastry bag with the new meringue mixture and pipe a ¾-inch ring on the outer rim of the meringue base. Set one of the baked meringue circles on top of it. If it cracks or breaks, it can be glued together with a little fresh meringue. Repeat the process, piping a circle of fresh meringue around the edge and placing the remaining meringue on top. Finally, pipe one more circle of fresh meringue and set the rosettes on it. Fill in any empty spaces along the sides with meringue.

Bake the completed shell for 30 minutes. Turn off the heat and leave it in the oven for a few hours or overnight.

Shortly before serving, whip the cream until stiff. Fill the meringue shell with the lemon curd. Spoon or pipe some of the whipped cream over it. Keep in a cool place but do not refrigerate. Serve with the remaining whipped cream passed separately.

LEMON CURD

Use as the filling for Meringue Shell with Lemon Filling (see preceding page), small individual meringue shells, tarts, or layer cakes. Leftover lemon curd keeps well in the refrigerator.

You will need a 2-quart heavy saucepan and a wooden spoon.

ABOUT 2 CUPS

6   large lemons
10 egg yolks
1   cup sugar
1   stick (¼ pound) sweet butter, cut into 8 slices, plus
     2 tablespoons butter

Soak the lemons in hot water to cover for 20 minutes. Dry them well and roll them, pressing down heavily with your hands. Grate the rind of two of the lemons into a medium-size bowl, avoiding all the white pith. Juice all the lemons, stir the juice into the rind and set aside.

Put the egg yolks and sugar in the saucepan. Cook over low heat, stirring with a wooden spoon until they are well combined. Stir in the lemon juice and rind. Add the slices of butter one at a time. Cook, stirring constantly to prevent sticking, until the mixture is thick enough to coat the spoon. Test by running your finger along the bowl of the spoon. If it leaves a visible trace, the lemon curd is ready. Transfer it to a bowl. Dot with the 2 tablespoons of butter to prevent a skin from forming on the surface. When it is cool, refrigerate it until ready to use.

PRALINE ICE-BOX CAKE

We are sentimental about this cake, which we often make for our friends' birthdays. In fact, they always call it Bobby and Arthur's Birthday Cake. Invented for Julia Child, we refer to it as Julia's Cake, and dedicate it to that delicious woman.

Both the praline powder and the chocolate icing can be made well in advance and stored in the refrigerator or freezer. Bring them to room temperature before using them. The filling, however, should be prepared and the cake assembled about 6 hours before serving time.

You will need a 9- or 10-inch springform pan with a removable rim 3 inches high.

16 SERVINGS

CHOCOLATE ICING

4 *ounces unsweetened baking chocolate*
1 *stick (¼ pound) sweet butter*
2½ *cups confectioners' sugar*
1 *egg yolk*
2 *tablespoons unsweetened cocoa*
2–4 *tablespoons powdered instant espresso coffee, to taste*
2–4 *tablespoons kirsch or rum*

FILLING

2 *sticks (½ pound) sweet butter*
2 *cups confectioners' sugar*

8   egg yolks
2   tablespoons kirsch, or more to taste
2   teaspoons vanilla
1   tablespoon powdered instant espresso coffee
2   cups heavy cream

Kirsch to taste
4   dozen lady fingers
¼   cup apricot, peach, or cherry jam
1   cup Praline Powder (see next page), prepared ahead
       of time and refrigerated
1   cup heavy cream

Icing: Melt the chocolate in the top of a double boiler and let it cool. Cream the butter and sugar together with an electric mixer until very smooth. Add the egg yolk, cocoa, powdered coffee, and 2 tablespoons of kirsch, beating until well blended. Then beat in the chocolate until well blended. (If made in advance, bring to room temperature before using.) Add a little more kirsch if needed, so that the icing will spread easily.

Filling: Beat the butter and sugar together until very smooth. Beat in the egg yolks one at a time. When well blended, gradually add the kirsch, vanilla, and powdered coffee, beating until well absorbed. In a separate bowl, whip the cream until stiff. Fold the whipped cream into the mixture. Taste and add more kirsch if desired.

To assemble the cake: About 6 hours before serving time, line the springform pan with foil or plastic wrap. Press it against the sides and bottom of the pan, allowing enough foil to hang over the sides so that you can fold it back later to cover the cake.

Pour in a shallow platter equal amounts of kirsch and water, about 2 tablespoons of each. Separate the lady fingers, so that you have strips of six connected tops and six connected bottoms. Dip each strip, flat side down, into the kirsch-water mixture for a few seconds so that it becomes moist but not wet. Press the lady fingers against the sides of the pan, flat sides out. (If they stick out above the top of the pan, they can be trimmed later with scissors.) Add more kirsch and water to the platter as needed, and continue dipping the lady fingers in the mixture before lining the bottom of the pan with them, flat sides down. Any gaps should be filled in with broken pieces of moistened lady fingers. The sides and bottom of the pan must be completely lined.

Put half the filling in the lined pan, spreading it evenly. Sprinkle with half the praline powder and dot with half the jam. Repeat the process: a layer of moistened ladyfingers, then a layer of the remaining filling, sprinkled with the remaining praline powder and jam. Press a final layer of moistened lady fingers on top, this time flat sides up. Fill in any gaps. Trim the lady fingers along the sides of the cake with scissors so that the top of the cake is even. Fold the overhanging foil to cover the top completely. Use more foil if needed. Set the cake in the refrigerator with a plate on top of it for 4 hours.

To decorate the cake: The icing must be at room temperature. Remove the cake from the refrigerator and carefully peel back the foil from the top of the cake. Invert the cake onto a round cake plate at least 2 inches wider than the cake. Carefully remove the springform pan and the foil. Whip the cup of cream until stiff. Spread it evenly on the top and sides of the cake, using a spatula to make it as smooth as possible.

Decorate the cake with icing in any way you wish. With a pastry bag and decorating tube, you can write loving messages or simply make rosettes and ribbons of chocolate icing. The cake should then be returned to the refrigerator for the icing to set. Remove it from the refrigerator about 30 minutes to 1 hour before serving. Prepare yourself for cheers and applause.

PRALINE POWDER

Praline powder is very useful to have on hand. Placed in a tightly covered jar, it can be stored in the refrigerator for days or in the freezer for months. Delicious in icings and over ice cream. Essential for our praline ice-box cake.

You will need a shallow metal baking pan, such as a jelly-roll pan.

ABOUT 2 CUPS

2 *cups sugar*
⅔ *cup water*
½ *teaspoon cream of tartar*
2 *cups blanched almonds*

Butter the baking pan and set it aside.

Combine the sugar, water, and cream of tartar in a pot with a heavy bottom. Stir until the mixture comes to a boil. Add the almonds. Cook without stirring until the almonds are lightly browned and the syrup is golden brown. Pour it into the pan to cool. (It does not have to cover the pan entirely.) Spread it with a spatula to about a ¼-inch thickness. When it is cool and hard, break it into pieces. (You now have praline, or almond brittle, a confection that can be eaten like peanut brittle.)

To make praline powder for Praline Ice-box Cake (see page 328), grind a few pieces of praline at a time in a food processor with the knife blade until they are coarsely chopped. (There should be some ¼-inch pieces.)

To make a more finely ground praline powder, simply process the praline until it is pulverized. It is useful in butter creams to fill and ice cakes.

RICE CAKE

ᔕᔕ

Wonderful for large parties. You will need a 12-inch springform pan with a removable rim 2½ inches high.

16–18 SERVINGS

6½	cups milk
1½	cups rice
	A pinch of salt
1	cup sugar
4	eggs, separated
½	cup finely chopped blanched almonds
	Grated rind of 2 lemons and ½ orange
½	cup currants
1	teaspoon almond extract
1	teaspoon vanilla
½	cup dry bread crumbs
5	tablespoons Grand Marnier, or more to taste
½	cup confectioners' sugar
	Optional: 1 cup heavy cream

Preheat the oven to 350°.

Bring the milk to a boil in a heavy pot. Stir in the rice, salt, and half the sugar. Simmer for about 15 minutes, or until the rice is almost tender. Remove it from heat and set it aside to cool.

In a large bowl, beat the egg yolks with the remaining sugar. Add the rice, almonds, the lemon and orange rind, currants, almond extract, and vanilla. Beat the egg whites until stiff and fold them gently into the rice mixture.

Butter the cake pan, coat it with the bread crumbs and fill it with the rice mixture. Bake for about 1½ hours, or until the top is nicely browned. Remove from the oven and let it cool in the pan. Make holes in the cake with a toothpick and pour the Grand Marnier over it.

The rice cake should sit for a few hours or, better still, overnight. Dust it with confectioners' sugar just before serving. Or whip the cream until stiff with the confectioners' sugar and spread it over the cake. Excellent accompanied by sliced fresh peaches or stewed fruit.

HUNGARIAN PANCAKES
(Palacsinta)

სა

You will need a 7- or 8-inch pan with sloping sides and a pastry brush.

6–7 SERVINGS (12–14 PANCAKES)

1   *cup milk*
2   *large or 3 medium-size eggs*
1¼ *cups flour*
¼   *teaspoon salt*
1   *teaspoon sugar*
½   *cup beer (do not open the beer until you need it)*
    About 1 stick (¼ pound) butter, melted
1   *tablespoon kirsch or rum*
1½ *cups apricot jam*
½–¾ *cup finely chopped walnuts*

Mix the milk, eggs, flour, salt, and sugar in a blender or food processor or by hand until smooth. Set the batter aside for 1 to 2 hours. When ready to make the pancakes, stir in the beer. Set the pan over medium-low heat and brush it with melted butter. When the butter is hot, pour in 2 to 2½ tablespoons of batter, tilting the pan quickly to coat the bottom with as thin a layer as possible. When bubbles appear in the top of the pancake, turn it over. Fry each pancake until it is very lightly browned on both sides. Remove it at once to a platter and keep warm, loosely covered with foil, in a low oven. Repeat the process until all the batter is cooked.

Stir the kirsch into the apricot jam. If the jam is lumpy, force it through a sieve or purée it in a food processor. Spoon about 1½ tablespoons of jam down the center of each pancake, then roll it up. Arrange the rolled pancakes side by side on the platter and keep them warm, loosely covered with foil, until ready to serve. Serve hot sprinkled with chopped walnuts.

AUSTRIAN PANCAKES, ALEXIS GREGORY
(Kaiserschmarrn)

One of the greatest desserts of Vienna, a city famous for its sweets. Named in honor of Emperor Franz Joseph I.

You will need one or two 8-inch omelet pans with sloping sides.

6–8 SERVINGS

⅔   *cup dried currants or raisins*
½   *cup brandy, Grand Marnier, or Calvados*
2   *cups milk*
4   *eggs, separated*
2   *tablespoons sugar*
½   *teaspoon salt*
1   *cup flour*
1½   *sticks (12 tablespoons) butter, melted*
1   *cup confectioners' or granulated sugar*

Soak the currants in the brandy for 30 minutes. Drain them. Set the currants and the brandy aside in separate bowls.

Put the milk, egg yolks, sugar. and salt in the container of a food processor or blender. Add the flour and process until the batter is smooth. (To make the batter by hand, beat these four ingredients together until smooth. Add the flour ½ cup at a time and beat until smooth.) The batter should have the consistency of heavy cream. Beat the egg whites until stiff. Carefully pour the batter over them and gently fold the egg whites into the batter with a rubber spatula until no whites are visible.

For each pancake, brush just enough of the melted butter to cover the bottom of an omelet pan and set the pan over medium-low heat. (Once you have made this recipe you will find that you can easily do two batches at once, using two pans.) Add enough batter to cover the bottom of the pan by ¼ inch. Cook over low heat for 3 to 4 minutes, or until the pancake has puffed up a little. Test by lifting the sides of the pancake with a spatula. When the bottom is lightly browned, slide it onto a plate. Brush the pan with a little melted butter. As soon as it is hot, invert the pancake into the pan and cook the other side until lightly browned. With two forks, tear it into eight irregular pieces and transfer them to a warmed serving platter and keep them warm in the oven while you cook the rest of the batter in the same way.

When all the pancakes have been cooked and torn apart, heat 3 to 4 tablespoons of the butter in a large frying pan. Add the pancakes and the currants. Sprinkle with 8 tablespoons of confectioners' sugar and cook over low heat, stirring and lifting the pieces with a spatula until they are all lightly coated with sugar and butter. Warm the brandy in the omelet pan, then carefully ignite it with a match. Pour the flaming brandy over the pancakes. When the flames die down, transfer everything to the warm serving platter, sprinkle generously with sugar, and serve at once.

These pancakes are delicious served alone or, as is often the case in Vienna, accompanied by a plum or other fruit compote. We sometimes serve it with tart apple slices lightly sprinkled with sugar and sautéed in butter. In that case, we use apple brandy (Calvados) in the preparation and the flambéing of the pancakes.

One of our favorite menus: Whitebait Provençal (see page 144), Sausages with Mushrooms (see page 250), and these wonderfully light Austrian pancakes.

RUSSIAN CHEESE PANCAKES
FOR GENIA

❧

You will need a pan with sloping sides and a spatula.

ABOUT 20 SMALL PANCAKES

BATTER

1   *stick (¼ pound) butter, melted*
1   *7½-ounce package farmer cheese or 1 cup dry pot cheese*
2   *eggs, lightly beaten*
1   *tablespoon sugar*
¼   *teaspoon salt*
½   *cup buttermilk or sour cream*
¼   *cup flour*

GARNISHES

1   *cup granulated sugar*
1   *cup sour cream*
1   *cup strawberry jam*

Set aside all but 1 tablespoon of the melted butter to use for frying. Put 1 tablespoon of melted butter in a bowl or food processor, add all the other ingredients, and mix until the batter is smooth.

Set the pan over medium-low heat and brush it with melted butter. When the butter is hot, drop in the batter by rounded tablespoonfuls widely spaced. Fry until bubbles appear in the tops of the pancakes. Turn them and cook a few seconds longer, or until the pancakes are browned on both sides. Keep them warm on a platter in a low oven until all the pancakes are ready.

Serve hot, sprinkled generously with sugar. Pass sour cream and strawberry jam separately.

FOOD PROCESSOR COOKIES

If you can turn your food processor on, you can make the cookies
that follow. They are as good to eat as they are simple to prepare.
Do not hesitate to add cinnamon, grated lemon peel, ground cloves, or
a bit of mace to any of these cookies if you are so inspired.

A great boon in recent years is the easy availability of kitchen
parchment paper. Cookie sheets lined with it require no greasing or
flouring.

BUTTER COOKIES

∽

ABOUT 36 COOKIES

¼　cup shelled almonds
2½　cups flour
2½　sticks (1¼ cups) cold butter, cut into ¼-inch slices
½　cup sugar
1　teaspoon vanilla
1　teaspoon finely grated lemon rind
1　teaspoon lemon juice
　About 1 cup apricot preserves

Preheat the oven to 350°.

Place the almonds in the container of a food processor with the
knife blade. Process for a few seconds, or until the nuts are ground.
Add all the other ingredients except the apricot preserves, and process
for 10 to 20 seconds, or until the dough is smooth. Refrigerate for
30 minutes.

Roll tablespoonfuls of dough into walnut-size balls. Press the center
of each ball with the tip of your finger to make a small depression,
and fill it with a bit of the apricot preserves. Bake on cookie sheets
lined with kitchen parchment paper for about 15 minutes, or until
the cookies are golden brown. Put the cookie sheets on cake racks to
cool. When the cookies are firm, remove them and put them directly
on the cake racks.

NUT THINS

ᖰᘯ

ABOUT 36 COOKIES

¼ cup sugar
1¼ cups shelled nuts (almonds, walnuts, or pecans)
    A pinch of salt
½ stick (4 tablespoons) cold butter

Put all the ingredients in the container of a food processor with the knife blade. Process until the nuts are ground and the batter forms a mass.

Shape the mixture into a roll on a sheet of waxed paper and roll it up. Refrigerate it until it is firm, or freeze it until you want to use it.

When ready to bake, defrost the batter if it has been frozen. Preheat the oven to 325°. Unwrap the roll while it is still cold and firm. Cut it into ⅛-inch slices. Place them four inches apart (as they spread during baking) on cookie sheets lined with kitchen parchment paper. Bake for 10 minutes, or until lightly browned. Cool on cake racks until firm. Remove the paper and cool the cookies again on racks. Store in airtight containers.

PECAN CARAMEL SANDWICHES

ᖰᘯ

24 SANDWICH COOKIES

1⅓ cups shelled pecans
1½ cups flour
2 sticks (½ pound) frozen butter
½ cup confectioners' sugar
½ teaspoon salt

CARAMEL FILLING

1¼ cups brown sugar
½ cup granulated sugar

1   tablespoon corn syrup
⅓   cup cream
    Ground pecans (the half portion reserved after
        processing the shelled pecans)
2   teaspoons bourbon

Grate the pecans in a food processor with the knife blade until finely ground. Pour into a bowl and divide into two equal parts, one half to be used for the cookies and the other half for the filling.

Without washing the food processor, place the flour in it. With a hot knife, cut the frozen butter into 16 slices and distribute them evenly over the flour. Process, on and off, for about 10 seconds, or until the mixture resembles coarse meal.

Add the sugar, salt, and half of the ground pecans. Process again, using the on-and-off pulse method, until the ingredients are well combined. It is important not to process the dough too long. To test, stop the machine and pinch some of the dough together with your fingers. If it sticks together, it is ready. If not, process it for a few seconds longer. Transfer the dough to a bowl and gather it together to form a large loaf-shaped mass. Divide the dough into four equal parts. Roll into balls, wrap them in waxed paper and chill them in the freezer for 10 to 15 minutes.

Preheat the oven to 375°. Roll out each portion of dough between two sheets of waxed paper to a thickness of ¼ inch. Cut into 12 rounds with a small cookie cutter. Bake on cookie sheets lined with kitchen parchment paper for 10 to 12 minutes, or until the cookies are browned around the edges. As each batch of cookies is baked, remove the cookie sheet to a cake rack to cool. As soon as the cookies are firm, carefully remove them from the cookie sheets with a metal spatula and place them directly on cake racks.

To make the filling, combine all the ingredients except the bourbon in a heavy-bottomed saucepan. Cook over low heat until a little of the mixture dropped into cold water forms a soft ball. Remove the saucepan from the heat and beat the filling until it cools and thickens somewhat. Beat in the bourbon. If the filling becomes too thick to spread, it can be thinned by beating in another teaspoon of bourbon or cream.

Spread the flat side of half the cookies with a thin layer of caramel filling not quite to the edges. Cover them with the remaining cookies, flat side down.

WALNUT ROLLS

❧

ABOUT 48 SLICES

PASTRY

2½ cups flour
2   sticks (½ pound) butter, cut into 16 slices
½   teaspoon cinnamon
1   egg, lightly beaten
⅓   cup milk

FILLING

¼   cup shelled walnuts
1   tablespoon candied orange peel
2   tablespoons raisins
1   teaspoon cinnamon
6   tablespoons sugar

GLAZE

1   egg, lightly beaten
½   cup sugar

Place all the pastry ingredients in a food processor fitted with a steel blade. Process for a few seconds, until a ball forms. (Some bits of butter should still be visible.) Divide the dough into four equal parts. Roll them into balls, wrap each one tightly, and refrigerate for 4 hours or overnight.

Place all the filling ingredients in the food processor. Process until coarsely chopped. Set aside.

Preheat the oven to 375°.

Roll out each ball of dough on a lightly floured board into a rectangle 10 or 12 inches by 5 or 6 inches. The dough should be no thicker than ¼ inch. (A little thinner would be even better.)

Sprinkle one-quarter of the filling on each rectangle, leaving a 1-inch border all around. Roll it up like a jelly roll and pinch the ends to seal the dough. Arrange the rolls seam side down.

Brush the rolls with the beaten egg, sprinkle them with sugar and transfer them to a buttered cookie sheet or a sheet lined with kitchen parchment paper. Bake each roll (two rolls will fit on a large cookie sheet) for 30 minutes, or until well browned. Cool on cake racks. Cut the rolls into slices and serve.

ALMOND CRISPS

You will need a 15½- by 10½-inch jelly-roll pan. Must be prepared a day in advance but will keep for several days.

32 LARGE OR 64 SMALL BARS

DOUGH

6   *tablespoons butter*
¼   *cup sugar*
1   *large egg yolk*
     Grated rind and juice of ½ lemon
½   *teaspoon vanilla*
1⅓   *cups flour*
2   *tablespoons heavy cream*

TOPPING

¾   *cup plus 2 tablespoons sugar*
¾   *cup slivered almonds*
4   *large egg whites*
½   *teaspoon each powdered ginger and cinnamon*

Preheat the oven to 375°.

Cream the 6 tablespoons of butter with the sugar until light in color. Add the egg yolk, lemon rind, juice, and vanilla. Beat until fluffy. Gradually stir in the flour and mix until well combined. Work in the cream and gather the dough into a ball.

Butter the jelly-roll pan or line it with kitchen parchment paper. Lightly flour your fingers and the heel of your hand, and press the dough into the pan to make a very thin even layer. Bake for 12 to 15 minutes. Remove the partially baked cookie base to cool, but leave the oven heat on.

Cook all the ingredients for the topping in a heavy saucepan over medium heat, stirring constantly, until the mixture comes to a boil. Let it boil for a minute or less. Remove it from heat as soon as it is a pale gold color. Pour it over the partially baked dough, spreading it evenly to cover the dough.

Return the cookie sheet to the 375° oven for 45 minutes, or until the topping is golden brown. Remove it from the oven and mark the topping with a sharp knife to indicate 4 bars across and 8 bars down for large bars or 8 bars across and down for small ones. Let the almond crisp harden for a day before you cut it. Use a sharp knife and lift the bars out with a spatula.

BETTY VREELAND'S COSMIC COOKIES

❧

ABOUT 36 COOKIES

1 *stick (¼ pound) butter, softened*
½ *cup plus 1 tablespoon sugar*
1 *egg, lightly beaten*
1 *teaspoon vanilla*
¾ *cup flour*

Preheat the oven to 400°.

With a wooden spoon, mix the butter and sugar together thoroughly; stir in the egg and vanilla. Add the flour and stir until well combined. Chill the batter in the refrigerator for 30 minutes. (It can be frozen until ready to use and then defrosted until soft but still cold.) Drop by teaspoonfuls at least 4 inches apart on a buttered cookie sheet and bake for about 7 to 10 minutes or until browned around the edges but still pale in the center. Remove at once with a spatula. Cool on cake racks. Store in airtight metal containers until ready to serve.

VARIATIONS: Stir 4 tablespoons of grated almonds into the batter. Or substitute 1 teaspoon of lemon juice for the vanilla and add the grated rind of a lemon to the batter.

LEMON SQUARES FOR ANNIK

ᕙᓫ

You will need two cookie sheets, 10 by 13 inches, with no rim on at least one side. One of our absolute favorite cookies.

MAKES 20 SANDWICH COOKIES

½   *pound butter*
⅞   *cup (1 cup minus 2 tablespoons) superfine sugar*
2   *egg yolks, at room temperature*
1   *teaspoon grated lemon rind*
1   *teaspoon vanilla*
2¼ *cups flour*
    Lemon Curd (see page 327)
½   *cup confectioners' sugar*

Preheat the oven to 375°.

Cream the butter and sugar together by hand or in an electric mixer. Mix until well combined. Add the egg yolks, lemon rind, and vanilla, and beat until well mixed. Add the flour gradually. Beat until it is thoroughly mixed in.

Divide the dough into two parts. Roll on a lightly floured board and then shape into rectangles about 8 by 10 inches. Butter two cookie sheets and transfer the dough to them. Roll each rectangle of dough out again, as evenly as possible, until it completely covers the cookie sheet. (Start from the middle and roll out in all directions, taking care of the corners. The edges should be as high as the rest of the dough. If necessary, push the edges back in with a knife to make an even rectangle.)

Bake for about 10 minutes, or just until very lightly colored around the edges. Remove each sheet from the oven and cut immediately into 20 squares.

Let them cool on the cookie sheets for 2 to 3 minutes. Then carefully remove them with a metal spatula to racks to cool and become firm.

Spread half the squares with lemon curd and top with the remaining squares. Sprinkle with confectioners' sugar.

VARIATION: Softened Chocolate Icing (see page 328) or Caramel Filling (see page 337) can be used in place of the lemon curd to make delicious chocolate or caramel squares.

LEMON TILES
(Tuiles au Citron)

❧

ABOUT 20 COOKIES

½   *cup sugar*
¼   *teaspoon lemon extract*
2   *egg whites*
5   *tablespoons flour*
4   *tablespoons butter, melted*
⅓   *cup ground blanched almonds*
    Rind of 1 lemon, grated
½   *cup slivered almonds*

Preheat the oven to 425°.

In a bowl, whisk the sugar, lemon extract, and egg whites for 1 to 2 minutes, or until foamy. Add all the remaining ingredients except the slivered almonds and mix gently.

Lightly butter three cookie sheets or line them with kitchen parchment paper. Drop the batter by half-teaspoonfuls at least 4 inches apart on the cookie sheets. Flatten the batter into 3-inch circles with the back of a spoon. (The batter will be so thin that the cookie sheet will show through in spots.) Sprinkle each cookie with a few slivered almonds.

Have ready at hand some wine bottles or rolling pins. You will need these to shape the cookies the instant you remove them from the oven. Bake the cookies, one sheet at a time, on the middle rack for 4 minutes, or until lightly browned around the edges. Remove them with a long, narrow spatula and drape them over the bottles at once. They will look strangely like Dali's melting watches, but do not worry. As they harden they turn into crisp cookies that resemble curved French roof tiles. If the cookies harden before you can remove all of them from one cookie sheet, put the sheet back in the oven for a few seconds and they will soften again. Store in airtight tin containers.

VARIATION: For ginger tiles, substitute 1 teaspoon of finely minced candied ginger for the lemon extract and rind.

GINGER MARMALADE COOKIES

༄

24 COOKIES

 1   cup finely ground almonds
1¾   cups flour
 ½   cup sugar
 ½   teaspoon salt
 4   teaspoons powdered ginger
1½   sticks (12 tablespoons) sweet butter, at room
       temperature, cut into 12 pieces
 1   teaspoon vanilla
2-3   tablespoons ginger marmalade
       Optional: 2 tablespoons confectioners' sugar

Put all the ingredients except the marmalade and the confectioners' sugar in a bowl. Knead them together until they are well combined. Gather the dough into a ball. Refrigerate for 30 minutes, or until firm.

Preheat the oven to 350°. Line a cookie sheet with kitchen parchment paper or butter it lightly. Pinch off pieces of dough and roll them into walnut-size balls. Place them on the cookie sheet. Press down the center of each cookie with your fingertip and fill the indentation with ginger marmalade. Bake in the upper third of the oven for about 20 minutes, or until the cookies are dry but not browned. Set them on cake racks to cool. If you like, dust them with confectioners' sugar. Store in airtight containers.

VARIATION: For orange marmalade cookies, substitute finely grated orange peel for the powdered ginger and 2 tablespoons orange or lemon juice for the vanilla. Use orange marmalade to fill the cookies instead of ginger marmalade.

OATMEAL LACE COOKIES

෧෴ॽ

36 3-INCH COOKIES

1½   cups rolled oats
¾   cup dark brown sugar
¾   cup white sugar
3   tablespoons flour
¼   teaspoon salt
⅔   cup sweet butter
1   egg, lightly beaten
1   teaspoon vanilla
½   cup finely chopped walnuts or pecans

Preheat the oven to 350°.

Combine the oatmeal, brown and white sugar, flour, and salt. Melt the butter. Make a well in the center of the dry ingredients. Add the melted butter, egg, and vanilla. Combine well. Fold in the chopped nuts. Drop the batter by teaspoonfuls about 3 inches apart onto un-greased cookie sheets or a sheet lined with kitchen parchment paper.

Bake 5 to 8 minutes until lightly browned on the edges and bubbling throughout. Let them cool *completely* on the cookie sheets set on cake racks before removing them with a spatula.

CRISP OATMEAL COOKIES

෧෴ॽ

Paul and Lisa D'Andrea, the owners of Simple Pleasures, that splendid bakery in Bridgehampton, N.Y., gave us this unusual recipe. You will need kitchen parchment paper to line the cookie sheets.

ABOUT 36 COOKIES

1   cup unsifted all-purpose flour
1   cup tightly packed dark brown sugar

½   *cup granulated sugar*
2   *cups quick-cooking oats*
¼   *teaspoon salt*
½   *cup (¼ pound) melted butter*
1   *teaspoon baking soda*

Preheat the oven to 350°.

Combine the flour, both kinds of sugar, oats, and salt. Stir in the melted butter. Combine the baking soda and ¼ cup of boiling water and add them to the batter. Stir until well combined. Drop by level tablespoonfuls onto parchment-lined cookie sheets, leaving 4-inch spaces between the cookies. (The batter spreads as it bakes.) Bake for 12 to 15 minutes, or until lightly browned. Transfer the cookies to cake racks as soon as they are firm enough to handle. Store in an airtight container.

NOTE: As an alternate procedure, place the batter on a sheet of waxed paper and shape it into a roll or rectangle 2 inches wide. Refrigerate until the batter is firm. Then cut into ⅛-inch slices, transfer to parchment-lined cookie sheets and bake.

MOCHA BROWNIES

〰

You will need a 15½- by 10½-inch jelly-roll pan.

36 LARGE OR 64 SMALL BARS

6   *ounces unsweetened baking chocolate*
1½   *sticks (⅜ pound) butter*
1   *tablespoon cocoa powder*
2   *tablespoons instant espresso coffee powder*
6   *eggs*
3   *cups sugar*
2   *tablespoons Kahlúa coffee liqueur, Grand Marnier*
       liqueur, or vanilla extract
1½   *cups flour*
½   *teaspoon salt*
       Optional: 2–3 tablespoons Kahlúa coffee liqueur or
          Grand Marnier

Preheat the oven to 325°.

Melt the chocolate and the butter in a heavy saucepan. Stir in the cocoa and coffee powder. Set aside to cool for a few minutes. Beat the eggs and sugar in a large bowl until light in color. Add the liqueur or vanilla. Stir in the chocolate mixture, flour, and salt until well combined. Do not overmix.

Butter the pan and dust it with flour. Pour the batter into the pan. Bake for about 40 minutes, or until the top is dry and a toothpick inserted in the batter comes out almost clean. Cool on a cake rack before cutting into bars.

For a more sophisticated taste, prick each brownie in two or three places with a toothpick while still warm and spoon a little liqueur over the surface.

DEVON FREDERICKS AND SUSAN COSTNER'S BLUEBERRY MUFFINS

ᕱᔈ

A recipe from two beautiful, gifted girls.

ABOUT 24 MUFFINS

3 *cups flour*
4½ *teaspoons baking powder*
1½ *cups sugar*
½ *teaspoon salt*
½ *teaspoon baking soda*
1 *tablespoon cinnamon*
2 *teaspoons grated lemon rind*
1¼ *cups milk*
2 *cups fresh blueberries*
2 *eggs, slightly beaten*
2 *sticks (½ pound) butter, melted*

Preheat the oven to 400°.

Sift the dry ingredients into a large bowl. Make a well in the center and put all the other ingredients into it. As quickly and lightly as possible, stir simply to blend, not to make a smooth batter.

Grease two 12-inch muffin pans and fill them three-quarters full with the batter. Bake for 20 to 25 minutes, or until golden brown.

ELIO'S ORANGE–NUT COOKIES

∽

Anne Isaak, one of the guiding spirits of Elio, that wonderful Italian restaurant in New York, makes these delectable cookies.

ABOUT 36 COOKIES

1   *cup hazelnuts*
2   *cups minus 2 tablespoons flour*
⅔   *cup sugar*
½   *teaspoon salt*
1½ *sticks (⅜ pound) cold unsalted butter*
1   *egg and 1 egg yolk, and 1 extra egg yolk if needed*
    Grated rind of 2 oranges
¼   *cup of orange liqueur, such as Grand Marnier or*
       Cointreau

Toast the hazelnuts over medium heat, shaking the pan, until the skins split. Wrap them in a towel and rub them to remove most of the skins. Let them cool. Chop them—not too fine—in a blender or food processor. Mix the flour, sugar, salt, and butter in a bowl until just a few streaks of butter are visible. Add the egg, egg yolk, orange rind, and liqueur, and work them into the cookie dough. If the dough is too dry to hold together, work in the extra egg yolk and a little more liqueur. Shape the dough into a long roll like a rolling pin 2 to 2½ inches in diameter. Wrap it in plastic and refrigerate until firm.

Preheat the oven to 375°.

Slice the dough into ¼-inch slices with a sharp knife. Bake the slices on a buttered or parchment-paper-lined cookie sheet for 10 minutes, or until lightly browned around the edges. Cool them on racks. Remove them from the cookie sheet with a spatula as soon as they are firm. Place them on racks again to cool and harden further.

These cookies are best eaten the day they are made. Unused cookie dough can be refrigerated or frozen until ready to use.

CRUSTLESS TARTE TATIN

6~9

4–6 SERVINGS

4 *tablespoons butter*
6 *tart apples, peeled, cored, and sliced thin*
3 *tablespoons dried currants*
   Grated peel and juice of ½ lemon
2 *tablespoons brown sugar*
1 *cup granulated sugar*

Preheat the oven to 450°.

Butter the bottom and sides of a pie plate. Put the apple slices in it, arranging them in layers. Sprinkle each layer with currants, grated lemon peel, lemon juice, and brown sugar, and dot with butter. Cover with foil pierced in a few places with a sharp knife. Set the pie plate on a cookie sheet and bake for 1 hour, or until the apple slices are tender. Remove the foil for the last 15 minutes. (If the apples seem in danger of burning, cover them again with the foil.) They should be moist but not sitting in liquid. If excess liquid accumulates, remove it with a bulb baster. Remove the apples from the oven and let them cool to lukewarm.

Melt the granulated sugar in a small heavy saucepan with ¼ cup of water over medium heat. If the sugar on one side of the pan begins to turn dark before the rest, stir it. Remove from heat as soon as the sugar syrup has become dark amber in color. Pour it over the apples to cover them evenly or use a pastry brush to paint a layer of caramel over them. Work quickly. If the caramel begins to harden, return it to the heat for a few seconds, then finish coating the apples. Let it cool for 30 minutes before serving.

QUICK GRAPE DESSERT

6~9

Should you not know that seedless grapes, sour cream, brown sugar, and kirsch mixed together and chilled make a superb, quick dessert, we urge you to try it. Equally good with blueberries or strawberries.

ANISE-FLAVORED MELON BALLS
(Melon à l'Anis)

◦~

4–6 SERVINGS

1 *large ripe melon, honeydew or cantaloupe*
4 *tablespoons confectioners' sugar or superfine sugar*
½ *cup anisette liqueur*
   Sprigs of mint for garnish

Cut the melon in half and discard the seeds. With a spoon or melon-ball cutter, scoop out the pulp in balls. Reserve the melon shells. Put the melon balls in a glass bowl and sprinkle them with the sugar and liqueur. Refrigerate for 3 hours, stirring from time to time. When ready to serve, put the melon balls into the shells and garnish with sprigs of mint.

MELON WITH SAUTERNE

◦~

4 SERVINGS

1 *tablespoon honey*
½ *cup Sauterne wine*
1 *large ripe melon*

In a glass bowl, mix the honey and Sauterne together. Add the melon balls made with a melon-ball cutter. Mix well. Refrigerate for 1 to 2 hours, mixing occasionally.

BAKED MELON

❧

12 SERVINGS

3   *ripe cantaloupes*
    Grated rind and juice of 1½ lemons
2   *tablespoons each vanilla extract, honey, and Cointreau*
1–1½   *cups heavy cream, whipped*

Cut each cantaloupe in half. Scoop out and discard the seeds and strings. Peel off and discard the rind and the unripe green part. Cut the pulp into strips. Put them in a baking dish and sprinkle them with grated rind. Mix together the lemon juice, vanilla, honey, and Cointreau and pour over the melon pieces. Bake in a moderate oven for 20 minutes. Serve cold with whipped cream.

OLD-FASHIONED ORANGE JELLY

❧

Packaged gelatin desserts have made most of us forget how good the real thing can be.

4 SERVINGS

1   *lemon*
4–6   *oranges (to make 1¾ cups juice)*
1   *envelope unflavored gelatin*
2   *tablespoons sugar*
½   *cup heavy cream*

Lightly grate the rind of the lemon and of 1 orange, avoiding the bitter pith. Put the grated rind in a medium-size bowl. Add the gelatin, sugar and 2 tablespoons of water. Mix well.

In a saucepan, heat 1¾ cups of freshly squeezed orange juice and 2 tablespoons of lemon juice just to the boiling point. Add to the bowl and stir until the gelatin is completely dissolved. Stir it from the bottom two or three times before it sets. Chill until firm (3 to 4 hours). Serve the jelly in the bowl or unmold it onto a round serving platter. Whip the cream until stiff and pass it separately.

VARIATION: Line a serving bowl or mold with sections cut from 1 or 2 navel oranges, cut with a sharp knife to avoid all pith and membrane. Carefully pour the hot gelatin-juice mixture over them. Chill until firm and serve with Oatmeal Lace Cookies (see page 345).

PEARS IN WINE

6 SERVINGS

18 *Seckel pears*
½ *bottle Barolo or other good Italian red wine*
1½ *cups sugar*
6 *whole cloves*
2 *cinnamon sticks*
3 *strips each lemon peel and orange peel (with none of the white pith)*

Preheat the oven to 400°.

Peel the pears, leaving them whole with their stems on. Cut a very thin slice off the bottom of each pear so that it will stand upright. Arrange the pears as close together as possible in a large baking dish. Put the rest of the ingredients into a saucepan and bring them to a boil. Stir until the sugar is dissolved. Pour over the pears and bake, basting often, for about 15 minutes, or until the pears are tender. (The cooking time depends on the ripeness of the pears.)

Arrange the pears on a deep platter. Strain the wine from the baking pan into a pot. Cook it over high heat until it is reduced by half. Pour it over the pears and serve hot, cold, or at room temperature.

STUFFED BAKED PEARS

6✑❜

4 SERVINGS

1   *tablespoon butter*
4   *large pears*
2   *tablespoons currants*
2   *tablespoons chopped walnuts*
¼   *cup honey*
1   *cup white wine*
2   *tablespoons red currant jelly*
    A pinch of powdered ginger

Preheat the oven to 350°.

Butter a flameproof baking dish just large enough to hold the pears upright. Peel and core the pears, leaving the bottoms intact. Combine the currants, walnuts, and honey. Spoon some of the mixture into each pear. Place the pears in the baking dish and pour the wine over them. Cover with foil. Bake for about 20 minutes, or until tender.

Remove the pears to a serving bowl. Place the baking dish over direct heat. Add the currant jelly and a pinch of ginger. Cook, stirring, until the sauce is thick and syrupy (about 5 to 7 minutes).

Pour the sauce over the pears and serve warm.

PRUNES IN PORT WINE

6✑❜

This unusual recipe from the Landes region of France has a most attractive feature: the prunes do not need to be cooked.

8–10 SERVINGS

1   *pound prunes*
1½   *cups sugar*
1   *vanilla bean*
¾   *cup port wine*
     Grated rind of 1 orange
1   *cinnamon stick*

Place the prunes in a bowl. Simmer 3 cups of water, the sugar, and the vanilla bean together in a saucepan, stirring occasionally, until the sugar is dissolved. Raise the heat and cook for 8 to 10 minutes until you have a thin syrup. Remove from heat and stir in the port, orange rind, and cinnamon stick. Pour over the prunes immediately. Let the prunes stand, covered, in a cool place for 24 hours. Drain the liquid into a saucepan and reduce it over high heat to half its volume. Pour it over the prunes again.

Delicious at any temperature. Serve with softened vanilla ice cream passed separately.

TIPS: Leftover prunes and syrup can be used in several ways. The prunes can be pitted, then puréed with their syrup in a blender or food processor. This purée can be used as the base for a prune soufflé, or it can be mixed into a vanilla ice cream mixture for home-made prune ice cream or layered into parfait glasses alternately with whipped cream or ice cream.

A RAISIN NIGHTCAP

For non-dessert-eaters or as a novel after-dinner liqueur.

Put heaping tablespoons of seedless raisins in small glasses. Fill the glasses three-quarters full with Grappa, Marc de Bourgogne, or Calvados. Let the raisins soak for several hours. Serve with demitasse spoons.

Eat the liqueur-soaked raisins and then sip the raisin-flavored liqueur. Heady and delicious!

RHUBARB FOOL

6–8 SERVINGS

2   *pounds young rhubarb, cut into small pieces*
1   *cup sugar*
    Juice of ½ lemon

1 *cup heavy cream*
1 *pint strawberries*
  Confectioners' sugar to taste

Put the rhubarb in a pot with ½ inch of water. Add the sugar and lemon juice. Mix well. Simmer, stirring occasionally, until the rhubarb is soft. Chill it in the refrigerator. Whip the cream until stiff and fold it into the rhubarb. Slice the strawberries, arrange them on top of the rhubarb-cream mixture, and sprinkle with confectioners' sugar. Lady fingers are fine with this English dessert.

STRAWBERRY MOUSSE, ALAIN CHAPEL

A dessert as beautiful as it is delicious from one of France's greatest chefs.

8–10 SERVINGS

2 *quarts ripe strawberries, cleaned and hulled*
  Juice of ½ lemon
  Sugar to taste (about 4–8 tablespoons)
2 *tablespoons kirsch*
1 *cup heavy cream*

Reserve 8 to 10 perfect berries for the garnish. Purée the remaining berries and lemon juice in a blender or food processor. Stir in the sugar and kirsch.

In a large bowl, whip the cream until stiff. Fold in half the strawberry purée. Put ½ cup of this pink mixture on each dish. Place ¼ cup of the kirsch-flavored red strawberry purée in the center of each serving and garnish with a whole strawberry. Or, just before serving, fill a bowl with the pink mixture, and place the red purée in the center and the strawberries all around.

STRAWBERRIES AND ORANGES
IN MARSALA

A delightful Sicilian dessert.

4 SERVINGS

1 *pint strawberries, cleaned and hulled*
3 *seedless oranges*
2 *tablespoons superfine sugar*
2 *tablespoons Marsala wine*
Optional: Fresh mint leaves for garnish

Stem the berries and halve them lengthwise. Grate the rind of 1 orange; then juice it. Place the rind and juice in a serving bowl, add the sugar and Marsala and stir until the sugar is dissolved. Add the berries. Peel the remaining oranges, cutting away the white pith. Slice them, quarter the slices and add them to the bowl. Stir gently. Taste and add a little sugar if desired. Chill until serving time. If you like, sprinkle with chopped fresh mint and garnish with sprigs of mint.

APPLE CRISP WITH HAZELNUT TOPPING

When we lived in Paris, there was no dessert we served our French friends that they enjoyed more than that old American favorite, apple crisp, unless it was *our* favorite, Quince Crisp (see page 370). With either, they liked to sip a bit of Calvados.

6 SERVINGS

6 *tart apples*
4 *tablespoons sugar*

½   teaspoon cinnamon
    Grated rind and juice of ½ lemon
1   cup hazelnuts
1   cup dark brown sugar
1   cup flour
    A pinch of salt
1   stick (¼ pound) butter
    Optional: ½ pint vanilla ice cream with 1 tablespoon
        Calvados

Preheat the oven to 400°.

Peel and core the apples and cut them into thin slices. Toss them in a bowl with the sugar, cinnamon, and lemon rind and juice. Butter a shallow baking dish and arrange the apple slices in it in an even layer.

Spread the hazelnuts in a single layer in a large pie plate and toast them in the oven for 5 to 10 minutes. Rub them vigorously between two towels to remove as much of their skin as possible. Grind them in a blender or food processor until finely chopped. (Do not overblend or they will turn into an oily paste.) Mix them with the brown sugar, flour, and salt. Work in the butter until the mixture is crumbly. Scatter it evenly over the top of the apples.

Bake for 50 to 60 minutes. Serve the apple crisp warm, accompanied, if you like, by a sauce made of softened ice cream with a little Calvados stirred into it.

APPLE-CRANBERRY TART FOR CAROL

∽

You will need a 9-inch tart pan with a removable rim.

6 SERVINGS

SWEET CORNMEAL PASTRY

¼   cup plus 2 tablespoons yellow cornmeal
¾   cup sifted all-purpose flour
¼   teaspoon salt

⅓   cup superfine sugar
5   tablespoons cold butter, cut into 5 pieces
2   small egg yolks, lightly beaten

1   egg, lightly beaten
2   cups tart apples, peeled, cored, and coarsely chopped
    Juice of 1 lemon
2   cups whole cranberries
½   cup brown sugar
¼   cup white sugar
2   tart apples, peeled, cored, and sliced
1   tablespoon butter
1   tablespoon sugar
½   cup currant or apple jelly

In a bowl, mix the cornmeal, flour, salt, and sugar till well combined. Cut in the butter until the mixture has the consistency of coarse meal. Work in the egg yolks, and a little ice water if needed, and gather the dough into a ball. Wrap tightly in plastic and chill until ready to use.

Roll out the dough ¼ inch thick and line a buttered tart pan with it. Cover the dough with foil and scatter rice or dried beans on top (so that it will hold its shape while baking). Refrigerate for at least 1 hour.

Preheat the oven to 400°.

Cover the tart shell loosely with foil and bake for 15 to 20 minutes. Let it cool on a rack. Brush the bottom with the beaten egg and return the shell to the oven for 5 to 8 minutes. Let it cool again.

Combine the chopped apples, lemon juice, and cranberries with both kinds of sugar in a heavy pot. Cover and cook over low heat for about 20 minutes, stirring occasionally, until the cranberries burst and the apples are fairly soft. Cool the mixture and pour it into the tart shell.

Arrange the apple slices in an overlapping pattern on top of the apple-cranberry mixture. Dot with butter and sprinkle with sugar. Bake for 30 minutes.

Melt the currant or apple jelly over medium heat for 3 to 4 minutes. Brush the tart with the jelly glaze while it is still warm.

APPLE ROLL

෴

You will need a 16- by 11-inch jelly-roll baking pan and a pastry brush.

8–10 SERVINGS

PASTRY

2½ cups flour
½ teaspoon salt
½ cup sugar
2 sticks (½ pound) cold sweet butter, cut into ¼-inch slices
2 egg yolks
¼ cup white wine, milk, or ice water
1 teaspoon vanilla

FILLING

6 greenings or other tart apples (or 6 ripe but firm pears)
  Grated rind of 1 lemon
  Juice of ½ lemon
½ cup sugar
1 tablespoon flour
1 tablespoon cinnamon (or ginger)
⅓ cup raisins (or currants)
⅓ cup coarsely chopped almonds or hazelnuts
¼ cup coarse bread crumbs mixed with 2 tablespoons
    sugar and a pinch of cinnamon
2 egg whites and 2 lightly beaten egg yolks
  About ¼ cup sugar (granulated or confectioners')

Mix together the flour, salt, and sugar. Work in the butter by hand or in an electric mixer set at low speed until the mixture resembles coarse meal. Beat the egg yolks lightly with the wine and vanilla and work them into the dough. Gather the dough into a ball. Roll it lightly in flour, wrap it in plastic wrap and refrigerate it for 1 hour or more.

Meanwhile, prepare the filling. Peel and core the apples and cut them into thin slices. Mix them with the lemon rind and juice. Combine the sugar, flour, and cinnamon, then stir in the raisins and nuts.

Preheat the oven to 350°. Roll the dough out on a lightly floured board into a rectangle 16 by 11 inches. (The normal procedure is to fill the roll, then transfer it to the baking pan. However, as it is a delicate operation once the roll is filled, you may prefer to transfer the dough to the baking pan at this point and then fill it.)

Sprinkle the seasoned bread crumbs down the center of the dough lengthwise, leaving a 3-inch border on each side and a 1½- to 2-inch border at each end. Lay half the apples over the bread crumbs. Cover with half the sugar-raisin-nut mixture. Repeat the process with the remaining ingredients. With a pastry brush, paint the edges of the dough with a little egg white and fold the sides of the dough over the filling, sealing the seam securely. Fold over the ends and seal them. Carefully transfer the apple roll to the baking pan (if you have not already done so). Brush it lightly with egg yolks. Bake it in the center of the oven for 45 minutes, or until it is golden brown. Serve warm, sprinkled with sugar.

GREEK CHEESE AND HONEY PIE

⁓

You will need an 8-inch tart pan with a removable rim.

6–8 SERVINGS

FILLING

10	ounces Greek Mizithra cheese or 2 ounces (about ¼ cup) mild goat cheese, such as Montrachet, plus 1 7½-ounce package of farmer cheese
1	egg plus 2 egg yolks
4	tablespoons thick honey, warmed slightly
4	tablespoons sugar, or a little more to taste
	A pinch of salt
	Grated rind of 1 lemon
1	teaspoon flour
¼	teaspoon cinnamon
	Pastry: Sour Cream Pastry (see page 372) or Sweet Cornmeal Pastry (see page 357)

Preheat the oven to 400°.

Beat together all the filling ingredients except the cinnamon by hand or in an electric mixer until well combined.

Roll out the pastry on a lightly floured board to a thickness of $\frac{3}{16}$ inch. Line the tart pan with it. Trim the edges. Prick the bottom with a fork and line the pastry dough with paper or foil, pressing it down and against the sides. Fill with metal pastry weights, rice, or dried beans so that the pie crust will hold its shape. Bake for 10 minutes. Remove to a rack, remove the weights and foil, and let the pie crust cool for a few minutes.

Lower the oven heat to 350°. Pour the filling into the partially cooked pie crust and bake for 20 to 30 minutes. Remove the pie from the oven when a sharp knife inserted in the filling comes out fairly clean. Serve warm or cool, sprinkled with cinnamon.

BLUEBERRY KUCHEN

⌒

You will need a 9- by 1½-inch round cake pan with a removable rim.

8 SERVINGS

PASTRY

1½ cups flour
¼ teaspoon salt
3 tablespoons sugar
1½ sticks (12 tablespoons) cold sweet butter, cut into 12 pieces
1½ tablespoons vinegar

FILLING

5 cups fresh blueberries
⅔ cup sugar
2 tablespoons flour
½ teaspoon cinnamon

Preheat the oven to 400°.

Put the flour, salt, and sugar in a bowl and mix well. Cut in the butter, using two forks or a pastry cutter, until the mixture resembles coarse meal. Sprinkle with the vinegar. Gather the dough into a ball. With lightly floured fingers, press the dough onto the bottom and up and around the sides of the cake pan. The dough should hang over the rim slightly in five or six places.

Put 3 cups of the blueberries into the pan. The berries should come right to the top along the edges to support the crust during baking. Mix the sugar, flour, and cinnamon, and spread the mixture over the berries. Bake for 50 to 60 minutes, or until the crust is well browned and the filling is bubbling up. Remove the pan to a cake rack. Cover it immediately with the remaining 2 cups of blueberries. Gently press them onto the cooked berries. Use a sharp knife to trim off any overhanging bits of crust. When the kuchen is cool, carefully loosen the crust around the sides. Remove the rim of the pan and serve.

LEMON TART LUTÈCE
(Tarte Citron Maman)

⁓

Monsieur André Soltner, the owner of New York's four-star restaurant Lutèce, told us a heartwarming story. One of his devoted clients, a rich and worldly Swiss gentleman, had always longed for a tart that his mother baked every Sunday during his childhood. He described it with such nostalgia that Monsieur Soltner decided to re-create it. After weeks of experiment, he presented it as a surprise to Monsieur X, who exclaimed, "*C'est ça! Voilà la tarte au citron de maman!*" The tart still appears on the menu from time to time. It is a lemon-and-almond meringue confection—the kind of dessert that dreams are made of.

You will need a 9-inch tart pan with a removable rim.

6 SERVINGS

TART BASE

3   *large eggs, separated*
¾   *cup sugar*
     Grated peel of 1 lemon

1 cup finely ground almonds (easily done in a food
    processor or blender)
1 tablespoon flour
¼ teaspoon salt
3 lemons

MERINGUE TOPPING

2 egg whites
  A pinch of salt
¼ cup sugar
½ cup finely ground almonds

Preheat the oven to 350°.

Butter and flour the sides and bottom of the tart pan. Shake out any excess flour. Beat the egg yolks and sugar in an electric mixer until the mixture is very pale and falls from the beater in a ribbon. Stir in the lemon peel, ground almonds, and flour until they are well combined. Beat the egg whites with the salt until they are stiff. Carefully fold them into the batter. Fill the tart pan with the batter. Set it on a cookie sheet and bake for about 25 minutes, or until the tart base is lightly browned and begins to come away from the sides of the pan.

While the tart base is baking, peel the lemons, removing all the white pith, and slice them with a sharp knife as thinly as possible. Discard any seeds. When the tart base is done, remove it from the oven and let it cool on a rack for 20 minutes. Cover it with the lemon slices, overlapping them slightly if necessary.

Make the meringue topping. Beat the egg whites with a pinch of salt until they form soft peaks when the beater is lifted, then add the sugar, a tablespoon at a time, beating after each addition. Fold in the ground almonds and, spatula dipped in cold water, spread this meringue over the lemon slices.

Return the tart to the 350° oven for 15 minutes, or until the meringue is lightly browned. Cool on a cake rack, and, using a spatula, remove the rim and the bottom of the tart pan. Transfer to a platter and serve.

AN ORANGE TART FOR TANNY

⌒〰

We immodestly claim that this is one of the best orange tarts you will
ever eat.

You will need an 8-inch tart pan with a removable rim, and a pastry
brush.

6 SERVINGS

PASTRY

 1 *cup plus 2 tablespoons flour*
    A pinch of salt
 ½ *cup sifted superfine sugar*
 1 *stick (¼ pound) butter*
 2 *egg yolks*

GLAZE

 2 *tart green apples, cored and quartered but not peeled*
 2 *juice oranges*
 1 *teaspoon grated orange rind*
 1 *cup plus 2 tablespoons sugar*

FILLING

 5 *navel oranges*
    Optional: 1 cup whipped cream; 1 tablespoon
       Cointreau or Grand Marnier; 2 ounces bitter
       chocolate, melted

Prepare the pastry several hours before you plan to use it. Sift the
flour, salt, and sugar together into a bowl. Cut the butter into 8 slices
and work them into the flour-sugar mixture with a pastry cutter or
your fingers until the mixture has the consistency of coarse meal.
Beat the egg yolks lightly with a fork and work them into the dough.
Form the dough into a ball, dust it lightly with flour, wrap it in
plastic wrap, and refrigerate it for several hours. (Or freeze it for 30
minutes.)

Make a glaze by boiling the apple quarters in 1½ cups of water for 15 minutes. Line a sieve with moistened cheesecloth; press the apples and liquid through the sieve into a fairly large saucepan. Add the juice of the 2 oranges, the grated rind, and the sugar. Boil, stirring, for 5 to 10 minutes, or until the sugar has dissolved. As soon as a bit of the glaze jells when dropped onto a dish, remove it from the heat and set aside in the saucepan.

With a sharp knife, peel the navel oranges, removing all the white pith. Cut the orange sections free of membrane. Drain them on paper towels while you prepare the tart shell.

Preheat the oven to 350°.

Press the dough into the bottom and sides of the pan with floured fingers. Prick the dough with a fork. Cover it with waxed paper and fill with rice (or beans) so that the tart shell will not puff up during baking. Bake the shell for 25 to 35 minutes. Remove it from the oven and discard the rice and the waxed paper. Paint the bottom of the tart shell with a little of the glaze. Return the tart shell to the oven and bake until the sides begin to come away from the pan. Remove it and let it cool. When it is completely cool, set the tart shell over a wide jar or coffee can to support the bottom and carefully remove the outer rim of the pan by lowering it. (It may be necessary to loosen the outer edges of the shell gently with a small knife before removing the rim.) Separate the tart shell from the bottom of the pan with a broad spatula and slide it onto a serving plate.

Working from the outer edge, arrange the drained orange sections in slightly overlapping concentric circles to fill the tart shell.

If the glaze has solidified, reheat it slightly. Brush or spoon it evenly over the oranges. Let the tart cool for a few minutes before serving.

If you can't resist, pass some whipped cream with a little Cointreau or Grand Marnier stirred into it.

We once dribbled some melted bitter chocolate over the top of the tart when the glaze had cooled. The result met with great approval.

PEAR TART
(Tarte aux Poires)

◦⌒⌐

You will need an 8-inch tart pan with a removable rim.

6 SERVINGS

PASTRY

1	*cup all-purpose flour*
1	*stick (8 tablespoons) sweet butter, chilled*
2½–3	*tablespoons ice water*
½	*teaspoon salt*

PEAR SAUCE

3	*large, ripe but firm pears*
3	*tablespoons sugar*
2	*tablespoons sweet butter, cut into a few pieces*

POACHED PEARS

6	*large, ripe but firm pears*
1	*bottle good red wine*
½	*cup sugar*
1	*egg, lightly beaten*
	Glaze: ½ cup apple jelly

Place the flour in a food processor with the knife blade. Cut the butter into 8 slices and arrange them on top of the flour. Process 5 to 7 seconds. Remove the mixture to a bowl. Add the ice water and salt to the processor. Place the flour-butter mixture *on top* of the water and process for 8 to 10 seconds. Do not overblend! The mixture should stick together, but there should be heavy traces of butter in the finished dough. If it does not stick together, process with a quick on-and-off pulse of the motor for a few seconds. (To make by hand, cut the cold butter, salt, and flour together with a pastry cutter or two knives until it has the consistency of coarse meal. Add the ice water; mix until the dough forms a ball. Add more water only if needed.)

Turn the dough out onto a lightly floured board and roll it into a ball. Wrap it in plastic and store it in the refrigerator for 3 to 4 hours or overnight. (It also keeps well in the freezer. Defrost it before using.)

Preheat the oven to 400°. Make the pear sauce. Peel and core the pears and cut them into small pieces. Place them in a buttered baking dish. Sprinkle them with sugar, dot with butter, and bake, uncovered, for 20 minutes. Remove from the oven and cool. The pears should have the consistency of heavy applesauce. Remove and discard any excess juice. Set aside to cool.

Peel the pears to be poached, but do not core them. Place them in an enamel-lined pot just large enough to hold them in one layer. Add the wine and the sugar. Cook over high heat until the liquid begins to boil. Lower the heat, cover, and simmer until the pears are tender but still quite firm when tested with the tip of a sharp knife. Remove from the heat and let them cool in the pot.

Roll out the dough on a lightly floured board into a 12-inch circle ⅛ inch thick. Place the tart pan on a baking sheet. Fold the dough over the rolling pin and center it over the tart pan. Unfold the dough carefully to cover the pan. Gently ease the edges of the dough down inside the pan so that the dough does not stretch. The sides of the tart should be slightly thicker than the bottom. Trim the edges of the dough, then pinch them so that the dough stands an even ⅛ inch higher than the pan. Press down with the back of a fork to decorate the edge of the tart. Prick the bottom with the fork in several places. Return to the refrigerator for 1 to 2 hours before baking.

Preheat the oven to 350°. Cut a 12-inch circle of parchment paper, then make 1½-inch cuts all around the edge at 1-inch intervals. Center the paper over the dough in the tart pan and press down to cover the bottom. The cut border of the paper will overlap nicely. Fill to the top with dried beans so that the tart shell does not puff up during baking. Bake for 30 minutes, then carefully remove the beans and paper. Brush the dough with a beaten egg and return it to the oven for 5 minutes. Cool on a wire rack.

Preheat the oven to 350°. Line the tart shell with the pear sauce. Carefully remove the poached pears from the wine syrup. Core them and cut each into 12 slices. Arrange them on top of the pear sauce, starting with a circle at the outer rim of the tart and overlapping them so that the wine-reddened edges are visible. Set the tart pan on a cookie sheet and bake for 30 minutes. Cool on a wire rack.

Make the glaze by heating the apple jelly over low heat until it has melted. Brush it evenly over the top of the tart.

Set the tart pan over a coffee can, loosen the outer rim with a knife, and remove the rim by sliding it down. Loosen the tart from the bottom with a broad spatula and slide it carefully onto a serving dish.

PECAN CHESS PIE

6–8 SERVINGS

FILLING

1 *cup brown sugar*
1 *egg*
1 *tablespoon flour*
¼ *cup milk*
¼ *cup butter, melted*
¼ *teaspoon vanilla*
1¾ *cups pecans, coarsely chopped and toasted 8–10
      minutes in a low oven*

*An uncooked pie shell, using pastry recipe in Our
      Favorite Strawberry Tart (see page 374)*
1 *cup heavy cream, whipped*
2 *tablespoons confectioners' sugar*
1 *tablespoon bourbon*

Preheat the oven to 375°.

Beat the first six ingredients together until smooth. Stir in the pecans. Spoon the mixture into the uncooked pie shell.

Bake for 40 minutes. Turn off the heat, but leave the pie in the oven with the door open for 1 hour.

Serve with whipped cream, flavored with confectioners' sugar and bourbon.

HILDE'S PLUM TART

❧

Hilde's Sweet Shop and Tea Room in Sag Harbor is a Long Island oasis of delicious food and exquisite pastry.

You will need an 8- or 9-inch cake pan with a removable rim 2 inches deep.

8 SERVINGS

PASTRY

1½ cups flour
    A pinch of salt
1   teaspoon baking powder
4   tablespoons sugar
1½ sticks (12 tablespoons) sweet butter, chilled and cut
        into 12 pieces
1   egg, lightly beaten
1   teaspoon vanilla

FILLING

2½ pounds Italian purple plums (usually available from
        late summer through early autumn)
½   cup sugar
1   tablespoon flour
½   teaspoon nutmeg
½   teaspoon cinnamon
2–3 tablespoons butter, cut into bits

GLAZE

½   cup apricot jam, forced through a coarse sieve

Combine the dry ingredients for the pastry in a mixing bowl. Cut in the butter with a pastry cutter or two knives until the mixture resembles coarse meal. Add the egg and vanilla and work them in. Gather the dough into a ball and roll it lightly in flour. Seal it tightly in plastic wrap and refrigerate it for 1 hour. With lightly floured fingers, pat it into place on the bottom and up the sides of the cake pan. Chill it again while you prepare the plums.

Preheat the oven to 350°.

Stem, wash and dry the plums for the filling. Cut them vertically, leaving the halves connected, pull out the pits and make small cuts in the middle at the top and bottom so that each plum can be opened out in one piece. Arrange them in circles, standing up side by side, skin sides out. Start at the outer edge, then fill in the center. Mix together the sugar, flour, nutmeg, and cinnamon and sprinkle over the fruit. Dot with butter. Bake for 45 minutes, or until the crust is browned and the fruit tender. Remove to a rack and paint with apricot glaze, made by bringing the apricot jam to a boil with 1 tablespoon of water. Brush the hot glaze over the fruit while the tart is still warm. When the tart has cooled, remove the rim and serve.

QUINCE CRISP

6 SERVINGS

4 *cups peeled, cored, and thinly sliced quinces (you may*
    need as many as 8–10 quinces)
½ *cup freshly squeezed orange juice*
    Juice of 1 lemon
½ *cup sugar*
4 *tablespoons butter*

TOPPING

1 *cup flour*
    A pinch of salt
1 *cup dark brown sugar*
1 *stick (¼ pound) sweet butter*

Optional: 1 cup heavy cream

Preheat the oven to 375°.

Spread the sliced quinces evenly in a lightly buttered baking dish. Pour the orange and lemon juice over them, sprinkle them with the sugar and dot with the butter. Bake until the fruit is almost tender.

(Depending on the ripeness of the fruit, the baking will take from 30 to 60 minutes.) Remove from the oven and cool to lukewarm, but keep the oven on.

Meanwhile, prepare the topping. Mix the flour, salt, and brown sugar until well combined. Work in the butter until the mixture is crumbly. Scatter it evenly over the partially baked quinces and return the baking dish to the hot oven immediately. Bake until the topping is brown and crisp and the fruit is soft. Serve warm with heavy cream, whipped or unwhipped, passed separately.

A RICOTTA PIE IN AN AMARETTO CRUST FOR ANNE

൭

The Italian macaroons give the pie crust its distinctive flavor. You will need a 10- or 11-inch pie pan.

6–8 SERVINGS

CRUST

24   *amaretti (Italian macaroons), or enough to make 1 cup of crumbs*
12   *graham crackers, or enough to make 1 cup crumbs*
1½   *sticks (12 tablespoons) butter*

FILLING

2   *cups (1 15-ounce container) fresh ricotta cheese*
3   *egg yolks*
½   *cup sugar*
½   *teaspoon salt*
  Optional: 1 teaspoon Amaretto liqueur or ½ teaspoon each almond and vanilla extracts

Garnish: ½–1 teaspoon cinnamon

Preheat the oven to 375°.

Pulverize the amaretti and graham crackers in a food processor. (You can, of course, make the crumbs with a rolling pin.) Put the

2 cups of crumbs in the pie plate. Melt the butter, pour it over the crumbs and mix thoroughly with your fingers. Pat the crumbs down firmly and spread them to cover the bottom and sides of the pie plate. Bake the crust for 10 minutes, or until it is lightly browned. Cool it on a cake rack while you prepare the filling.

Beat all the filling ingredients together, by hand or in an electric mixer, until smooth. Carefully spoon the mixture into the cooled pie crust and spread it evenly. Bake for 50 to 60 minutes, or until a toothpick inserted in the filling comes out dry. Remove to a cake rack to cool. Sprinkle the cinnamon over the pie and serve.

RUSSIAN CHEESE PASTRIES
(Baked Vareniki)

The traditional Russian *vareniki* are boiled dumplings filled with cherries and served with sour cream. But in the Fizdale family, Grandmother invented a baked cheese-filled version served with cherry or strawberry preserves and, of course, sour cream. Try them. They are exquisite and can be prepared—except for the baking—well in advance.

The dough and filling can be prepared ahead of time and refrigerated for several hours or overnight. The pastries can also be rolled out, filled, set on well-buttered cookie sheets, and refrigerated for several hours or overnight. *Vareniki* should be served warm, so plan to put them in the oven just before you begin your meal.

6 SERVINGS (ABOUT 12 PASTRIES)

SOUR CREAM PASTRY

2   *cups flour*
1   *teaspoon baking powder*
¼   *teaspoon baking soda*
¼   *teaspoon salt*
1   *tablespoon sugar*
1   *stick (¼ pound) very cold, firm sweet butter, cut into 8 slices*
3   *tablespoons sour cream or crème fraîche*
2   *eggs, lightly beaten with a fork*

FILLING

12 ounces (1½ packages) farmer cheese or
   three-quarters of a 16-ounce carton dry
   cottage cheese
3 ounces Philadelphia cream cheese
1 egg
½ teaspoon salt
2 tablespoons sugar

Garnish: 1 cup sour cream; 1 cup good strawberry or
   cherry preserves

Put the flour, baking powder, baking soda, salt, and sugar in the bowl of a food processor with the metal blade. Mix by flicking the motor on and off three or four times. With the motor running, add the butter quickly, a piece at a time, until the mixture resembles coarse meal. Then quickly add the sour cream and the beaten eggs. Process for a few seconds until the dough begins to stick together. Remove it to a bowl and form it into a ball. Roll it lightly in flour and refrigerate for 30 to 60 minutes or longer before rolling it out. (If you are making the dough by hand, sift the first 5 ingredients together and mix them well. Cut in the butter until the mixture looks like coarse meal. Stir in the sour cream and eggs. Work them in lightly with your fingers, then gather the dough into a ball.)

Prepare the filling. Cream together the two kinds of cheese until well combined. Mix in the egg, salt, and sugar. Chill for 30 minutes or longer.

Preheat the oven to 375°.

Roll the dough out on a lightly floured board until quite thin, about ¼ inch. Cut into 4-inch rounds with a floured cookie cutter. Put a tablespoon of the filling on one side of each round. Dip a pastry brush in ice water and lightly brush the rim of the dough. Fold it over the filling to form half-circles. Pinch the edges to seal them. (If you like, you can pull the two outer points together—rather like tying a kerchief—and pinch them together. The pastries will then look like Italian tortellini.)

Transfer the pastries to well-buttered cookie sheets. When ready to bake, brush them with melted butter and bake them for 20 to 30 minutes, or until lightly browned. Keep them in a warm place. Serve with sour cream and preserves, passed separately.

OUR FAVORITE STRAWBERRY TART

〜

You will need a 9-inch tart pan with a removable rim.

6 SERVINGS

PASTRY

1½ cups flour
6   tablespoons butter, chilled
3   tablespoons sugar
     A pinch of salt
1   egg, lightly beaten

FILLING

¼   cup finely ground almonds or hazelnuts
¾   cup heavy cream, beaten until thick with 1 teaspoon
        sugar
2–3 cups ripe strawberries

GLAZE

½   cup currant jelly
2   tablespoons sugar
1   tablespoon eau de vie de framboise (raspberry brandy)

Prepare the pastry several hours in advance. Sift the flour into a large bowl. Make a well in the center. Cut the butter into 6 slices and put them in the well with the sugar and salt. Work in the flour with your fingers or two forks until the mixture has the consistency of coarse meal. Add the egg and just enough ice water to hold the mixture together. Shape into a ball, dust with flour, wrap in plastic wrap and refrigerate for at least 3 hours.

When ready to bake the tart, preheat the oven to 400°. Roll out the dough on a lightly floured board to ¼-inch thickness. Line the tart pan with the dough. Prick the dough with a fork in several places. Line the dough with foil and fill it with dried peas or beans so that the dough will hold its shape during baking. Bake for 20 minutes, then carefully remove the foil and dried peas. Return the tart shell to the oven for 8 minutes, or until it is golden brown. Let it cool on a cake rack.

Cover the bottom of the tart shell evenly with the ground almonds, then with a layer of whipped cream. Wipe the strawberries clean with a damp cloth, remove the stems, and arrange them in the tart shell over the whipped cream, starting at the outer edges.

Heat the jelly, sugar, and ¼ cup of water. Bring to a boil, then simmer for 5 minutes. When cool, stir in the raspberry brandy. Reheat. Spoon over the berries to glaze them.

(This tart is equally delicious made with raspberries or *fraises des bois*; and surprisingly satisfying made with seedless grapes.)

SHERBETS, ICES, AND ICE CREAM

Just as we make instant iced soups with frozen vegetables (see page 65), we make fruit ices and sherbets in no time at all. When really ripe fruit is available, peel it, cut it up, wrap tightly and freeze it. Then—or later—remove it from the freezer at the beginning of a meal. At dessert time, process the still partially frozen fruit for a few seconds and serve it immediately. If you like, process it with a little lemon juice and sugar or an appropriate fruit brandy—*eau de vie de poire* with ripe pears, for example. You might purée an egg yolk, a whole egg, or a little cream with the frozen fruit if you are not counting calories.

For best results, ice creams and sherbets should be made in an ice cream machine following the directions carefully. However, they can be made in metal pans in the freezing compartment of your refrigerator or in a home freezer. In that case, when the mixture begins to freeze around the edges, it should be put in a bowl, whipped vigorously for a minute and returned to the freezer for 2 hours or until firm.

POINTS TO REMEMBER

1. All the ingredients should be refrigerated until ready to use.
2. If stored in the freezing compartment of a refrigerator, ice cream must be placed in the coldest part of the freezing compartment, that is, on the metal shelf at the bottom. If stored on the rack or in the door, it may not harden sufficiently.

INSTANT BANANA BLITZ

❧

4–6 SERVINGS

4 *ripe bananas*
2–4 *tablespoons rum*
1 *tablespoon chopped ginger*
½ *cup heavy cream*
  Optional: sugar or honey to taste

The day before making this recipe, peel the bananas and discard any fibrous strips. Cut each banana into four pieces and wrap them tightly in plastic wrap. Freeze them overnight.

Put the bananas, rum, chopped ginger, and cream in a food processor with the knife attachment. Process until well blended. If you add sugar or honey, process for 2 to 3 seconds longer. Serve immediately.

INSTANT PINEAPPLE ICE

❧

3–4 SERVINGS

1 *very ripe pineapple (make this ice only if you find a*
  really ripe pineapple—fragrant, with leaves that
  pull out easily)
2 *tablespoons rum or kirsch*
  Optional: 1–2 tablespoons powdered sugar; 2–4
  tablespoons heavy cream

The day before making the ice, prepare the pineapple. With a heavy knife, cut it into quarters lengthwise. Cut off and discard the hard core. Working over a platter to catch the juice, use a curved, serrated grapefruit knife to separate the pineapple from the outer rind. With a sharp knife, cut 1-inch-wide wedges against the rind. Place the pineapple wedges and their juice in a freezer container. Freeze overnight.

Remove the pineapple from the freezer about 15 minutes before making the ice. Separate the frozen wedges with a knife dipped into hot water. Place them, still frozen, in a food processor with the knife blade. Process with the rum until smooth and frothy. After 10 seconds, stop and scrape down the sides of the bowl with a spatula. Process again. Taste. Add powdered sugar or cream or both if you like, although this ice is exquisite as it is. Serve at once.

INSTANT STRAWBERRY ICE

ᖚ

4–6 SERVINGS

1   *16-ounce package of frozen whole strawberries packed without sugar or syrup (if you can find only frozen berries packed in sugar or syrup, omit the optional sugar in this recipe)*
1–2   *tablespoons kirsch, or more to taste*
4–6   *tablespoons sugar*
   Optional: 4–6 tablespoons cream

Keep the berries in the freezer until 10 or 15 minutes before preparing the ice. With a large heavy knife dipped in hot water, cut the frozen berries into chunks.

Place them in a processor with the knife blade, add the kirsch and purée until smooth. Stop the machine every 10 seconds and scrape down the sides with a rubber spatula.

Taste, add more kirsch, sugar, and cream if you like. Process 5 seconds longer. Serve as soon as possible, as ices taste best when eaten immediately.

PEAR SHERBET WITH PEAR BRANDY

❧

A classic French dessert following the traditional procedure.

6 SERVINGS

1 *cup sugar*
Juice of 1 lemon
A 1-inch piece of vanilla bean
5–6 *ripe pears*
1 *egg white, lightly beaten*
⅓ *cup pear brandy (eau de vie de poire) or more if desired*

Boil the sugar with 2 cups of water for 5 minutes, stirring until the sugar is dissolved. Stir in the lemon juice and add the vanilla bean.

Peel, core, and quarter the pears. Poach them in the sugar syrup until tender, about 10 minutes. With a slotted spoon, remove the pears, except for four pieces to be used as a garnish, to a blender or food processor and purée them. Boil down the sugar syrup to 1 cup and discard the vanilla bean. Combine the syrup with the puréed pears and cool. Fold in the egg white and freeze according to the directions on your ice cream maker. Serve in parfait glasses, ice cream dishes, or large wine glasses, each portion topped with thin slices of the reserved poached pear and a tablespoon of pear brandy.

NOTE: If made in ice trays, freeze the pear mixture to a mush before adding the egg white. Remove it from the trays to a bowl, beat it well, fold in the stiffly beaten egg white, and refreeze before serving.

STRAWBERRY ICE

❧

6–8 SERVINGS

1½ *cups fresh strawberries, cleaned and stemmed*
¾ *cup superfine sugar*
Juice of 1 orange, strained
Juice of 1 lemon, strained

Do not wash the strawberries. Simply clean them by wiping them with a slightly dampened paper towel. Purée the strawberries in a food processor. Put them in a large bowl and set them aside.

In a saucepan, cook the sugar and ⅔ cup of water over medium heat until the syrup reaches 219° on the candy thermometer. If you do not have a candy thermometer, cook for exactly 5 minutes after the mixture comes to a boil. Pour this syrup over the strawberries, mix well, and let stand until cool. Add the orange and lemon juice and mix well. Refrigerate until well chilled.

Fill metal ice trays with the puréed mixture and freeze until almost solid. Place the mixture in a chilled bowl and beat it with a chilled rotary beater or process it in a food processor until smooth. Return it to the trays and freeze until solid. Transfer from the freezer to the refrigerator 30 minutes before serving.

If necessary, purée once again. Serve accompanied by unsweetened whipped cream mixed with a little kirsch.

ROSAMOND RUSSELL'S STRAWBERRY-PAPAYA ICE

ᔕ∾

8 SERVINGS

1   box ripe strawberries, sliced (to make 2 fully packed
    cups)
1   large ripe papaya, sliced (to make 1 cup)
2   cups superfine sugar mixed with 1 cup water
3   tablespoons lime juice
    Optional: 1–2 tablespoons Cointreau or Grand
    Marnier

Make the ice mixture following the procedure for Strawberry Ice (see above). Purée the strawberries and papaya together. Add the lime juice and Cointreau just before putting the mixture in the freezer.

Serve in chilled stemmed glasses. Any leftover ice kept in the refrigerator instead of the freezer for an hour or so makes a delightful sauce for unsweetened sliced strawberries.

CAPPUCCINO ICE CREAM

❦

A rather soft ice cream, quickly prepared because the eggs do not have to be cooked.

ABOUT 5 CUPS (6–8 SERVINGS)

3   cups heavy cream
¾   cup superfine sugar
3   egg yolks
2   tablespoons instant espresso coffee powder
1   teaspoon powdered cocoa
½   teaspoon cinnamon
1   teaspoon Kahlúa coffee liqueur, Grand Marnier, or
        brandy

Whip the cream until stiff. Toward the end, gradually whip in half the sugar. Set aside. Beat the remaining sugar with the egg yolks until light in color. Add all the other ingredients and stir until well combined. Fold in the whipped cream and mix well.

Freeze the mixture in an ice cream maker following the directions. Serve at once or store in the coldest part of a freezer. Excellent with Hot Chocolate Sauce (see below) and superb in Elizabeth Torstenson's Ice Cream Cake (see page 324).

HOT CHOCOLATE SAUCE

❦

1   cup dark brown sugar
½   cup granulated sugar
     A pinch of salt
2   squares unsweetened chocolate
1   tablespoon unsweetened cocoa
1   tablespoon instant espresso coffee
⅔   cup milk
1   tablespoon butter
1   tablespoon corn syrup
2   teaspoons brandy or vanilla or 1 teaspoon of each

Put all the ingredients except the brandy and vanilla in a heavy pot. Cook, stirring, over low heat until the chocolate melts. Raise the heat and boil, covered, for 2 minutes. Remove the cover and cook until a little of the mixture dropped into cold water forms a soft ball. Remove from the heat and beat vigorously for a minute. Let cool for a few minutes, then beat in the brandy.

Before serving, place in a double boiler over simmering water to reheat.

CHRISTOPHE DE MENIL'S PERNOD ICE CREAM

A decadently delicious dessert. You will need a heavy-bottomed 2-quart saucepan, a wire whisk and a wooden spoon.

6 SERVINGS (ABOUT 1 QUART)

5   *egg yolks*
2½ *cups heavy cream*
1   *cup milk*
⅔ *cup sugar*
1   *teaspoon aniseed, pulverized*
6   *tablespoons Pernod*

Whisk the egg yolks lightly in a large bowl and set them aside. Warm 1½ cups of the cream, the milk and sugar over medium heat. Stir occasionally until the sugar is dissolved. Just before the mixture comes to a boil, remove it from the heat. Whisking the egg yolks constantly to prevent curdling, slowly and gradually pour in the hot cream.

Pour the mixture back into the saucepan. Cook over medium heat, stirring constantly with a wooden spoon, for about 8 to 10 minutes. Do not let the custard come to a boil. It is ready when the custard coats the spoon and your finger, run along the spoon, leaves a visible path. Pour the custard into a bowl immediately and stir in the aniseed. When it is cool, strain it through a fine sieve. Whip the remaining heavy cream until stiff and stir it into the mixture. Refrigerate for 1 hour. Freeze it in an ice cream machine. When the mixture begins to thicken, gradually add the Pernod and freeze until it is firm.

FIG ICE CREAM

∽

You will need a heavy-bottomed 2-quart saucepan, a wire whisk, and a wooden spoon. And you must buy the kind of dry figs, available in specialty shops, that are rather plump and moist.

ABOUT 1 QUART

1 *cup (½ pound) plump, moist dried figs*
½–¾ *cup cognac (or port)*
⅓ *cup slivered almonds*
2 *egg yolks*
2 *cups heavy cream (or half-and-half)*
½ *cup sugar, or a little less to taste*

A few hours before you make the ice cream, cut off and discard the stems of the figs. Chop the figs rather fine. Put them in a small container and cover them with the cognac.

Toast the almonds in the oven until they are lightly browned. Let them cool, then chop them coarsely in a food processor or blender.

In a bowl, beat the egg yolks lightly. Warm the cream and the sugar in a heavy-bottomed saucepan over medium heat, stirring with a wooden spoon until the sugar has dissolved and the cream is hot (do not let it boil). Remove the pan from the heat and pour 1 cup of the hot cream into the eggs, whisking constantly to prevent curdling. Then pour it all back into the saucepan and whisk until well mixed. Return the saucepan to the stove over medium heat. Cook for 8 to 10 minutes, stirring constantly with the wooden spoon to prevent sticking. When the custard coats the spoon lightly and your finger run along the spoon leaves a visible path, it is ready. Pour it into a bowl and let it cool. Then chill it in the refrigerator.

Reserve ¼ cup of the figs and 2 to 3 tablespoons of the chopped almonds for the garnish. Stir the remaining figs and almonds into the cold custard, pressing the lumps of chopped figs against the side of the bowl with the back of a spoon to break them up. The fruit must be well mixed into the custard.

Freeze in an ice cream maker following the directions. Store in the freezer or serve at once. Garnish each portion with a little of the chopped figs and almonds.

MANGO ICE CREAM

6 SERVINGS

8   *egg yolks*
1   *cup granulated sugar*
2½ *cups heavy cream*
3–4 *ripe mangoes, peeled and sliced (enough to make*
      3 cups of purée)
    Optional: 6 tablespoons confectioners' sugar

Beat the egg yolks and the sugar together until thick and light in color. Heat the cream (do not let it boil) and pour it gradually into the egg mixture, beating constantly so that the eggs do not curdle. Purée the mangoes through a food mill or in a food processor. Fold 3 cups of this purée into the egg mixture. Add up to 6 tablespoons of confectioners' sugar to taste. Chill the mixture in the refrigerator, then freeze it in an ice cream machine or in ice trays. (If you have any leftover mango purée, serve it over the ice cream.)

RASPBERRY SAUCE

4 SERVINGS

1   *pint ripe raspberries*
    Confectioners' sugar to taste, depending on the tartness
      of the berries
    Optional: 1 teaspoon kirsch

Purée the ingredients in a blender or food processor. Push the sauce through a fine mesh strainer to get rid of the seeds. Chill until ready to serve.

VARIATION: Substitute strawberries for the raspberries.

INDEX

Arthur Gold and Robert Fizdale are internationally known as duo pianists and as the authors of *Misia: The Life of Misia Sert.* They also, as *The New Yorker* wrote recently, "cook formidably." In fact, for ten years they delighted the readers of *Vogue* with articles on food. They live in New York City and Water Mill, New York.